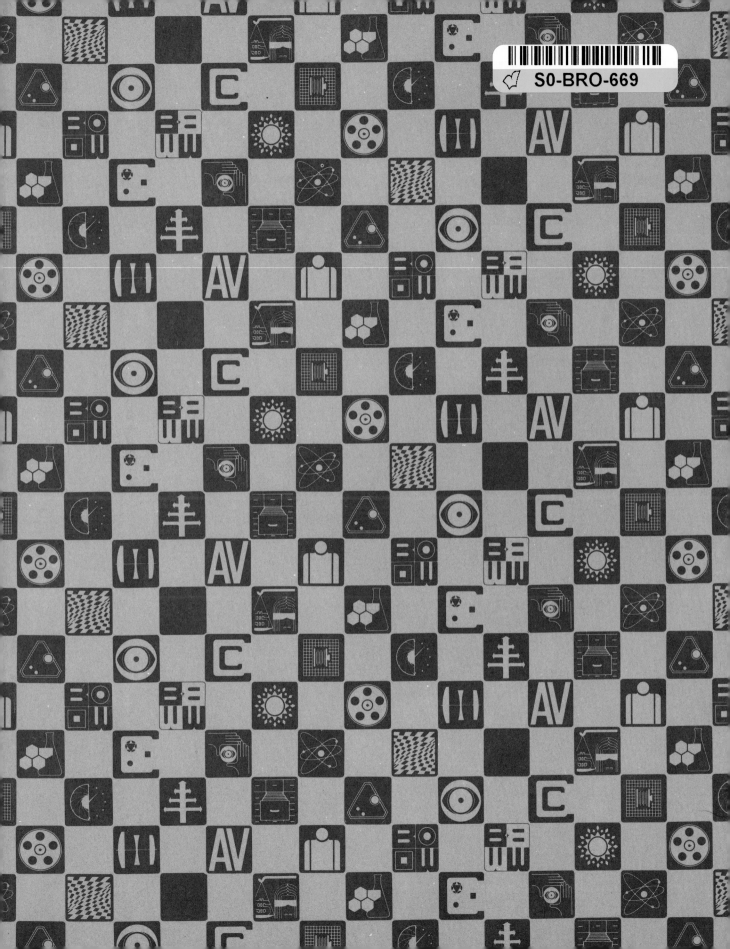

Encyclopedia of Practical Photography

Volume 3

Che-Contact

Edited by and published for
EASTMAN KODAK COMPANY

AMPHOTO
American Photographic Book Publishing Company
Garden City, New York

Note on Photography

The cover photos and the photos of letters that appear elsewhere in this encyclopedia were taken by Chris Maggio.

Copyright © 1978 by Eastman Kodak Company and American Photographic Book Publishing Company, Inc.

Library of Congress Cataloging in Publication Data

Amphoto, New York.
    Encyclopedia of practical photography.

    Includes bibliographical references and index.
    1. Photography—Dictionaries. I. Eastman
Kodak Company. II. Title.
TR9.T34   770'.3   77–22562

ISBN 0–8174–3050–4 Trade Edition—Whole Set
ISBN 0–8174–3200–0 Library Edition—Whole Set
ISBN 0–8174–3053–9 Trade Edition—Volume 3
ISBN 0–8174–3203–5 Library Edition—Volume 3

Manufactured in the United States of America

Symbol Identification

 Audiovisual

 Color Processing and Printing

 Picture-Making Techniques

 Biography

 Equipment and Facilities

 Scientific Photography

 Black-and-White Materials

 Exposure

 Special Effects and Techniques

 Black-and-White Processing and Printing

 History

Special Interests

 Business and Legal Aspects

 Lighting

 Storage and Care

 Chemicals

 Motion Picture

 Theory of Photography

 Color Materials

 Optics

 Vision

Guide for the Reader

Use this encyclopedia as you would any good encyclopedia or dictionary. Look for the subject desired as it first occurs to you—most often you will locate it immediately. The shorter articles begin with a dictionary-style definition, and the longer articles begin with a short paragraph that summarizes the article that follows. Either of these should tell you if the information you need is in the article. The longer articles are then broken down by series of headings and sub-headings to aid further in locating specific information.

Cross References

If you do not find the specific information you are seeking in the article first consulted, use the cross references (within the article and at the end of it) to lead you to more information. The cross references can lead you from a general article to the more detailed articles into which the subject is divided. Cross references are printed in capital letters so that you can easily recognize them.
Example: *See also:* ZONE SYSTEM.

Index

If the initial article you turn to does not supply you with the information you seek, and the cross references do not lead you to it, use the index in the last volume. The index contains thousands of entries to help you identify and locate any subject you seek.

Symbols

To further aid you in locating information, the articles throughout have been organized into major photographic categories. Each category is represented by a symbol displayed on the opposite page. By using only the symbols, you can scan each volume and locate all the information under any of the general categories. Thus, if you wish to read all about lighting, simply locate the lighting symbols and read the articles under them.

Reading Lists

Most of the longer articles are followed by reading lists citing useful sources for further information. Should you require additional sources, check the cross-referenced articles for additional reading lists.

Metric Measurement

Both the U.S. Customary System of measurement and the International System (SI) are used throughout this encyclopedia. In most cases, the metric measurement is given first with the U.S. customary equivalent following in parenthesis. When equivalent measurements are given, they will be rounded off to the nearest whole unit or a tenth of a unit, unless precise measurement is important. When a measurement is considered a "standard," equivalents will not be given. For example: 35 mm film, 200 mm lens, 4″ × 5″ negative, and 8″ × 10″ prints will not be given with their customary or metric equivalents.

How Articles are Alphabetized

Article titles are alphabetized by letter sequence, with word breaks and hyphens not considered. Example:

> Archer, Frederick Scott
> Architectural Photography
> Archival Processing
> Arc Lamps

Abbreviations are alphabetized according to the letters of the abbreviations, not by the words the letters stand for. Example:

> Artificial Light
> ASA Speed

Contents
Volume 3

Chemistry of Photography

The photographic process, from the manufacture of the light-sensitive materials to the processing of the final print, is based on a series of chemical reactions. Some of the reactions are comparatively simple; others are quite complex.

Photographic material has a mechanical support, such as film, glass, or paper base, with a light-sensitive coating, or emulsion, made up of minute silver halide crystals (usually silver bromide) suspended in gelatin. Exposure to light in a camera, printer, or enlarger gives no visible effect, but there is an invisible change that produces a latent image. This is a physical action. To obtain a visible, usable image then requires chemical action. The exposed material is treated with various chemical solutions in order to be developed, fixed, and washed.

When exposed photographic material is placed in a developer solution, the developer reacts with the exposed grains that contain the latent-image material, freeing the silver from its compound and depositing it as tiny, irregular grains of metallic silver. Multitudes of these minute grains form the black silver image. The developer will also react with unexposed grains, but much more slowly, so that only a relatively small amount of silver (fog density) is formed in the unexposed areas during normal development.

After development, the undeveloped silver halide crystals in the emulsion must be removed to keep them from darkening and obscuring the image. This "fixing" is done by treating the emulsion in a solution of sodium or ammonium thiosulfate. Either forms a soluble compound with the silver halide but has practically no effect on the silver image under normal conditions.

After the undeveloped silver halide has been dissolved, the emulsion is still saturated with chemicals of the fixing bath. If the hypo-plus-silver compounds remained, they would slowly decompose and attack the image, making it discolor and fade. Thus the hypo is removed by washing.

Other chemical reactions are also important in photography. Dyes may be formed or released as a silver image is being developed, in order to produce an accompanying color image. A silver image may be bleached to a colorless state; this is required in black-and-white and color reversal processing. The color of a visible silver image may be changed, or a bleached image may be redeveloped in a single color; such reactions are the basis of toning processes. However, it is the chemical reactions involved in the manufacture of photographic materials, and in the development and fixation of a silver image that are common to all of photography. Those reactions are discussed here. The others are discussed in the articles BLEACHING; COLOR FILM PROCESSING; and TONING.

Reactions in Manufacture

The manufacture of photographic materials starts with the production of silver nitrate, made by dissolving silver in nitric acid.

This is not a simple replacement between the hydrogen ion of the acid and the silver atoms. It involves an oxidation reaction in which part of the acid takes electrons from the silver atoms to form silver ions, which then combine with some of the other acid molecules. This crude silver nitrate is purified by repeated recrystallizations from water solutions.

The light-sensitive emulsion layer is made by mixing a solution of silver nitrate with a solution of the desired halide, such as potassium bromide, in the presence of gelatin, to produce this reaction:

$$AgNO_3 + KBr \rightarrow AgBr\downarrow + KNO_3$$

Thus silver bromide (AgBr) is formed by a double decomposition. Since it is practically insoluble, it is precipitated. The soluble potassium nitrate (KNO_3), which is the other product of the reaction, can be washed away.

The gelatin keeps the tiny crystals of silver bromide from clumping together, and helps to keep the unexposed grains from being attacked by the developer. It supplies minute quantities of sulfur compounds, which react with the grains and increase their sensitivity to light. Finally, when the emulsion is coated on the support and dried, it provides a mechanical binder that holds the silver halide grains in place but which is water-permeable, allowing the developer and fixer solutions to penetrate and act on the grains.

Development

Chemical, or direct, development is carried out by bringing the exposed photographic emulsion into contact with a developing solution that contains a developing agent but no silver salt. The silver formed in the developed image is the result of the chemical reduction of the individual exposed silver halide grains. This reduction starts in the tiny particles of silver that are formed during exposure, and proceeds from these "development centers" until the entire grain is reduced to metallic silver.

There are many different formulas for developer solutions, but almost all practical formulas have five primary constituents: water, developing agent, preservative, accelerator, and restrainer.

Solvent. Water is the primary solvent in photographic developers. It can dissolve and ionize the different chemicals; it can penetrate the emulsion layer; and it can swell the gelatin, thus providing the developing agent with ready access to the exposed silver halide crystals. A second solvent is used occasionally in concentrated liquid developers to keep all of the chemicals in solution.

Developing Agent. A developing agent is a chemical substance that must be a reducing agent for silver ions, and must show a preference for reducing the silver halide grains that have been exposed. Usually, organic developing agents are employed.

The most popular developing agents are: (1) Kodak Elon developing agent (methyl-p-aminophenol sulfate); (2) Amidol (dihydrochloride of 2,4-diaminophenol); (3) Phenidone® (1-phenyl-3-pyrazolidone); and (4) hydroquinone. Most developer formulas call for more than one developing agent to impart the desired characteristics to a developer. Combinations of Elon and hydroquinone have been most successful in black-and-white photography.

The developing agent in the developer solution is ionized, and during development, these developer ions supply electrons to the silver ions in the exposed silver bromide grains, thus reducing them to atoms of metallic silver. This action simultaneously oxidizes the developing agent.

Preservative. The oxidation products of the developing agents are usually dark colored and rather unstable. A preservative in the developer solution reacts with these oxidation products to form practically colorless compounds and thus keeps the solution from turning dark and staining the emulsion. The preservative also protects the developing agent from being oxidized by the oxygen in the air. By far the most common preservative is sodium sulfite (Na_2SO_3). It is a component of almost all developers.

Activator. A solution of developing agent in water makes a poor developer because it does so little actual developing. An alkali is needed to get things moving. The degree of alkalinity is controlled by the choice of alkali and the quantity used. Common alkalies in developing solutions are borax, Kodalk balanced alkali, sodium carbonate, and sodium hydroxide (listed in order of increasing alkalinity). Sodium sulfite is slightly alkaline and, with some developing agents, provides all the alkalinity needed. Generally speaking, developing activity is proportional to the alkalinity.

Restrainer. Even though the developing agents usually employed show a strong preference for developing the *exposed* silver halides, all show some tendency to reduce the *unexposed* silver halides also. A restrainer is usually added to discourage the action of the developer on the unexposed silver halide. The restrainer thus restricts the chemical fog. Potassium bromide is almost always the restrainer used, although sodium bromide, potassium iodide, and sodium iodide are occasionally used in developer formulas.

Miscellaneous Ingredients. Some developer formulas call for one or more special ingredients to impart a special property to a developer or to permit a developer to be used under a special condition. Sometimes sodium sulfate (Na_2SO_4) is added to a developer to permit developing at a higher-than-normal temperature. The sulfate prevents the gelatin from swelling too much. Without the sulfate, very high temperatures soften and swell the gelatin so much that physical damage to the image can result. Those photographic materials designated as designed for high-temperature, rapid processing have an emulsion that has been hardened in manufacture to prevent such physical damage.

It is sometimes desirable to add an *antifoggant* to minimize the growth of fog.

Stop Bath

A stop bath is an acid solution generally composed of acetic acid and water. Its function is to stop development quickly, and to protect the fixer. It may contain a hardener to protect the gelatin of the emulsion, a buffer to maintain its level of acidity during use, and a visual indicator that changes color as the stop bath loses strength.

After the desired degree of development has been obtained, it is necessary to halt the action of the developer. This is accomplished almost immediately when the alkaline developer is neutralized by the acid stop bath. This fast neutralization prevents continued action on the emulsion, and it prevents aerial oxidation of the developing agent, which otherwise could produce stains or fog in the emulsion layer of the product.

A water rinse is sometimes used in place of a stop bath, but it works simply by diluting the developer in the emulsion to a point where it is no longer effective. But that may take one to three minutes. A fresh acid stop bath completes its job in 10 to 20 seconds; its chemical action is far more positive and effective.

Because fixer solutions are acidic, they can become less effective if there is an excessive carry-over of alkaline developer solution. The acid stop bath neutralizes the developer, which matches the state of the photographic emulsion more closely with the acid nature of the fixer solution.

The gelatin in an emulsion is subject to various degrees of swelling, depending upon the relative alkalinity or acidity of the processing solutions through which it passes, and how much the gelatin was hardened in manufacture. When an emulsion is subjected to large changes in the degree of swelling, a defect called reticulation can be produced. Reticulation is the formation of a pattern of ridges, valleys, and cracks in the surface of the gelatin layer. This pattern is caused when the gelatin actually buckles under the great stresses imposed on it by swelling. An acid stop bath helps to control the amount of emulsion swelling and allows the emulsion-hardening properties of the fixer to do a better job.

Fixing

After the latent image is developed to produce a visible image, the emulsion still contains unexposed and undeveloped silver halides, which would darken if exposed to light. The main purpose of the fixing bath is to remove the unexposed silver halides without affecting the developed image, and to

thereby help make the image permanent. This permanent image is said to be "fixed."

A suitable fixing bath must meet several requirements: (1) It must dissolve the unexposed silver halides completely. (2) It must form salts with the dissolved halides that are soluble in the fixing bath itself and in the later wash, and that are stable when diluted (so that they will not decompose during washing). (3) It must not attack the gelatin or the emulsion support. (4) It must not seriously affect the silver grains of the developed image.

Although silver bromide is practically insoluble in water, it can be dissolved in a solution of sodium or ammonium thiosulfate. This action occurs because the thiosulfate combines with silver ions to form complex ions that are soluble even in the presence of small quantities of bromide.

$$Ag^+ + 2(S_2O_3)^{--} \rightarrow Ag(S_2O_3)_2^{--}$$

Although a fixing bath can be simply a 30 percent solution of a fixing agent in water, most formulas call for a number of other ingredients in order to provide longer life, greater capacity, and more effective action.

Solvent: Water.

Fixing agent: Either of two compounds may be used. Sodium thiosulfate ($Na_2S_2O_3 \cdot 5H_2O$) is commonly called hypo; it has been the standard fixing agent since 1839. Ammonium thiosulfate [$(NH_4)_2S_2O_3$; example: Kodak rapid fixer] is a liquid concentrate that is faster acting and has greater capacity. Although it costs more than hypo, only about half as much is required to make a given quantity of fixing bath.

Acid: Usually acetic acid is added to the fixing bath to neutralize any alkaline developer that might remain in the emulsion, and to help maintain the acidity of the fixer at a desired level.

Preservative: In acid solution, the thiosulfate tends to break down and form free sulfur, according to the equation:

$$S_2O_3^{--} + H^+ \rightleftarrows HSO_3^- + S$$

Since this action is reversible, the decomposition can be prevented by the presence of sufficient quantities of one of the substances on the right-hand side. Therefore, sodium sulfite is used as a preservative since in acid solution it forms the bisulfite ion HSO_3. This preservative action of sulfite in the fixing bath is due to an entirely different chemical action than its preservative effect in developers.

Hardener: Practical fixing baths usually contain a hardening agent to harden, or tan, the gelatin so it will not become too soft or swollen during washing. Potassium alum, $KA1(SO_4)_2 \cdot 12H_2O$, is a common hardener. It requires a slightly acid solution to harden the gelatin effectively.

Buffer: A fixing bath must not have too much acidity, but it must be able to withstand the addition of a considerable amount of alkaline developer. A "buffered" solution has acidity in reserve, so that as some is used up in neutralizing developer, a compensating amount is released to keep acidity of the solution at the desired level. To achieve this, acetic acid is used in combination with sodium sulfite. When a hardener is also used in the solution, it has a decided effect on the buffering. Boric acid is often added to improve buffering and to prevent the formation of by-product sludge in a hardening fixing bath.

Washing

Washing films and papers is largely a preventive measure. Chemicals from the fixing bath left in film or paper will, in time, cause discoloration through sulfiding of the image:

$$Na_2S_2O_3 + 2Ag = Ag_2S + Na_2SO_3$$

The resultant silver sulfide, when exposed to high relative humidity and high temperatures for extended times, may be oxidized slowly to silver sulfate, and the image begins to disappear.

Thorough washing will dissolve out the complex silver compounds formed in the fixing bath so that only insignificant traces remain in the material, and sulfiding will not occur. Compounds such as Kodak hypo clearing agent make the complex compounds dissolve more readily in water and thus increase the effectiveness of washing.

• *See also:* BLEACHING; COLOR FILM PROCESSING; DEVELOPMENT; FIXING; STOP BATH; TONING.

Further Reading: Carroll, John S. *Photographic Lab Handbook,* 4th ed. Garden City, NY: Amphoto, 1977; Rhode, Robert B. and Floyd H. McCall. *Introduction to Photography,* 2nd ed. New York, NY: Macmillan Publishing Co., 1971.

Chevalier, Charles Louis

(1804–1859)
French optician

In 1826, Chevalier introduced Louis Daguerre to Joseph Nicéphore Niépce. In 1839, he built the first Daguerreotype camera with a cemented achromatic lens. This lens was a meniscus in shape, with its concave side facing the subject, and a diaphragm in front, thus fulfilling the conditions required for flatness of field. Similar lenses were used for many years thereafter and have never been surpassed for box cameras, even to the present day. High-quality portrait lenses that provide a variable degree of image softness with changing *f*-numbers, are similar in structure.

Children, Photographing

Only photography provides an enduring record of the continuing growth and the varied activities of the very young. Because intimate picture records of babies and children become priceless as time passes, you should take each new photograph with the utmost care to ensure the very best portrayal of childhood. To do so, you must combine a knowledge of child psychology with a definite camera-handling approach to achieve this goal.

Capturing Natural Expressions

Successful child photography involves capturing the natural spirit of childhood. Almost all pictures of infants have this natural quality. Babies are unaware of the camera as they are pictured during the normal course of their daily routine. But as children reach four or five years of age, they become acutely conscious of the presence of the camera. Self-conscious poses and expressions usually replace the normal youthful interests. Too often, the photograph shows this artificiality. Only after the shutter has been released and the camera put away does the child's naturalness return.

Most children are unable to respond to posing directions. Asking a child to pose in a specified way invariably results in a loss of naturalness. The young

If a child is enjoying an activity, the natural enthusiasms or absorption can be recorded without need for posing instructions.

and eager often overact in their effort to please. Some may respond with a lackadaisical, let's-get-it-over-with-quickly attitude. Attempting to correct these attitudes generally produces an even less satisfactory response. So unless you are photographing a professional model, do not give posing directions.

But if a child is enjoying an activity of his or her own choosing, the natural enthusiasm can be recorded on the film without the need for any posing instructions. The normal progression of the activity will create many opportunities for picture-taking that will be superior to those situations which might have been contrived. The unplanned and the unexpected provide chances for capturing an exceptional photograph. Your objective should be catching the fleeting expression or the momentary situation rather than attempting to direct the action.

The Picture-Series Method

To photograph a child of camera-conscious age, select an activity that the child enjoys, such as listening to a bedtime story or playing in a pool of water. Then plan a number of photographs to tell the complete picture story of the event. This picture-series method can also be used if you want only a single photograph near the end of the activity. Allow the child to enjoy the activity from the beginning rather than be instructed to start with a preconceived pose that might be part of the later action. Make exposures from the beginning also, so that picture-taking becomes part of the activity. The picture-series approach produces a storytelling set of photographs, the most striking of which can be used as an outstanding single photo.

The picture series should show a complete story: the first photograph sets the scene, several others show the continuing action, and a final picture concludes the activity. The opening photograph should show the child or children and all essential toys or work materials in detail. This establishes the location of the activity. Make certain that the backgrounds are simple and compatible with the story to be pictured. The photographs that follow in the series may be close-ups, especially of facial expressions. Catch any action at its peak intensity. The final photograph should complete the story by showing the end result of the previous activity.

Finding Picture Opportunities

Everything a child does during waking hours is a new adventure in the continuing story of childhood. Observe this great variety of daily activities for situations that might be suitable for a picture series. Immediately write down any picture possibility, because chance observations are often difficult to remember at a later time.

Children, Photographing

For posed photos, an assistant is often essential to help with details and to provide a second source of attraction for the child's attention.

Most children will repeat an enjoyable activity, so pictures may be taken at that time. But you need not limit your picture opportunities to situations that can be repeated. You can create new diversions by using gifts to provide the interest that brings out the most animation in a child. For example, giving an artistically inclined girl a set of paints would provide the situation for picturing the artist at work. Or presenting a pumpkin to a boy could result in a series on decorating a Halloween jack-o'-lantern.

Make all photographic preparations before presenting the gift. The first time the child sees the gift will be the time of maximum enthusiasm. That is the time to get a complete set of pictures. The child's interest will be diminished the second or third time the gift is used, although such repeat sessions can be photographically productive. However, the child may exhibit much less animation than occurred the first time.

Some situations pass by so quickly that you cannot get all the pictures you want. So repeat the situation. You can present a child with a new birthday cake on three different days with great success. Cake frosting seldom loses its appeal.

Photography and fun will become associated in the mind of a child who is allowed to enjoy the activity while the camera is present. Future photographic sessions will be welcomed by the youngster. But you should carry the psychology of securing child cooperation at least one step further. Photographic modeling is a paid profession, regardless of the age of the model, and you should reward your young models as a regular practice. A small reward, such as a snack treat, a small toy, or a picture book, should be given immediately after the last shutter click. If the reward is always given immediately afterward, without fail, the taking of photographs becomes associated with a most pleasant experience, thus ensuring the child's favorable attitude the next picture-making time. Of course, if you plan to sell or publish the pictures, arrangements with a parent or guardian will be necessary—including a properly signed model release.

Working with an Assistant

A happy, animated child is the first requirement for outstanding child photography. But there

Young teenagers are particularly camera-shy. Here, use of natural backlighting eliminated the need for more elaborate setups, thus requiring only minimal intrusion.

Children, Photographing

High shutter speeds are needed to stop the action of children at play, and may require a reflector or fill-in flash for proper lighting.

Lighting

Photography of children under conditions of only slight control often makes it difficult to obtain sufficient lighting. Outdoors, use a reflector or fill-in flash near the camera, with the sun behind the picture subject, to secure good facial rendition. The sun provides the backlight to help separate the subject from the background. This is especially important for pictures of children with dark hair that might blend into a shaded or tree-filled background.

Rapid-recycling electronic flash is also an excellent source of fill-in lighting for outdoor use. Regular or improvised reflectors permit you to observe just how much light is being directed into the shadows. Reflectors are especially useful with cameras having focal-plane shutters. The high shutter speeds needed to stop action of children at play won't synchronize with electronic flash in a focal-plane camera, so reflectors may be used to supply the necessary lighting.

Indoors, use bounce flash to give a soft, even illumination that is both natural-appearing and effective over a wide area. To give a sparkling high-

For interior shots, bounce flash gives a soft, even illumination that is effective over wide areas.

are many discordant details that may mar the finished photograph. An assistant is invaluable for detecting and correcting many of these deficiencies, thus freeing the photographer's attention for the selection of the best possible picture composition or for catching a fleeting moment of action. The child's mother can often provide such help by keeping stray wisps of hair in place, smoothing wrinkles from clothing, or, in the case of an infant, providing other necessary services. A regular assistant who has become familiar with your own particular working methods is the most efficient.

During the actual time of picture-taking, your assistant should be near, or even slightly behind, you. Two moving persons, widely separated, provide a divided source of attraction for the child's attention. Sometimes happy expressions can be coaxed from a tired or self-conscious child by having your assistant engage in a pantomime behind your back, such as a clownlike attempt to hit you on the head with any available object. Crazy antics should be used sparingly and only as a desperation measure for totally unresponsive children.

Children, Photographing

383

light to the eyes, use a weak fill-in flash at or near the camera. But you will have to determine by test the correct exposure for the bounce lighting under the actual conditions of use. Be sure to record the exact placement of the lights, the camera and subject location, the lens settings, and all other important information. Even better, write the details down before making the exposures. You can sketch a map of the floor arrangement with the distances marked and the height of the lights noted. It's amazing how much you can forget by the time the processed film is available for study.

The diffused lighting given by bounced flash produces a feeling of softness that is characteristic of childhood. However, you may wish to have pictures that show maximum detail and texture. Direct flash gives this type of rendition. For best results, use at least two lighting units: one for the off-camera main light, the other for the fill-in light on or near the camera. The two-light triangle lighting arrangement avoids the overly dark shadows and the flat lighting given by a single source of light near the camera. Cameras with a permanently attached flash unit may be used to trigger a slave lighting unit at some distance away. A non-wired slave unit can supply the main source of off-camera light, with the on-

camera flash being used as the fill light. An electronic flash with two flash heads can be used for the same lighting arrangement. Place the stronger, off-camera light so that the illumination will come from the direction in which the child is facing. But shadow areas should be well illuminated too, in case the child does not look in the anticipated direction.

Some Helpful Techniques

Photograph the Child's Possessions. Tell the child that you want to take a photograph of her doll or favorite stuffed toy, or of his block house or sand castle; do not mention taking the child's picture at the same time. Children are much less self-conscious if they think you are photographing their possessions, even though they are in the picture too. You can stage a birthday party for a child's favorite doll and invite the child to attend. Dolls have birthdays too, you know!

Use a Flash Decoy. Some of the younger children will smile wondrously at the light from a flashbulb after the picture has been taken. If you observe any amazement on the part of the child to a flash, have an extra hand-triggered flash unit available.

Flash it first, and then when the child reacts, take the picture with the regular lights.

Photograph from the Child's Level. Lower the level of your camera so that it is even with the child's eyes or lower. Children, especially those just beginning to walk, live in a world of huge (to them) furniture and giant adults. By photographing from a low level, you can show some of the child's perspective in your photographs. You can also picture some of the difficulties encountered by children as they attempt to cope with gigantic surroundings, such as the problem of climbing into a chair.

Children are best photographed in the security of their own home or in the familiar surroundings where they are the most relaxed. But providing a child with an interesting diversion will permit you to photograph anywhere. When children have fun, they forget the immediate surroundings, even though these may be strange. Some professional photographers have adopted a walk-around technique of child portraiture, in which the film exposures are made as the unrestricted child is allowed to investigate a number of play areas in the same bounce-lighted studio. By photographing children naturally, at home or away, you can capture the spirit of youth in your pictures.

• *See also:* BABY AND CHILD PHOTOGRAPHY.

Further Reading: Editors of Time-Life Books. *Photographing Children.* New York, NY: Time-Life Books, 1971; Fearnley, Bernard. *Child Photography.* Garden City, NY: Amphoto, 1972; Lahue, Kalton C., et al. *Photographing Children.* Los Angeles, CA: Petersen Publishing Co., 1974; Szasz, Suzanne. *Child Photography Simplified.* Garden City, NY: Amphoto, 1976.

Chlorhydroquinone

Chloroquinol, 2-chloro-1,4-benzenediol, Adurol

Developing agent, producing brown tones on papers, formerly used in negative developers also, but has no particular advantage in this use.
Formula: $ClC_6H_3(OH)_2$
Molecular Weight: 144.56

White crystalline powder, readily soluble in hot water. As a developer, its properties roughly correspond to a mixture of hydroquinone and about five percent of Metol. Reduction potential 7.0. Chlorhydroquinone has a very low fog tendency, particularly in developing equipment where the film is exposed to air a part of the time.

Chloroform

Trichloromethane

Used as a nonflammable solvent; it not only dissolves oils and greases, but many plastics, gums, and resins as well, and thus can be used in film cements and mountants.
Formula: $CHCl_3$
Molecular Weight: 119.38

Clear, colorless, very volatile liquid with a characteristic odor. Slightly soluble in water, mixes with alcohol, benzene, ether, petroleum solvents, and oils. Protect from light and keep cool.
DANGER: Very poisonous. The vapors are poisonous in large amounts, anesthetic in small concentrations. Use only with good ventilation.

Chretien, Henri

(1879–1956)
French mathematician and optician

In 1927, Chretien demonstrated the Hypergonar, said to be the first anamorphic lens intended for motion-picture photography. At the time, it aroused little interest, though a similar lens was marketed for a short while in the early 1930s by C. P. Goerz, New York, for 16 mm amateur cameras and projectors. About 1953, the Chretien lens and system was used by Twentieth Century-Fox for a full-length feature film entitled *The Robe,* which introduced the Cinemascope system of wide-screen presentation.

Citric Acid

2-hydroxy-1,2,3-propanetricarboxylic acid;
β-hydroxytricarballylic acid

A mild acid used in certain toning baths, in clearing baths, and in the making of paper emulsions.
Formula: $C_6H_8O_7.H_2O$
Molecular Weight: 210.14

Crystals, slightly deliquescent in moist air, but tend to lose water of crystallization in dry air or when heated. Very soluble in water, freely soluble in alcohol, soluble in ether.

Clayden Effect

Local desensitization of an emulsion caused by a very short exposure to a high-intensity light prior to an overall exposure to a lower intensity for a longer time. One example, seen on occasion, occurs during long time exposures at night in capturing lightning strokes; if the lightning occurs early in the exposure, followed by a fairly long exposure to dim night illumination, the result will be a reversed image of the lightning bolt, because the first, very high intensity exposure *desensitizes* the emulsion to the second exposure. Instead of a heavy black image of the lightning on the negative, it will produce a clear area, which in turn will cause the lightning to appear black on the print instead of white, giving rise to the so-called "black lightning" phenomenon; the remainder of the image is correct in tonality. A similar effect is produced when a film is first exposed to x-rays and then to visible light; in this case, it is known as the Villard Effect.

Clerc, Louis Philippe

(1875–1959)
French scientist

Clerc was a professor of photographic chemistry and physics at the University of Paris from 1898 to 1937. He is best known for his book *Photography, Theory and Practice.* The most comprehensive work of its kind when first published in 1926, it passed through many revisions and editions. A completely revised two-volume edition was published in the U.S. in 1973 by Amphoto. Clerc also was the founder and editor of the journal *Science et Industries Photographiques* and author of the book *The Technique of Photomechanical Reproduction.*

Clinical Photography

Clinical photography is one branch of medical photography. Clinical photographs are still photographs and motion pictures made to show the condition of patients undergoing treatment. In some cases, the photographs are required as an aid in analyzing and diagnosing a condition. Most often, they are made to provide a record of the original state of a condition, and its response to treatment at various stages. Clinical pictures may be used to communicate essential information about a patient to others, such as specialists. They may also be used to help train clinic personnel and to teach medical students.

Most photographers who do clinical photography are employed in hospitals as medical photographers; clinical pictures are just one aspect of their job. However, in small communities, professional photographers may be requested by physicians to do some clinical photography for them.

Medical photography is a rewarding occupation for those who experience a personal satisfaction from a dedication to the welfare of people. The field offers ample challenges in techniques and communications to make it an interesting and creative career. This opportunity to function as both an illustrator and a communicator adds continual variety to the field of medical photography. First and foremost, however, the clinical photographer must remember that he or she is not dealing with objective medical specimens, but with people. Patients are people with problems. They are often in pain and are usually apprehensive.

The clinical photographer has to put patients at ease as much as possible and quietly impress them with the importance of clinical photography. The best way to do this is to really feel a genuine empathy toward the patients. The photographer should be understanding, but not openly over-sympathetic because that may seem to indicate an undue seriousness in the condition. He or she must be patient but firm, particularly with hesitant older people and rebellious children. Forced cheerfulness and cold indifference are both out of place.

It goes without saying that the clinical photographer must be efficient. He or she can then speed up the sessions for the comfort of the patients as well as provide the medical staff with informative photographs. The clinical photographer needs to have a humane temperament and to be proficient in camera work. Apprenticeship in the photographic department of a hospital, university, or research institution provides the best means for gaining a faculty for working with patients.

In addition to knowing the technical aspects of the job, the clinical photographer must learn hospital procedures and become familiar with a certain amount of medical and anatomical terminology. This and other aspects of medical photography become easy when the photographer is motivated by an interest in medicine rather than in the art of photography alone.

Types and Purposes of Clinical Photography

Clinical photography includes producing "before-and-after" photographs—records of afflicted areas and the same areas when they are healed. However, this is only a small part of the scope of the field. A progress record has many more purposes than just showing that the treatment was successful. For one thing, the "after" picture is unnecessary from most medical standpoints. It is merely necessary to state that the diseased condition cleared up.

Kinds of Photographs. A "before" picture depicts a condition as it appears when first seen by the physician. This type of photograph is a common one and is made whenever the case is distinctive enough to merit study or inclusion in the patient's history folder. It is the basic record. The number and the nature of follow-up pictures that are made depend upon the specific needs arising for following the progress of treatment or for supplying illustrations for lecturing and publication.

Progress Records. A progress record is a series of pictures that show the location and extent of an involvement before treatment, various stages of change, and the appearance after cure. When accompanied by dates, the rate of remission is indicated.

In addition to the general purposes for medical photographs, the progress record has specific uses. Often, the remission of a condition is slow, and sometimes it becomes worse. The busy physician cannot remember the exact appearance of every patient on previous visits. Serial photographs can chart slow changes. They enable the physician to decide whether to continue, modify, stop, or change the treatment. The physician can convincingly discuss the difficult case with the patient. He or she may even elect to show the photographs to the patient in order to justify and to encourage continuation of the treatment.

Apparatus Demonstrations. The clinical photographer is often called upon to record appliances, such as braces, casts, splints, exercisers, and prostheses. His or her duty is to show how they are worn by the patient and their function in modifying posture and mobility.

Most photographs of equipment alone are made in the photographic laboratory. But recording scenes of technicians manipulating equipment is within the scope of the clinical photographer. Such scenes may be either staged in the studio, or photographed on location.

Patients undergoing therapy in special baths and other appliances in the department of physical medicine would be photographed on location. So, the photographer must know the rudiments of lighting an indoor scene.

Photo-Diagrams. A challenging phase of clinical photography is the production of photo-dia-

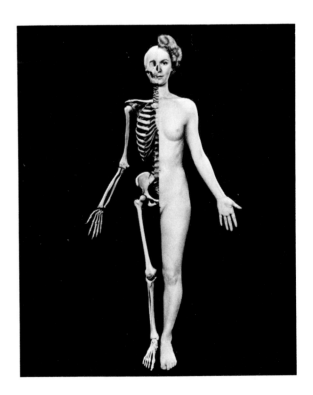

Photo-diagrams provide more concise and clear information than do photographs alone. They may be made by cutting and mounting two or more photographs, or by adding artwork directly on unferrotyped prints.

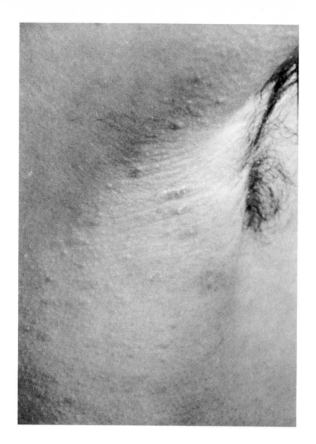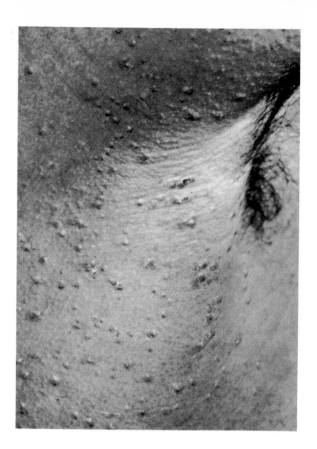

Orthochromatic films are often preferable to panchromatic films for emphasizing certain features of the skin, such as rashes, vein patterns, and variations in pigmentation. In photo at right, faint pink lesions of pityriasis rosea were made more apparent by employing orthochromatic film, which provides darker than normal images of reddish subject colors.

grams. Photographic prints form the basis of such illustrations. The photographer can draw pertinent coordinates, angles, fiducial marks, and limits on the prints. Combinations of photography and the work of an artist are often effective as diagrams. For other applications, several photographs can be cut and mounted together. These types of illustration can easily be designed to present more concise and clearer information than could be shown by photographs alone.

Modified Renditions. In general, photographs will be expected to render skin tones and the appearance of lesions as naturally as possible. Nevertheless, emphasis of certain features is sometimes needed for "mapping" faint rashes, venous patterns, and pigment patches. A common method of modifying skin

tone rendition in black-and-white photography is to use an orthochromatic rather than a panchromatic film.

Infrared and ultraviolet photography are other techniques frequently used to obtain modified renditions that are more informative than visual inspection. These techniques are covered in separate articles.

If backgrounds are not chosen carefully, tonal rendition will be changed when it is not desired. The accompanying three photographs show the effect created with backgrounds of various tones. Paleness of the skin can be accentuated with a black background; a significant swarthiness, as in jaundice, becomes emphasized with a white background. Both surrounding tones clearly outline body contours.

For general work, a gray background presents the most natural appearance. For black-and-white photography, a 2-to-1 or a 1-to-2 brightness ratio in background-to-skin meter values gives satisfactory results. The first yields a background tone a little lighter than the skin rendition; the second, a little darker. For color work, a 1-to-1 ratio is usually best.

Group Pictures. Most group photographs in clinical photography will include patients in locations such as rehabilitation centers, psychology clinics, laboratories, and therapy classes. Another nonclinical photographic activity is the preparation of simple class portraits of students to serve as reference rosters for instructors. Similar photos of hospi-

Background color is important to maintain proper tonal rendition in black-and-white photography. (Left) A black background tends to lighten skin tones but presents no shadow problem. (Center) Shadows on a light-toned background can be eliminated by supplementary light. A meter reading from the background was twice that from the patient. (Right) Background was half as bright as the skin. For black-and-white photography, the subject should be either slightly lighter or slightly darker than the background for good tonal separation.

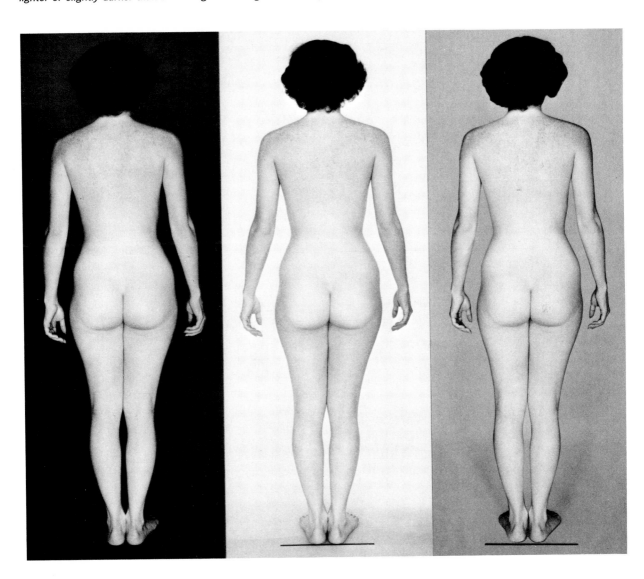

tal personnel and informal portraits of staff members are often made by the clinical photographer.

Action Studies. Broadly, this field covers people in motion or people exhibiting reactions. It deals with making records for studying gait, body movements, and facial expressions as these functions are affected by physical and behavioral irregularities. A series of still photographs is valuable in many applications. Other occasions will call for motion pictures. The photography of surgical operations records the actions of the surgeon, rather than those of the patient.

Specialized Photography. An endoscope is an optical instrument designed for looking inside the body, either through natural orifices like the bronchial tubes with a bronchoscope, or through incisions. Some surgical manufacturers make camera attachments for their scopes so that photographs can be taken inside body cavities. Photography of the retina of the eye is a special type of internal photography, as are the techniques for oral photography and dental photography.

Extreme close-ups of details and images that are life-size or larger are frequently required. Fingernails, capillary beds, and skin textures are common subjects for the clinical photographer. Some techniques for this kind of work are described in the article PHOTOMACROGRAPHY.

The medical photographer often has to prepare large prints for scientific exhibits at medical meetings. Slides and larger transparencies also are often required for conferences and exhibitions, as well as for teaching purposes.

There is also a need for visual material for television. With the increasing use of video presentations in medical teaching institutions, the photographer will often be called on to supply slides, prints, and motion pictures to meet this need.

Equipment and Materials

The Simple System. A clinical photography department will have a well-equipped studio area in most cases. However, there will be frequent calls for immediate pictures in a ward, clinic, receiving room, or laboratory. Elaborate equipment cannot be transported there, and the photographic staff may not even be free at that instant.

The answer is a simple system that can be taken to any location at a moment's notice, and that can be used easily even by those who are not experienced photographers. A number of such simple systems can be placed throughout the institution, so personnel in clinical departments and medical offices can do all their own routine photography. This arrangement ensures that photographs will be taken whenever they are needed, but that the photographic staff can concentrate on the work that demands their special capabilities.

Basic Setup. The basic arrangement for the simple system is a hand-held camera with accessories for focusing and viewfinding at close range, and a portable flash unit.

Portable lighting makes the photographer independent of electrical outlets and cords; it eliminates the need for estimating lens and shutter settings; and it provides sufficient illumination for obtaining a great depth of field with a small lens aperture.

An elaborate camera can be set for the simple system. This should be done by an experienced photographer, who can calibrate the lighting and then note the few settings for the inexperienced.

Although instant print cameras provide immediate results, they are not always the best choice for a simple system. They produce only a single, small print. Other prints can be made by copying the original, but of course, this requires giving up the original for a time. Instant print records do permit immediate comparison of color rendition or other pertinent details in the picture with the actual subject. This is especially valuable when the subject is irretrievable.

Versatility. To accomplish the greatest variety of clinical photography, a single-lens reflex camera that makes 2″ × 2″ slides and 35 mm negatives is the best choice. Such cameras are convenient to use at normal distances under all conditions, and they can be fitted with a variety of accessories for specialized work and close-ups when required. A camera with a built-in metering system and automatic diaphragm lenses—which present the brightest image for viewing and focusing—will be most convenient. Although 35 mm cameras with fully automatic exposure control are available, a semi-automatic model that gives the photographer more control over exposure may be more suitable for this type of work.

For close-up photographs the camera lens can be fitted with supplementary lenses, or extension

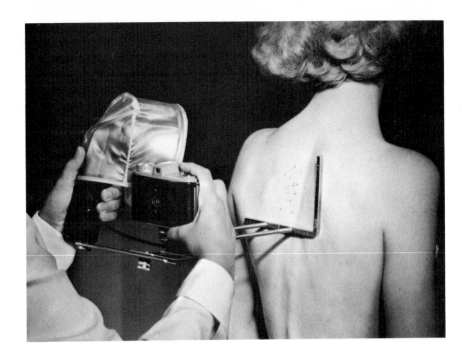

For cameras that do not permit through-the-lens viewing, a focusing frame may be used to delineate working distances and field sizes. As shown in this photo, when the focal frame is L-shaped in a sidelighted setup, there is no danger of casting a shadow of the frame across the subject. Directions for making focusing frames are in the article on Close-up Photography.

tubes or a bellows can be used to focus from about two feet down to six inches. A bellows is the most convenient way to obtain extreme close-ups. To focus close-ups with a single-lens reflex camera, set the focus so that the lens covers the field size desired. Then move the entire camera-plus-bellows setup back and forth until the main area of interest in the subject is in focus in the viewfinder. Usually, the depth of field is slight. In most cases, it is better to favor the front of the field and sacrifice some rear sharpness. Whenever possible, the use of a tripod will improve sharpness by eliminating camera movement and permitting use of a smaller f-stop setting.

Close-up Lighting. To adapt a manually controlled flash unit for close-up work, it may be necessary to reduce the intensity of the illumination. First, calculate exposures by dividing fractions of a foot (from the flash-to-subject distance) into the guide number for the film in use and make a series of test exposures. Units with low power outputs may be suitable without adjustment. If some reduction of illumination is required, some manufacturers offer plastic diffusers to be placed over the unit. Otherwise, you can use one or two layers of white handkerchief, or improvise a baffle by drilling suitable holes in a sheet of aluminum.

Auto-flash units solve most close-up as well as normal-distance exposure problems by monitoring their own output as reflected back from the subject. When proper exposure has been achieved, they cut themselves off instantly.

Any system of close-up lighting you work out should be based on an aperture of $f/22$, with an aperture of $f/16$ reserved for the far limit of a given lamp-subject range. These apertures provide the depth of field needed for most close-ups.

When the light comes from above and to the side of the camera lens, there is a definite lighting angulation. This provides a good delineation of the subjects. Such lighting is the best all-around one to adopt when it is not practical to arrange the lighting specifically for each subject. Even complexly shaped regions, such as hands, can be recorded satisfactorily.

Focal Frames. Instead of selecting cameras inherently capable of working at close range, the photographer can adapt a non-elaborate camera for focal-frame operation. Most amateur cameras can be focused close up with positive supplementary lenses. However, many viewfinders are not similarly adaptable for close ranges. The addition of a focal frame is required when the viewfinder does not indicate close-up fields. Focal frames should be made to delineate the working distances and field sizes provided by the supplementary lenses to be used. Supplementary lens data and methods for constructing focal frames are covered in the articles CLOSE-UP PHOTOGRAPHY and SUPPLEMENTARY LENSES.

The average close-up field required is often about 5″ × 7″. Any camera adapted for close-up photography should also be capable of providing larger fields. Most cameras focus as close as two-and-one-half feet without any special attachments. At this distance, approximately a half-length portion of the body is encompassed by miniature cameras. A working distance of eight feet suffices for most full-length shots. However, a six-foot man requires nine feet. Standardization at a closer distance can be adopted for children. A large proportion of patient photography can be accommodated by standardizing with these field sizes. The pertinent details of most conditions are revealed by one, two, or all three views.

Clinical Studio Photography

The simple-system approach enables personnel in various departments to meet some of their own photographic needs without special training. The staff clinical/medical photographer will most often work in a designated studio location to which patients come or are brought.

Maintaining the patient's physical and mental comfort is the paramount concern of the photographer. The posing procedure should be as short as possible. Films, cameras, accessories, and lights for a shot ought to be ready before the patient is asked to go over to the background. The lighting arrangement can usually be roughly estimated as soon as the area of interest is noted at the reception desk or on the request slip. A measurement made from the camera field to the floor, with the patient standing or sitting in the waiting area or nearby, will guide the approximate placement of the camera and establish the height of the lamps in standard plans.

Both in the studio and in other locations, electronic flash illumination is not only best for photographing moving patients but it is also cool. Therefore, it does not subject the quieter patients, especially those with burns and other painful skin conditions, to uncomfortable heat, nor does it expose those with weak eyes to steady bright lights.

Such lamps should have low-power tungsten bulbs for arranging the lighting and focusing.

Positioning. It is desirable to obtain the cooperation of the patient so that the best position for steadiness and for adequate lighting of a specific area can be achieved. The location of the patient as it affects shadows on a suitable background must be considered, too.

Records of plastic surgery, particularly, must be carefully positioned for accurate comparison. The surgeon should decide which anatomical plane should be generally presented to the camera. The angle between the subject-lens axis and the plane selected should then be determined and noted for subsequent records. In any event, it is desirable for the photographer to study the planes and aspects of the entire body. He or she can then direct the camera perpendicularly to such planes or at standardized angles to them.

The basic approach to posing is to decide upon the aspect and then to arrange the patient and camera in the manner most suitable from the standpoints of comfort, convenience, and background. Nevertheless, the photographer should be alert to other needs. Whenever possible, anatomical landmarks should leave clues as to the locality of close-up regions. In general, this is easy—the neckline, shoulder, axilla, nipple, umbilicus, elbow, knee, wrist, and ankle all provide readily identifiable areas. The back presents some difficulties, but the cervical prominences, the scapula, and the gluteal fold help to overcome them.

Viewpoint. In the majority of cases, the camera viewpoint will be easy to decide once the photographer has been told the significant features. The lens should take approximately the same general visual viewpoint as that required for seeing the condition. However, the patient is visually observed from several viewpoints, whereas the photograph is made from only one. Therefore, it is wise to select the camera viewpoint systematically. In that way all the photographs made in the department have a basis for comparison.

Serial Records. Reproducibility is the keynote of making serial records; otherwise, they do not provide valid qualitative or quantitative comparisons. A minor, but sometimes important, consideration is the size or location change that may occur in the area of interest. Treatment, such as radiation therapy, may involve a larger area than the original lesion. Or, since an extensive flap may be raised in plastic surgery, the donor area should be included in the first record of the procedures. In other cases, a lesion may be expected to extend its margins. Provision for such changes should be made in selecting the initial field of view.

For reproducibility in viewpoint, scale, and modeling, a careful record of patient, camera, and light positions is imperative. When standard lighting plans are suitable, the technical part of the record need not be as detailed. A check with previously made photographs should always be made.

Another help to serial study is the indication of anatomic landmarks by marking the skin. These indications, when accurately placed after careful physical examination can photographically depict a condition that does not clearly appear superficially, even to the eye. They offer an excellent way to follow changes.

Perspective. In most instances, the "normal" lens for the camera serves to provide a suitable perspective—the visual and photographic effect caused by a near object appearing larger when close than it does when farther away. However, for informal portraiture and for facial records for the plastic surgeon, a long-focus lens is required. It is generally accepted that a subject-lens distance of five feet is desirable. Perspective at this distance gives an "average" impression of the person—similar to his appearance during normal social contact and conversation. Features are not studied as intently from greater distances. And at closer distances, the features are distorted even to the eye; this is called foreshortening.

Obviously, the lens used must be capable of producing an image, say of the face and shoulders, that is of ample size. This is particularly necessary when color slides are made. With a 35 mm camera, an 85 mm lens would be practical for black-and-white prints, since they could be enlarged as required from the negatives. But a 135 mm lens would be needed for slides because the required magnification must be achieved on the film.

Parallax Error. The anatomical configurations of torso and full-figure photographs will vary considerably at different lens-subject distances. It is best to use a 4″ × 5″ studio camera for this kind of work. For a field only as large as the figure of a child, a record made from five feet will show body foreshortening. A record made from about 14 feet will provide a more suitable morphological record. For somatic measurement, however, a working distance of 33 feet (with a 20-inch lens) is recommended for adults. The parallax error is about one percent. A distance of 28 feet (with a 14-inch lens) entails a slightly higher error, but it is practical for depicting children in growth studies.

The parallax error arises because the lens "sees" each part of the body from a different angle. In practical terms, the error is the difference between a measurement made from an actual subject and the slightly smaller one obtained from the photograph.

Clinical Studio Lighting

Lighting is often the chief component of photographic style. Glamour and dramatic lighting are well known in pictorialism, but they are out of place in clinical photography. Even so, emphatic lighting can be used for the purpose of "underlining the information" contained in the photograph. Emphatic lighting that comes from above appears natural, because indoors and out, we are accustomed to that being the dominant light direction. The lighting contrast must make the clinical conditions inescapably clear. Dramatic lighting usually comes from other directions, frequently from below. The effect is theatrical rather than natural, and is unsuitable for clinical purposes. Even flat clinical lighting should have a basic downward component. The only exceptions are special lightings for cavities. Since these are often illuminated mainly with an inspection light for visual viewing, the same type of lighting is utilized for photography.

Types of Lighting. There are three basic types of lighting: flat, contour, and texture. They are related to the nature of the clinical condition. The photograph of the freckled arm demonstrates all three. The large freckles are flat lesions. If they were the main feature to be shown, flat lighting would record them to better advantage and not bury some of them in shadow. It is their dark tone, not their contour, that separates them from their intrinsically light-toned, textured surroundings. Of secondary clinical interest is the good physical condition of the arm—this is not a wasting disease. Modeling (plastic) lighting has shown the contour or roundness of the arm. The characteristic texture of the skin in

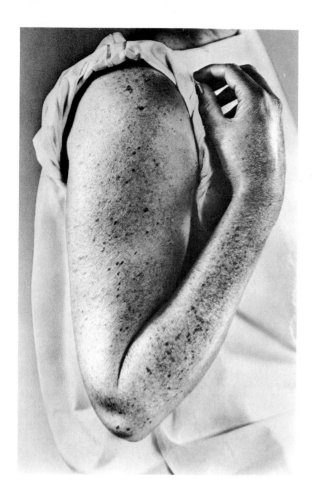

Choice of type of lighting to be used varies with the nature of the clinical condition to be photographed. This subject is somewhat unusual in that it required two types of lighting: contour lighting to show the well-developed arm and forearm, and texture lighting to depict the characteristics of the skin problem. The characteristically scaly texture of the skin, the main feature of the photograph, is clearly rendered by the glancing texture lighting. Where the lighting was relatively flat on certain parts of the curved surfaces, the abnormal, large freckles were recorded in good contrast.

summer is the main feature to illustrate. To do this, a texture (glancing) lighting is needed. It should not be overlooked that skin textures vary not only in roughness, but also in sheen. The arm in the accompanying illustration was lit to exhibit both types of surface as well as tone and contour contrasts.

Flat Lighting. This type of lighting is evenly distributed over the subject. Its main intensity is in a direction from above the camera, whether it is the result of one light or the combined result of more lights. It is achieved by using light units of equal intensity, equally spaced on both sides of the camera, and at equal distances from the subject.

The arrangement shown can be standardized so that even photographically inexperienced personnel can easily make many of the routine records, particularly of dermatological conditions and of stance and body outline. The positions of lamps,

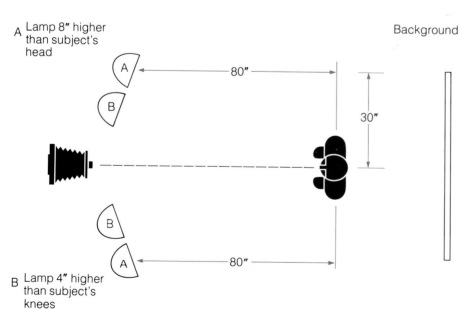

A Lamp 8" higher than subject's head

B Lamp 4" higher than subject's knees

Background

Standardized setups such as this one for flat lighting are useful. Mark positions of patient, tripod, and lamps with tape on the floor. Lamp locations for other arrangements can also be marked to make changes without delay.

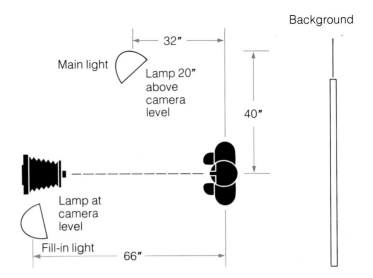

Unbalanced illumination is required for photographing rounded subjects. The main light should be more intense than the fill-in illumination.

tripod, and patient can be marked on the floor with tape. A suitable exposure can be worked out; then there are no lens adjustments to make.

Of course, flat lighting, standardized or not, does not serve to depict all conditions; contour lighting is often needed. But *optimum* contour lighting requires photographic experience. When a photographer cannot always be at hand, it is better to work out some form of standardized flat lighting and a simple arrangement for a basic contour lighting.

Contour Lighting. An uneven light balance is required to reveal the volume and contour of body forms. A main light and a weaker fill-in light are used. The easiest way to change from flat to contour lighting is to move one light closer to the subject; the resulting increase in intensity makes it the main light.

The main light is directed at the best angle to model the condition; the fill-in light is used to increase the luminosity of the shadows. The major concern is to avoid destroying the effect of the main light with unsuitable fill. Double shadows can result when the latter is too strong or wrongly directed. Also, the main shadow is lost when the fill is too great.

In general, the fill-in light should be placed as close to the camera as possible and directly over the lens, in order to minimize the shadow it produces. Since this is not always mechanically possible, the fill light has to be to one side of the camera (but still just a little higher than the lens). When the modeling angle is not small, the fill light can be on the same side as the main light. However, the fill light should be moved to the other side for balancing strong modeling at a smaller angle, because the shadow edge of the patient is quite dark under such a main lighting.

Texture Lighting. When the lighting angle is made very small, that is, when the light beam is glanced across the surface being photographed, texture becomes emphasized. Texture is a sort of "micro-morphology"—each little element presents a rounded or ridged contour. But the purpose is not to show each contour but rather the pattern of light and shade made by the elements.

Exposures. With texture lightings in particular, and for most optimum lightings, exposures can best be gauged with an exposure meter. Automatic cameras for exposing color film should be of the type having a manual override. The reason for this is that very pale skins may otherwise be overcompensated and record too dark; or black skins may record too light. About half a stop less exposure than that used for average skins usually renders very white skin correctly; a half stop more serves for dark skin. But for very black skin, a full stop more may be needed, especially when detail in the skin is to be recorded.

Care must be taken that a strongly contrasting background does not influence the light measurements unduly. It is for this reason, apart from image aesthetics, that in color photography the background should be lit to about the same intensity as the patient.

• *See also:* Dental Photography; Electron Micrography, Medical Photography; Photomacrography; Photomicrography; Radiography; Scientific Photography; Stereo Photography; Thermal Photography; Ultraviolet and Fluorescence Photography.

Close-Up Movies

When you're watching a movie, it's exciting to see the screen suddenly filled with a close-up picture of a small subject, such as a flower, a butterfly, or a model railroad engine. Close-up movies are exciting and fun—and they are easy to make.

Close-Up Lenses

Most 8 mm and super 8 movie cameras allow you to make sharp movies no closer than about 3½ feet from the subject. But that just isn't close enough to get really big pictures of small subjects. You can get closer by putting an inexpensive close-up lens over your camera lens. Close-up lenses, like filters, come in various sizes to fit different camera lenses. With most cameras, you will also need an adapter ring to hold the close-up lens in place. Usually, your camera manual will tell you what series-size or what diameter close-up lens your camera accepts and what adapter ring, if any, is required. Or your photo dealer can measure the camera lens to determine what series close-up lens and adapter ring you need.

The ability to move in on the activities of small and delicate creatures is one of the most exciting features of close-up moviemaking.

Clinical Photography

Close-up lenses in different strengths, or powers, offer a variety of subject-to-lens distances and picture areas. Higher powers let the camera focus at closer distances, providing images much bigger than normal.

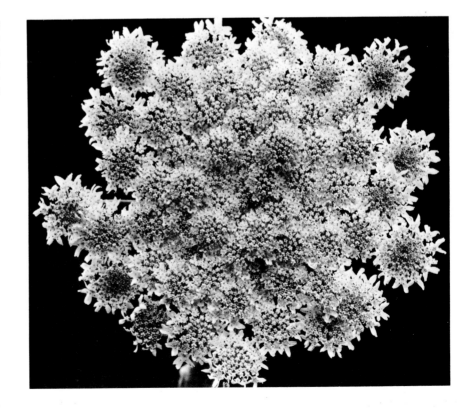

Close-Up Movies

At the very close distances required for close-up photography, depth of field is very shallow. Even with careful measurement and focusing, out-of-focus elements, such as the leaves at upper right hand corner of this photograph, may almost always be expected.

Close-up lenses are available in different strengths, or powers, such as +1, +2, and +3. The higher the number, the stronger the lens, and the closer you can get to your subject. The close-up lenses most commonly used in movie-making are +2 and +3. The tables indicate the subject distances and picture areas (called field sizes) for different close-up lenses on various cameras.

Subject Distance is Critical

When you make close-up movies, it is important to measure the distance to the subject quite accurately, because depth of field is very shallow when the camera is very close to the subject. Also, unless you have a camera with a reflex viewing system, the viewfinder isn't accurate at close ranges. That's because the viewfinder is some distance above the camera lens and therefore doesn't see exactly the same area the camera lens sees. (With a reflex camera, when you look through the viewfinder, you are looking directly through the lens.) At normal shooting distances, this variance (called parallax) is so slight that it can be ignored. However, at very close distances, parallax becomes a very important consideration.

Close-Up Movies

8 mm CAMERA WITH FOCUSING LENS

Camera Lens	Camera Focus Setting (in feet)	+2 Close-Up Lens		+3 Close-Up Lens	
		Close-Up Lens-to-Subject Distance (in inches)	Approximate Field Size (in inches)	Close-Up Lens-to-Subject Distance (in inches)	Approximate Field Size (in inches)
9 mm	Inf	19⅝	7¼ × 9½	13⅛	4¾ × 6⅜
	25	18½	6¾ × 8⅞	12⅝	4⅝ × 6
	10	16⅞	6⅛ × 8⅛	11⅞	4⅜ × 5⅝
	6	15½	5⅝ × 7⅜	11⅛	4 × 5⅜
13 mm	Inf	19⅝	5 × 6⅝	13⅛	3⅜ × 4⅜
	25	18½	4⅝ × 6⅛	12⅝	3⅛ × 4⅛
	10	16⅞	4¼ × 5⅝	11⅞	3 × 3⅞
	6	15½	3⅞ × 5⅛	11⅛	2¾ × 3⅝
27 mm	Inf	19⅝	2⅜ × 3⅛	13⅛	1⅝ × 2⅛
	25	18½	2¼ × 3	12⅝	1½ × 2
	10	16⅞	2 × 2¾	11⅞	1⅜ × 1⅞
	6	15½	1⅞ × 2½	11⅛	1⅜ × 1¾

FIXED-FOCUS 8 mm CAMERA WITH 13 mm LENS

+2 Close-Up Lens		+3 Close-Up Lens	
Close-Up Lens-to-Subject Distance (in inches)	Approximate Field Size (in inches)	Close-Up Lens-to-Subject Distance (in inches)	Approximate Field Size (in inches)
17½	4⅜ × 5⅞	12⅛	3⅛ × 4

FIXED-FOCUS SUPER 8 CAMERA

Camera Lens	+2 Close-Up Lens		+3 Close-Up Lens	
	Close-Up Lens-to-Subject Distance (in inches)	Approximate Field Size (in inches)	Close-Up Lens-to-Subject Distance (in inches)	Approximate Field Size (in inches)
9 mm	17½	7¾ × 10¼	12⅛	5⅜ × 7⅛
13 mm	17½	5⅜ × 7⅛	12⅛	3¾ × 4⅞
14 mm	17½	5 × 6½	12⅛	3½ × 4½

16 mm CAMERA WITH 25 mm LENS

Camera Focus Setting (in inches)	+2 Close-Up Lens		+3 Close-Up Lens	
	Subject-to-Film Plane Distance (in inches)	Approximate Field Size (in inches)	Subject-to-Film Plane Distance (in inches)	Approximate Field Size (in inches)
24	Close-up lens not needed;		11⅜	2⅜ × 3¼
20	use focusing adjustment.		10⅝	2¼ × 3
16	11⅛	2¼ × 3⅛	9⅞	2 × 2⅝
12	9½	2 × 2½	8½	1⅝ × 2¼

SUPER 8 CAMERA WITH FOCUSING LENS

Camera Lens	Camera Focus Setting (in feet)	+2 Close-Up Lens		+3 Close-Up Lens	
		Close-Up Lens-to-Subject Distance (in inches)	Approximate Field Size (in inches)	Close-up Lens-to-Subject Distance (in inches)	Approximate Field Size (in inches)
9 mm	Inf	19⅝	8¾ × 11½	13⅛	5⅞ × 7⅝
	25	18½	8¼ × 10¾	12⅝	5⅝ × 7⅜
	12	17⅜	7¾ × 10⅛	12	5⅜ × 7
	6	15½	6⅞ × 9	11⅛	4⅞ × 6½
9.5 mm	Inf	19⅝	8¼ × 10⅞	13⅛	5½ × 7¼
	25	18½	7¾ × 10¼	12⅝	5¼ × 7
	10	16⅞	7⅛ × 9⅜	11⅞	5 × 6½
	6	15½	6½ × 8½	11⅛	4⅝ × 6⅛
12 mm	Inf	19⅝	6⅝ × 8⅝	13⅛	4⅜ × 5¾
	25	18½	6⅛ × 8⅛	12⅝	4¼ × 5½
	10	16⅞	5⅝ × 7⅜	11⅞	3⅞ × 5⅛
	6	15½	5⅛ × 6¾	11⅛	3⅝ × 4⅞
13 mm	Inf	19⅝	6⅛ × 8	13⅛	4 × 5⅜
	25	18½	5¾ × 7½	12⅝	3⅞ × 5⅛
	10	16⅞	5¼ × 6⅞	11⅞	3⅝ × 4¾
	6	15½	4¾ × 6¼	11⅛	3⅜ × 4½
21 mm	Inf	19⅝	3¾ × 5	13⅛	2½ × 3¼
	25	18½	3½ × 4⅝	12⅝	2⅜ × 3⅛
	12	17⅜	3¼ × 4⅜	12	2¼ × 3
	6	15½	2⅞ × 3⅞	11⅛	2⅛ × 2¾
28 mm	Inf	19⅝	2⅞ × 3¾	13⅛	1⅞ × 2½
	25	18½	2⅝ × 3½	12⅝	1¾ × 2⅜
	10	16⅞	2⅜ × 3⅛	11⅞	1⅝ × 2¼
	6	15½	2⅛ × 2⅞	11⅛	1⅝ × 2
36 mm	Inf	19⅝	2¼ × 2⅞	13⅛	1½ × 1⅞
	25	18½	2 × 2¾	12⅝	1⅜ × 1⅞
	10	16⅞	1⅞ × 2½	11⅞	1¼ × 1¾
	6	15½	1⅝ × 2¼	11⅛	1¼ × 1⅝
45 mm	Inf	19⅝	1¾ × 2¼	13⅛	1⅛ × 1½
	25	18½	1⅝ × 2⅛	12⅝	1⅛ × 1½
	10	16⅞	1½ × 2	11⅞	1 × 1⅜
	6	15½	1⅝ × 1¾	11⅛	1 × 1¼

Fortunately, it's easy to make a cardboard measuring device to measure the subject distance as well as indicate the picture area. Consult the appropriate table to find the distance to the subject and the field size for your combination of camera lens, close-up lens, and focus setting (if your camera has a focusing lens). The larger of the two dimensions listed in the table under "Approximate Field Size" represents the *width* of the subject area, and the smaller dimension represents the *height* of the subject area. Then cut the cardboard as shown in the accompanying diagram.* You will need a different cardboard measuring device for each close-up lens and focus setting, because the subject distance and picture area vary, depending on the close-up lens and focus setting you use.

---

*Some cameras, usually 16 mm, require that the subject distance be measured from the film plane rather than from the close-up lens. The film plane is usually marked by φ on the camera body just behind the lens. If this is true of your camera, cut out the end of the cardboard that fits against the camera so that the edge of the cardboard is even with the film-plane indicator on the camera.

Close-Up Movies

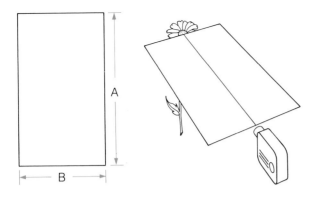

"A" indicates distance between subject and lens. "B" is the width of the area included in the picture at subject distance "A".

CARDBOARD MEASURING DEVICE DIMENSIONS

Dimension	+3 lens		+2 lens	
	Super 8	8 mm	Super 8	8 mm
A	12⅛	12⅛	17½	17½
B	4⅞	4	7⅛	5⅞

Draw a heavy line down the center of the cardboard as illustrated. To make a close-up shot, hold the center line on the cardboard up to the center of the close-up lens. Be sure to hold the cardboard straight out from the camera. Do not use the camera viewfinder to frame the subject. Line up the subject so that it just touches the end of the card and fits within the width of the card. Make sure the subject fits within the height of the field size too. Then drop the card and make the movie.

The accompanying table gives measurements (in inches) for a cardboard measuring device for use with either a fixed-focus super 8 or 8 mm camera, each equipped with a 13 mm lens.

It's a good idea to use a tripod for your close-up shots. A tripod makes it easier to hold the camera at the correct subject distance. It also helps to eliminate camera movement, which is much more noticeable in close-ups than in normal movies.

A tripod is especially useful for taking close-up movies, because accidental camera movement is more noticeable than in normal movies. The tripod also makes it easier to keep the camera at the exactly correct distance from the subject.

A zoom lens allows the photographer to visually move in on the subject while a shot is in progress, without having to move the camera. This is particularly important when photographing larger subjects, which tend to move from place to place more quickly than small creatures such as insects. The zoom lens also provides a variety of focal lengths without having to change lenses or add close-up lenses.

Close-Ups with a Zoom Lens

The important factor in making close-ups with any camera is the subject distance. If you have a close-up lens on a camera with a zoom lens and have accurately measured the subject distance, maintain that distance and you can zoom the lens to any position and still get sharp pictures. (Notice in the table "8 mm Camera with Focusing Lens" that the subject distance is the same for a specific close-up lens, regardless of the focal length of the camera lens.) Of course, when you use the wide-angle posi-

tion, you will photograph more of your subject; when you use the telephoto position, you will photograph less of your subject.

Depth of field is shallower when the zoom lens is in the telephoto position than when it's in the wide-angle position. Since the depth of field may be even less than one inch, try to keep the subject in one plane, parallel to the front of the camera, so that as much of the subject as possible will be in sharp focus. Always measure the close-up lens-to-subject distance as accurately as possible, and be especially accurate when the camera lens is in the telephoto position.

The data in the accompanying tables are applicable to zoom lenses. For example, the data for a 36 mm lens on a super 8 camera applies to a zoom lens on a super 8 camera when the lens is in the 36 mm (telephoto) position; the data for a 12 mm lens applies when the zoom lens is in the 12 mm (wide-angle) position.

A photo dealer can help you select a close-up lens and adapter for your camera. They are available from many companies including Ponder & Best, Inc., Spiratone Inc., and Tiffen Industries Inc.

Further Reading: Gulliver, Ann W. and William C. *A Guide to Creative Filmmaking.* West Haven, CT: Pendulum Press, Inc., 1974; Roberts, Kenneth H. and Win Sharples, Jr. *A Primer for Film-Making.* New York, NY: Bobbs-Merrill Co., 1971; Young, Freddie and Paul Petzold. *The Work of the Motion Picture Cameraman.* New York, NY: Hastings House, 1972.

Close-Up Photography

A close-up photograph takes in only a small object or portion of an object—perhaps a single detail or a group of just a few details. The resulting magnifica-

A close-up photograph directs attention to aspects of the subject that might normally go unnoticed. As this picture of a slice of red cabbage illustrates, the photographer must look for and learn to recognize the visual power of details in small, and often quite commonplace objects. Photo by William W. Cates for Editorial Photocolor Archives.

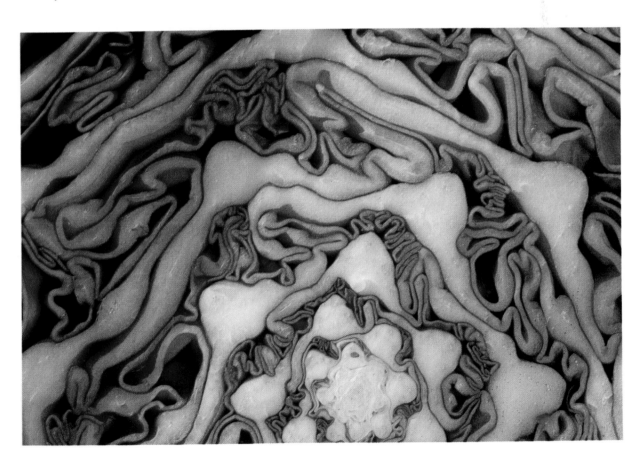

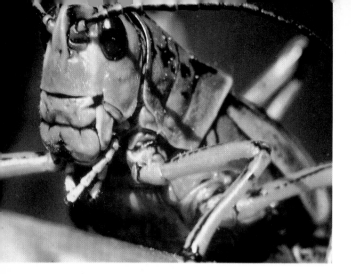

tion directs attention to aspects of the subject that might normally go unnoticed. It permits minute examination of the portion of the subject included, and it may convey a sense of psychological closeness or intimacy.

There is no precise definition of what constitutes a close-up. Generally, the term includes the range of images from one-tenth the actual size of the subject (a reproduction ratio of 1:10, or a magnification or scale of $0.10\times$), to those images that are the same size as the subject ("life-size," 1:1, or $1.0\times$) or slightly greater. Making images at greater magnification, "photomacrographs," requires precision lenses and careful optical techniques. Even greater magnification is possible by coupling a camera to a compound microscope for photomicrography.

In a general sense, magnification may indicate that the image is larger than the object (scale greater than 1:1). Actually, an image smaller than the object is a reduction. However, a reduction may be considered the same as a fractional magnification. An object reduction of four times produces an image one-fourth the original object size. This may be expressed as a scale of 1:4 or as $0.25\times$. In close-up

Making images at magnifications greater than actual size requires precision lenses and careful optical techniques. With objects of a size that may be difficult to gauge out of context, such as this sound pickup component from a movie projector, it is advisable to include in the photograph other objects of known sizes for comparison.

photography, "magnification" is commonly used to denote the scale of the image even when it is smaller than the object photographed.

Although it is common to take large, apparently close-up images from a distance (for example, in telephotography and when taking pictures through binoculars), true close-up photography is achieved by bringing the camera closer than usual to the subject. The image size or magnification produced by a lens of a given focal length is determined by the lens-to-subject distance. There are several ways to adapt a lens so it will give focused images of objects located closer than the usual minimum focusing distance.

The simplest way is to add a positive supplementary lens or "close-up attachment" in front of the camera lens. This has the effect of shortening the focal length of the camera lens. As focal length decreases, so does the minimum focusing distance. Therefore, the lens can be brought nearer the subject, and the image will be proportionately larger.

A far more versatile way to get close-ups is to increase the extension between the camera lens and the film plane. This also enables the lens to focus objects at closer than normal distances, and is the method used for virtually all serious close-up photography. It provides the greatest degree of control;

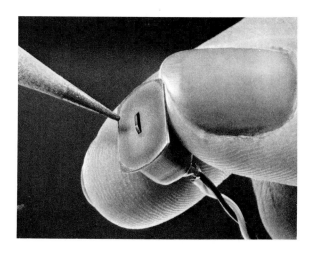

Close-Up Photography

The most versatile way to get close-ups is to increase the distance between the lens and the film. This method provides the greatest degree of control and is likely to produce better image quality than that achieved with supplementary lenses. Note relative sharpness even in the background details of this photograph.

it permits a variety of magnifications using only a single camera lens; and it is likely to produce somewhat better image quality than that achieved with supplementary lenses.

Triple-extension bellows view cameras are used to take close-up large-format pictures. Depth of field is a serious problem with all close-up photography, and is even more so with the longer focal-length lenses used on view cameras. However, the swing and tilt adjustments on view cameras are used to focus different subject distances in different field areas. Professional close-up pictures of food, jew-

elry, clothing details, small mechanical parts, and so forth are often photographed with view cameras.

A third approach, better in many ways than the other two, is the use of special lenses called *macro lenses.* Such lenses have two advantages:

1. They are optically corrected for close distances, so produce sharper images than regular lenses, which are optically corrected for greater distances.
2. Some are manufactured with built-in lens extension focusing, so that they focus up to magnifications of $0.5\times$ or $1.0\times$ without the need for accessory extension devices.

Some zoom lenses have close-up or macro ranges built into their focusing mechanism. While these are convenient and generally work fairly well, the optical quality is not usually quite as good as single-focal-length macro lenses.

These approaches to close-up photography are discussed in this article, along with some considerations of close-up lighting. A few simple methods for taking close-ups with non-adjustable cameras are also covered. More detailed information on close-ups with increased lens extension is included in the article PHOTOMACROGRAPHY. There is more about using lens attachments in the article SUPPLEMENTARY LENSES.

Close-Ups with Extensions

The type of camera most widely used for close-up photography is the 35 mm single-lens reflex. Because viewing is through the lens, a close-up may be framed and focused with great precision. Such cameras have rigid bodies. To extend the lens enough to focus on objects at very close distances, you must insert an extension ring, a tube, or a bellows between the lens and the camera body. Extension rings and tubes are often available in sets of various lengths, so they may be used singly or in combination for a number of different extensions. There are also telescoping or so-called "zoom" extension tubes.

The 35 mm single-lens reflex camera is the type most widely used for close-up photography, because through-the-lens viewing permits the greatest precision in framing and focusing. Extension rings and tubes of various lengths may be used singly or in combination for a number of rigid extensions—an important consideration in hand-held close-ups.

Close-Up Photography

An accessory bellows provides the greatest range of extension with rigid-body cameras. Generally, a bellows will do a better job than long tubes of supporting the lens securely without excess strain on the camera mounting ring. This is especially true of double-rail bellows. A bellows has one major disadvantage: if only a small amount of extension is required, the bellows length, even when totally collapsed, may be too great. Only a short tube or a ring will do.

Bellows-type cameras can also be given extra extension by adding rings or tubes to their fully extended length. However, some cameras have dou-ble- or triple-extension bellows that permit close-up photography without accessories. A double-extension bellows is one that is long enough to place a normal-focal-length lens (for the film format in use) at a distance of two focal lengths from the film plane. For example, a double-extension bellows for a 75 mm lens can put it up to 150 mm from the film; a triple-extension bellows could put it up to 225 mm away. Even if a bellows camera does not have additional built-in extension for a normal lens, it effectively becomes twice as long when used with a lens of half normal focal length.

For close-ups in the 0.1X to 1.0X range of magnifications, the maximum amount of extra extension required is equal to the focal length of the lens.

In any case, not a great deal of extra extension is required for close-ups in the 0.1× to 1.0× range of magnifications. A lens must be located only 1.1 focal lengths from the film plane to produce an 0.1× image, and two focal lengths from the film to produce a 1.0× image. Since the lens must be one focal length from the film simply to focus objects at infinity, the maximum additional extension required for images up to 1:1 is equal to one focal length—and some of that would be provided by the normal focusing mechanism of the camera or the lens.

Thus, with a normal (50 mm) lens on a 35 mm camera, less than two inches (50 mm) of extra extension is needed for close-ups when the built-in focusing capability of the lens is taken into account.

However, there is another important factor in close-up photography that affects the extension required for a given image size. That factor is working distance—the distance from the lens to the subject. You may want to use a deep lens shade or to place a light unit or a reflector between the camera and the subject. Close-ups involve close working distances,

and if the focal length of the lens is short the resultant working distance may not provide sufficient room for such setups. In that case, a lens of twice the focal length would provide the same image magnification at twice the working distance, but it also would require twice as much extension between lens and film.

For example, for an 0.5× image, a 50 mm lens must be 75 mm (3 inches) from the film and 150 mm (6 inches) from the subject. To gain more working distance, you could get an 0.5× image with a 100 mm lens placed 300 mm (11¾ inches) from the subject, but you would need a total of 150 mm (6 inches) extension from lens to film.

The relationship between close-up working distance and lens-to-film distance for all lenses is summarized in the previous table. For the method of figuring distances see the text on extensions in the box in this article.

Exposure with Extensions

The f-numbers for lens apertures are computed for a lens focused at infinity. As closer objects are focused, the f-values become less accurate because the effective focal length of the lens is changing slightly. When a lens must be extended more than 1.25 times its own focal length from the film (which is the case for magnifications of 0.25× and larger), the f-values change enough so that extra exposure is required to achieve proper results. Most through-the-lens metering systems automatically provide the required compensation in their readings. Otherwise, you must compute how much additional exposure is needed. The method is given in the text on extensions in the accompanying box; however, the following table provides sufficient data for almost all close-up situations. The exposure increases given apply to all lenses and all film sizes. The field sizes in the table tell how much subject area is included when using a 35 mm camera. See the text on extensions in the box for the method of computing close-up field sizes for other formats.

Note that if you compensate exposure by increasing the time (in order to use a small f-stop for increased depth of field), you may need additional exposure and adjusted development to compensate for reciprocity effect. Carefully consult the data for the film you are using whenever exposures are longer than 1/10 sec.

DISTANCE RELATIONSHIP FOR CLOSE-UPS

| Magnification | Number of focal lengths (F) in | |
	Lens-film distance*	Lens-subject distance*
0.10×	1.10F	11.00F
0.25×	1.25F	5.00F
0.30×	1.30F	4.30F
0.40×	1.40F	3.50F
0.50×	1.50F	3.00F
0.60×	1.60F	2.70F
0.75×	1.75F	2.30F
0.80×	1.80F	2.25F
0.90×	1.90F	2.10F
1.00×	2.00F	2.00F

*To obtain the actual distances, multiply the focal length of the lens in use by the factor given. With normal lenses, measure these distances from the iris diaphragm of the lens. With telephoto lenses, first focus on an object at infinity with the lens mounted normally on the camera. Measure forward from the film plane a distance equal to the focal length of the lens and mark the lens barrel at that point. Measure the close-up distances from that reference mark. Short-focal-length wide-angle lenses are seldom satisfactory for close-up photography because of the very short working distances involved.

FIELD SIZE AND EXPOSURE COMPENSATION FOR CLOSE-UPS WITH EXTENSIONS

| Magni-fication | Reproduction Ratio (Image: Object) | Approx. Field Size for 35 mm negative or slide | | Exposure Increase | |
		mm	inches	Open aperture	OR Multiply time by
0.25×	1:4.00	96 × 144	3¾ × 5⅝	½ stop	1.6
0.33×	1:3.00	73 × 109	2⅞ × 4¼	⅔ stop	1.8
0.40×	1:2.50	60 × 90	2⅜ × 3½	1 stop	2.0
0.50×	1:2.00	48 × 72	1⅞ × 2¾	1 stop	2.3
0.66×	1:1.50	36 × 55	1½ × 2¼	1⅓ stops	2.8
0.80×	1:1.25	30 × 45	1¼ × 1¾	1⅔ stops	3.3
1.00×	1:1.00	24 × 36	⅞ × 1⅜	2 stops	4.0

Extensions

1. Amount of Extension.

(a) With a rigid-body camera, the length of the ring or tube required or the length of accessory bellows extension is a fraction of the lens focal length. The fraction to use is the desired reproduction ratio or image-to-object scale (½, ¼, ⅕, etc.).

$$\text{Required extension} = \text{Reproduction ratio} \times \text{Lens focal length}$$

(b) With a bellows-type camera, the total distance from lens to film is the focal length plus the required extension, as determined in (a). Measure from the lens diaphragm to the film plane.

$$\text{Lens-film distance} = \text{Lens focal length} + \left(\text{Reproduction ratio} \times \text{Lens focal length} \right)$$

2. Magnification; Scale; Reproduction Ratio.

When a subject is sharply focused, the scale of reproduction is related to lens and film distances and focal length.

$$\text{Magnification} = \frac{\text{Lens-film distance}}{\text{Lens-subject distance}} \quad \text{OR} \quad \frac{\text{Lens-film distance} - \text{Lens focal length}}{\text{Lens focal length}}$$

$$\text{OR} \quad \frac{\text{Lens focal length}}{\text{Lens-subject distance} - \text{Lens focal length}}$$

Close-Up Photography

3. Focused Distance.

The distance at which the lens is focused, or at which the subject must be located, may be measured (a) from the center of the lens (diaphragm)* or (b) from the film plane.

(a)

$$\text{Lens-to-subject distance} = \frac{\text{Lens-film distance} \times \text{Lens focal length}}{\text{Lens-film distance} - \text{Lens focal length}} \quad \text{OR} \quad \frac{\text{Lens focal length} \times \text{Magnification} + 1}{\text{Magnification}}$$

(b)

$$\text{Film-to-subject distance} = \frac{\text{Lens focal length} \times \text{Magnification} + 1}{\text{Magnification}} \quad \text{OR} \quad \frac{\text{Lens-film distance} \times \text{Magnification} + 1}{\text{Magnification}}$$

4. Field Size.

The subject area is proportional to the negative size. For field width, use negative width; for field height, use negative height. (A 35 mm negative is 24 × 36 mm.)

$$\text{Field dimension} = \frac{\text{Negative dimension} \times \text{Lens-subject distance}}{\text{Lens focal length}} \quad \text{OR} \quad \frac{\text{Negative dimension}}{\text{Magnification}}$$

5. Exposure.

Close-ups using extensions require a larger aperture or a longer time than called for by a separate meter reading. (A through-the-lens meter reading requires no compensation.) If exposure is compensated for by lengthening the time, additional compensation for reciprocity effect may be required.

(a)

$$\text{Exposure increase factor} = (\text{Magnification} + 1)^2$$

Multiply the meter-indicated exposure time by this factor, or increase the aperture by an equivalent amount.

(b)

$$\text{Effective } f\text{-number} = \text{Marked } f\text{-number} \times (\text{Magnification} + 1)$$

The marked f-number is the aperture called for by the meter reading. Increase this setting by the number of stops difference between the marked f value and the effective (or actual) f value, or increase the exposure time as in (a).

---

*This is an approximation that is close enough for most purposes except when using telephoto lenses.

6. Depth of Field.

The depth of field *on either side* of the focused distance depends on magnification, the effective *f*-number, and a circle of confusion. Use the values for the circle of confusion shown .

Format Size	Diameter Circle of Confusion	
	mm	*inches*
35 mm or 126	.05	.002
2¼ × 2¼	.08	.003
2¼ × 3¼	.10	.004
4 × 5	.15	.006
5 × 7	.20	.008
8 × 10	.30	.012

First find the hyperfocal distance.

$$\text{Hyperfocal distance} = \frac{(\text{Focal length})^2}{f\text{-number} \times \text{Diameter of circle of confusion}}$$

Then, to find the limits of the depth of field:

$$\text{Near limit} = \frac{\text{Hyperfocal distance} \times \text{Distance for which camera is focused}}{\text{Hyperfocal distance} + \left(\text{Distance for which camera is focused} - \text{Focal length}\right)}$$

$$\text{Far limit} = \frac{\text{Hyperfocal distance} \times \text{Distance for which camera is focused}}{\text{Hyperfocal distance} - \left(\text{Distance for which camera is focused} - \text{Focal length}\right)}$$

Example: 2-inch lens at *f*/8, focused at 26 in., circle of confusion diameter = .002 in.

$$\text{Hyperfocal distance} = \frac{2^2}{8 \times .002} = \frac{4}{.016} = 250 \text{ in.}$$

$$\text{Near limit} = \frac{250 \times 26}{250 + 26 - 2} = \frac{6500}{274} = 23¾ \text{ in.}$$

$$\text{Far limit} = \frac{250 \times 26}{250 - 26 + 2} = \frac{6500}{226} = 28¾ \text{ in.}$$

Close-Ups with Supplementary Lenses

A supplementary lens or "close-up attachment" is a single-element lens used in combination with a camera lens.* It screws in or attaches to the front of the camera lens just like a filter. Positive (+) supplementary lenses are used for close-ups. They shorten the effective focal length of the camera lens so that objects at closer distances can be focused. When positive supplementary lenses are used for close-up photography, the *f*-values on the camera lens can be used directly with no exposure compensation.

Supplementary lenses are available in different strengths, or powers, such as +1, +2, and +3. The

*A few supplementary lenses of higher powers are made by cementing two elements together to give improved color correction.

higher the number, the stronger the lens and the closer you can get to the subject. You can use two close-up lenses together to work at even closer distances. For example, a +2 lens and a +3 lens equals a +5 lens. When you use two supplementary lenses together, place the stronger lens closer to the camera. Using more than two lenses together may result in poor image quality and may cut off the corners of the image.

It is easy to use a supplementary lens on a reflex or other camera that lets you view through the lens to frame and focus the picture. But with rangefinder viewing and non-reflex cameras, you must measure the lens-to-subject distance carefully to make sure the subject will be at the point the lens is focused on. It is especially important to measure accurately be-

cause the depth of field in close-up situations is very shallow. When the camera lens is set at infinity focus, the actual focused distance is equal to the focal length of the supplementary lens in use. Refer to the following table and to the text on supplementary lenses in the box in this article.

Data for Supplementary Lenses on 35 mm Cameras

The lens-to-subject distances given in the table on p. 415 apply to supplementary lenses used with any camera. The field sizes apply only to the focal lengths shown when used on a 35 mm camera. To compute field sizes for other focal length lenses, see the text on supplementary lenses in the box in this article.

Supplementary Lenses

1. Focal Length.

Supplementary-lens power (magnifying strength) is rated in diopters: +1, +2, +3, etc. To determine focal length, form a fraction by placing 1 over the power; the focal length is that fraction of a metre. When using two supplementary lenses together, add their powers (for example, (+2) + (+3) = +5) before forming the fraction.

Lens Power	Focal Length
+1	1 m = 1000 mm
+2	½ m = 500 mm
+3	⅓ m = 333 mm
+4	¼ m = 250 mm
+5	⅕ m = 200 mm

2. Combined Focal Length.

The focal length of the camera lens plus a supplementary lens:

$$\text{Combined focal length} = \frac{\text{Focal length of supplementary lens}}{\text{Focal length of supplementary lens} + \text{Focal length of camera lens}} \times \frac{\text{Focal length of camera lens}}{\text{Distance between lens diaphragm and supplementary lens}}$$

When using two supplementary lenses together, use the focal length of their combined powers. Mount the stronger of the two closest to the camera lens.

Example: A $+5$ diopter lens is placed on a 6-inch lens. When the supplementary lens is attached to the camera lens, there is 1 in. between the supplementary lens and the camera lens diaphragm. Assume the focal length of the $+5$ lens to be 8 in.

$$\frac{\text{Combined}}{\text{focal length}} = \frac{8 \times 6}{8 + 6 - 1} = \frac{48}{13} = 3\tfrac{5}{8} \text{ in.}$$

The following graph can be used to find the combined focal lengths of a number of combinations.

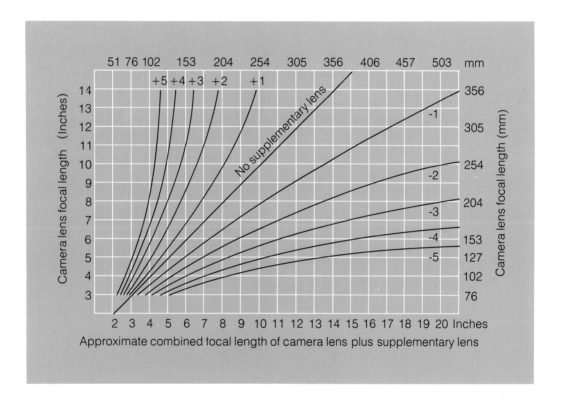

3. Focused Distance.

The distance from the combined camera and supplementary lenses to the point of sharpest focus is measured from the face or the rim of the supplementary lens.

(a) When the camera lens is focused at infinity, the actual focused distance is equal to the focal length of the supplementary lens.

(b) When the camera lens is focused at a nearer distance:

$$\text{Focused distance} = \frac{\text{Distance on camera lens scale} \times \text{Focal length of supplementary lens}}{\text{Distance on camera lens scale} + \text{Focal length of supplementary lens}}$$

4. Field Size.

The subject area is proportional to the negative size. For field width, use negative width; for field height, use negative height. (A 35 mm negative is 24 × 36 mm.)

$$\text{Field dimension} = \frac{\text{Negative dimension} \times \left(\text{Focused distance*} - \text{Combined focal length**} \right)}{\text{Combined focal length**}}$$

*As determined in No. 3
**As determined in No.2

5. Magnification; Scale; Reproduction Ratio.

The ratio between the size of the image and the actual size of the subject:

$$\text{Magnification} = \frac{\text{Focal length of camera lens}}{\text{Focal length of supplementary lens}}$$

6. Exposure.

No exposure correction is required for close-ups using supplementary lenses. Set the camera lens at an aperture called for by a meter reading of the subject.

7. Depth of Field.

The depth of field *on either side* of the focused distance depends on magnification, a corrected *f*-number, and a circle of confusion.

$$\text{Corrected } f\text{-number} = \frac{f\text{-number set on lens} \times \text{Focal length of supplementary lens}}{\text{Focal length of camera lens} + \text{Focal length of supplementary lens}}$$

First find the hyperfocal distance.

$$\text{Hyperfocal distance} = \frac{(\text{Focal length})^2}{\text{Corrected } f\text{-number} \times \text{Diameter of circle of confusion*}}$$

*See the table of the values for the circle of confusion in the box on extensions in this article.

Then, to find the limits of depth of field:

$$\text{Near limit} = \frac{\text{Hyperfocal distance} \times \text{Distance for which camera is focused}}{\text{Hyperfocal distance} + \left(\text{Distance for which camera is focused} - \text{Combined focal length}\right)}$$

$$\text{Far limit} = \frac{\text{Hyperfocal distance} \times \text{Distance for which camera is focused}}{\text{Hyperfocal distance} - \left(\text{Distance for which camera is focused} - \text{Combined focal length}\right)}$$

SUPPLEMENTARY LENS DATA FOR 35 mm CAMERAS

Supplementary Lens and Focus Setting of Camera Lens (in feet)		Lens-to-Subject Distance* (in inches)	Approximate Field Size (in inches) 50 mm Camera Lens
+1	Inf	39	18 × 26¾
	15	32¼	14¾ × 22
	6	25½	11¾ × 17¼
	3½	20⅜	9⅜ × 13¾
+2	Inf	19½	9 × 13½
	15	17¾	8⅛ × 12
	6	15½	7⅛ × 10½
	3½	13⅜	6⅛ × 9⅛
+3	Inf	13⅛	6 × 8⅞
	15	12¼	5⅝ × 8⅜
	6	11⅛	5⅛ × 7½
	3½	10	4⅝ × 6¾
+3 plus +1	Inf	9⅞	4½ × 6⅝
	15	9⅜	4¼ × 6⅜
	6	8⅝	4 × 5⅞
	3½	8	3⅝ × 5⅜
+3 plus +2	Inf	7⅞	3⅝ × 5⅜
	15	7½	3½ × 5⅛
	6	7⅛	3¼ × 4⅞
	3½	6⅝	3 × 4½
+3 plus +3	Inf	6⅝	3 × 4½
	15	6⅜	2⅞ × 4¼
	6	6	2¾ × 4⅛
	3½	5⅝	2⅝ × 3⅞

*Measure lens-to-subject distance from the front rim of the supplementary lens.

The head of a beetle photographed at f/22 (left) and f/8 (below). The smaller aperture provided sufficient depth to accommodate the head, but as the other photograph shows, this depth was obtained at the expense of sharpness.

Depth of field

Depth of field is very shallow at close distances, so you should use as small a lens opening as possible when you take close-ups.

Usually the closest part of your subject should not be closer than the near limit of the depth of field, but the more distant portions of the subject can lie beyond the far limit. When the background detail is out of focus, it will not usually detract from the main subject.

The following table gives some idea of the depth of field you can expect with supplementary lenses. In general, the camera should be focused on a plane one-third of the depth farther away than near subject details.

DEPTH OF FIELD IN INCHES WITH SUPPLEMENTARY LENSES ON 35 mm CAMERAS WITH 50 mm LENSES AT INFINITY FOCUS*

Diop-ters	f/8			f/16		
	Near	Far	Total	Near	Far	Total
1+	5¼	7⅜	12⅝	9¼	16¾	26
2+	1½	1¾	3¼	2⅞	4⅛	7
3+	⅝	¾	1⅜	1⅜	1⅞	3¼
4+	⅜	½	⅞	⅝	⅞	1½
5+	¼	¼	½	½	½	1
6+	⅛	¼	⅜	¼	¼	½
8+	⅛	⅛	¼	⅛	¼	⅜
10+	—	—	⅛	⅛	⅛	¼

*At the 3-foot focus setting, depth figures are very close to those for the infinity setting with a supplementary lens of the next higher power.

Simple Close-Ups

If you plan to take a number of close-ups using supplementary lenses and a non-reflex viewing camera, it will probably be worthwhile to make an accessory to help you put the camera at the proper distance and to frame the picture correctly. You can use a string, cardboard, or a wire frame to make devices of increasing versatility.

String "Rangefinder." You can use a ruler to measure close-up lens-to-subject distance, but it's much easier to carry a piece of string that you have measured ahead of time. Tape or tie one end of the string to the lens adapter ring and measure from the rim of the supplementary lens. Tie a knot in the string at the correct focusing distance for each close-up lens you plan to use. For example, if you plan to use a +2 and a +3 lens, simply tie one knot at 17 inches for the +2 lens and another at 12 inches for the +3 lens. This works for any camera, with any lens. If you have a focusing camera, leave the camera lens set at infinity. The knots are tied at distances equal to the focal length of the supplementary lenses. (See the supplementary lens information in the accompanying box.) You can make knots for as many distances as you have lenses. With the string held out straight from the front of the camera toward the subject, move your camera until the string is taut when the knot is at the subject. Then drop the string and take the picture.

The string method is simple and convenient for determining the proper focusing distance, but it does not show exactly what will be in the picture because the viewfinder is located above or beside the camera lens. This phenomenon is called "parallax." To correct for parallax, tip the camera slightly in the direc-

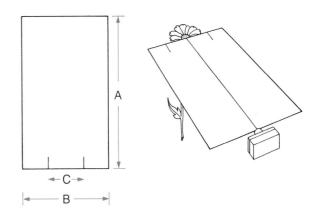

(A) Subject distance. (B) Width of the area included in the picture at subject distance "A". (C) Height of the area included; turn card vertically to see how much of subject will be included.

tion of the viewfinder after you have composed the picture. The closer you get to the subject, the more you need to tip the camera in order to get in the picture what you first saw through the viewfinder.

Cardboard Measuring Device. To make a simple measuring device from a piece of cardboard, determine the subject distance and the field size for your camera, close-up lens, and focus setting. Then cut the cardboard as shown in the accompanying illustration, and draw a line down the center. You need a different cardboard measuring device for each close-up lens because the subject distance and picture area vary with each close-up lens you use.

The following diagrams show how the dimensions of the measuring card can be found. First make a small card: *a* is the focal length of the lens, *b* is the film-format length, and *c* is the film-format height. Draw this out on a card, the length of which is *a* and the width is *b*. Next cut the large measuring card the length of the diopter power as shown below.

Power	Length—*a*	
	mm	inches
+1	1000	39⅜
+2	500	19¾
+3	333	13⅛
+4	250	9⅞
+5	200	7⅞

Parallax: At close subject distances, the viewfinder of a nonreflex camera does not show exactly what will be in the picture.

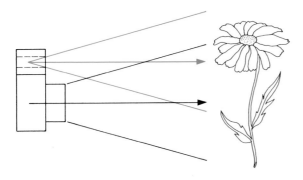

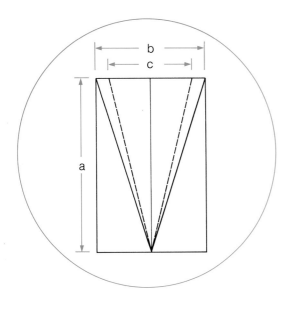

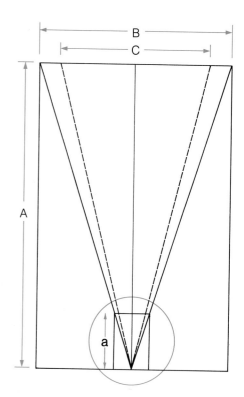

These diagrams show how to find the dimensions of the measuring card. (Left) First make a small card: a is the focal length of the lens, b is the film format length, and c is the film format height. (Right) Draw this out on a card whose length is A and whose width is B. Next, cut the large measuring card the length of the diopter power as shown on the preceding page. Place the small card along one end of the measuring card and line up the two center lines. Tape the small card in place and extend the heavy solid and broken lines as shown.

Place the small card along one end of the large measuring card and line up the two center lines. Tape the small card in place and extend the heavy solid line and the dashed line as shown.

Focal Frame

A focal frame is made from a piece of wood and a metal rod. The rod measures the distance to the subject and frames the area that will be in the picture. Each focal frame measures just one working distance and picture area, so you'll need a different focal frame for each close-up lens and focusing distance you plan to use.

To make the focal frame, you'll need some metal rod (⅜-inch aluminum stock is good), a hardwood board, and a few screws. If your camera has a 50 mm lens, find the dimensions for your focal frame in the

following instructions. If the focal length of your lens isn't in the table, take a test picture of two yardsticks crossed at right angles at the proper distance from the close-up lens (see table of data for supplementary lenses on 35 mm cameras). When you see the test picture, you will know the proper width (CC′) and height (BC and B′C′) for your frame.

Focal frames can also be used with close-up attachments on such larger format, fixed-focus cameras as instant print cameras. A version of the focal frame is used with movie cameras for titling.

When you use a focal frame, you can make a test to determine depth of field for your close-up equipment. Attach your camera to the focal frame, and slip the close-up lens over the camera lens. Set the lens at the opening you will be using for most of your

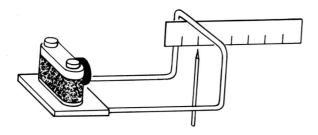

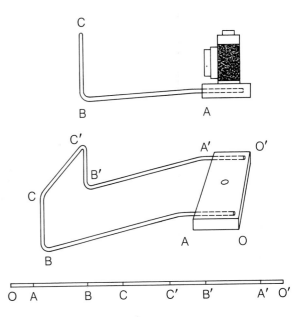

Test to determine depth of field for close-up equipment, using focal frame.

The letters in this diagram correspond to the letters in the table.

close-up work. Position a ruler near one inside edge of the frame as illustrated in the accompanying diagram. Point a pencil at the ruler in the plane of the frame, and take a picture. The results will indicate the area on the near and far side of the frame that will appear sharp in your close-ups.

For photographing three-dimensional objects, the focal frame is most practical if the focusing distance it measures is located slightly on the near side of the range of sharp focus. For this reason you should locate the frame about ten percent closer than the subject distance in the table "Data for Supplementary Lenses on 35 mm Cameras" in this article. The dimensions in the table for constructing a focal frame do this for you. If you want the sharpest focus right at the frame position, as for copying pictures, set the focusing scale of your camera at 15 feet instead of infinity.

Mark the rod with a hacksaw or file at all the bending points (see table: Focal-Frame Dimensions in Inches for 35 mm Cameras Focused at Infinity). To bend the rod, clamp it in a vise. Allow the mark to remain $\frac{3}{16}$ inch out from the jaws. Bend the rod with a wrench. Finish the bend with a hammer. Follow these steps to make your focal frame:

1. Bend A; check the angle against the drawing.

FOCAL-FRAME DIMENSIONS (INCHES)—35 mm CAMERAS FOCUSED AT INFINITY

50 mm Lens					40 mm Lens				
Sup. Lenses	Total Length	AB A'B'	BC B'C'	CC' OO'	Sup. Lenses	Total Length	AB A'B'	BC B'C'	CC' OO'
+3 & +3	31¼	6¼	3½	5¼	+3 & +3	33½	6¼	4⅛	6¼
+3 & +2	35⅞	7½	4⅛	6⅛	+3 & +2	38⅜	7½	4⅞	7⅛
+3 & +1	41½	9	4⅞	7¼	+3 & +1	45	9	5⅞	8¾
+3	52⅝	12⅛	6¼	9⅜	+3	56⅜	12⅛	7¼	11⅛
+2	77¼	18¾	9½	14¼	+2	82¾	18¾	11	16¾

Lens axis is about 1¼ inches above the base. For all frames, OA and O'A' are 3¼ inches. Close-up lens-to-frame distances given on the drawing apply to all cameras.

2. Bend B so that BC is at right angles to AO. Check with a square.
3. Bend a right angle at C.
4. Bend C′, B′, and A′ in the same manner as C, B, and A. Check with a square. AO and A′O′ should be parallel, and the distance between them should be equal to CC′.
5. Cut the wooden base to the outside dimensions (about 2 inches wider than the distance between C and C′).
6. Drill two ⅜-inch holes in the base for the rod ends.
7. Clamp the rod in a vise and drive the base onto both rod ends.
8. Clamp a straight board across the base so that a line along one edge comes where the lens axis will be (usually about 1¼ inches above the base).
9. Measure from this axis to the top bar of the frame, and check the distance against the table (this distance should equal one-half distance BC). Put a level on top of the top bar. Bend A or A′ up or down to make the top level. Rebend B or B′ to bring BC or B′C′ at right angles to AO and A′O′.
10. Now install four round-head screws in the base to position the camera. Install a ¼″ × 20 (20 threads per inch) stove bolt in the base, located so that it fits into the camera's tripod socket and holds the camera in place.

Close-Up Calculations

With a pocket calculator and the formulas in the accompanying boxes, you can determine factors for close-ups with supplementary lenses or with extensions. The formulas apply to the use of normal camera lenses. For retrofocus, and wide-angle and telephoto lenses, see alternate data in the articles, LENSES; PHOTOMACROGRAPHY; OPTICS; and SUPPLEMENTARY LENSES.

When making calculations, be sure that all measurements are in the same units.

1 metre	= 1000 mm	= 39⅜ inches
1 foot	= 30.5 cm	= 305 mm
1 inch	= 2.54 cm	= 25.4 mm

Close-Up Lighting

Establishing suitable lighting for revealing the form and texture of objects is an important technique in close-up photography. This is basically true in any kind of photography. The chief difference is that for close-up work the lamps have to be smaller.

Types of Lamps. Compactness is the key in choosing light sources for close-up photography. Because close-up photography in the field usually has to be done at $f/22$ for sufficient depth of field, exposures by direct sunlight are practical only with the fastest films, and then at relatively slow shutter speeds. To make faster speeds possible for moving or wind-blown subjects, artificial light is needed.

Synchronized photoflash units and compact electronic flash equipment are available for placing on the camera. Flashcubes, and AG-1B, 5B, 25B, and M3B photoflash bulbs supply adequate illumination. The blue bulbs should be used because of ambient daylight. Electronic flash lamps that yield a guide number of 35 to 50 for an ASA 25 film (daylight) are sufficiently powerful for most close-up lighting purposes.

There is a major consideration in selecting and arranging lighting units. They should provide enough light to permit photography at around $f/22$ at the greatest working distance, in order to permit sufficient depth of field. When photoflash bulbs are used, they should be synchronized at 1/250 or 1/500 sec. if at all possible to minimize subject movement.

Most small, portable electronic flash units have a flash duration of about 1/1500 sec. This is fast enough for most applications. However, for the close-up photography of rapidly moving creatures such as hummingbirds, 1/10,000 sec. is required.

Electronic flash lights are very much suited to the photography of living specimens. They are cool and permit short exposure times. Non-moving subjects can be photographed with tungsten illumination.

The usual photographic light sources produce beams that are too broad for close-up photography. They "wash out" fine detail and shape. Small sources provide much better modeling. Miniature desk lamps (high intensity) on flexible supports can serve to illuminate most close-up subjects. For ultra close-up photography, it is often better to use bare, clear-glass bulbs without reflectors. With such bare,

Because close-up photography in the field usually must be done at small apertures for sufficient depth, artificial light sources are almost always needed. Bare-bulb flash produces raw illumination for good close-up modeling.

Note the excellent three-dimensional rendition of shape and texture attainable with bare bulb alone. This results from the small size of the source and its architectural angulation—about 45 degrees above and to one side of the subject–lens axis.

Close-Up Photography

This live beetle was photographed in the field with only a bare bulb as a light source.

Once the record shot was made, a reflector was carefully moved up to within five inches of the subject. The beneficial effect of the fill-in illumination is quite apparent.

unfrosted lamps, the filament represents a compact light source.

The color temperature at which the lamps burn should be determined from manufacturers' data. Filters such as Kodak light balancing filters, or the equivalent, can be placed over the lens to provide the correct balance for color photography with various indoor color films.

Matte reflectors, such as a piece of the protective wrapping around Kodak sheet films, and small mirrors are better means for fill-in and accent illumination than additional lamps.

Measuring Exposures. Because of the small size of most close-up subjects and their proximity to the lens, it is often difficult to make exposure readings directly from them. A practical way to gauge an exposure is to make a closely approximate lighting setup. Then with the subject temporarily removed, put your hand or a Kodak neutral test card (gray side), or the equivalent, in its place. Make a reflected-light meter reading off the stand-in surface from a location as near to the lens as possible. Then replace the subject and make final adjustments in the lighting without appreciably changing the distance of the lamps. Alternatively, you can make a reading with an incident-light meter at the subject position.

Flash exposures usually have to be found by trial. Testing can be aided by calculating the lens and shutter settings from guide numbers. Data obtained for subject-lamp distances of fractions of a foot are reasonably close for indicating the range to be tested. Sample exposures for an ASA 25 film are: bare 15B photoflash bulb at 15.4 cm (6 inches), 1/500 sec. at a diaphragm setting of $f/22$, or 2500 BCPS electronic flash unit at 25.6 cm (10 inches), 1/60 sec. at $f/22$.

When the exposure cannot be adjusted by changing the shutter speed, other means for reducing the illumination are needed as working distances are

In order to properly display the silver, mirror-like bands on this scarab without picking up colors from other objects in the area, it was necessary to use another silver-colored object as a reflector. A crumpled, shiny, lead-foil cage was placed at the scarab's right, and light was thrown into the cage from the left; what the camera recorded was the reflection of the bright foil in the bands.

shortened. Sometimes the reflector on the flash holder can be omitted or blackened; this yields a bare-bulb exposure. Placing one or more thicknesses of handkerchief or translucent white plastic sheeting over the bulb is effective. Another expedient method is to partly cover the front of an electronic flash lamp with an improvised aluminum baffle. Some photographers use black tape for this purpose, but there is a likelihood that the tape will bake onto the lamp.

The accompanying table gives exposures for close-ups with flash using an ASA 64 film. For an ASA 25 film, use a lens opening one stop larger than the table indicates. For faster films, close down one stop for each doubling of film speed, or double the number of layers of handkerchief called for. With flashbulbs, use a shutter speed of 1/30 sec. With electronic flash, or between-the-lens shutters, use the synchronization speed called for with your camera.

Outdoor Exposure Measurement. When making flash close-ups outdoors during daylight hours, a small portion of the exposure effect on the film comes from the sky. This requires the use of daylight film. In order to avoid mixed illumination, photo-flash bulbs must be of the blue type; electronic flash illumination also has daylight quality. Daylight conditions, except full sunlight, do not produce enough ambient light to affect the dominant lighting from the flash. Therefore, exposures are the same regardless of the amount of daylight. However, under bright sunlight it is important to cast a shadow over the area photographed. You can usually shade the field with your body.

When possible, select a viewpoint from which the rays of the sun cause backlighting only. Then the sunlight need not be blocked, if separation of the subject from the background is desirable. A half-stop less exposure will be required. A lens hood should be used to avert flare from the sun.

When white flowers or other light-toned specimens are photographed, a half-stop reduction in the basic exposure is advisable. Another refinement that is often useful is to place a reflector opposite the flash to provide fill-in exposure. Slave lamps can also be utilized to provide supplementary illumination.

Using Slave Lamps. Backlighting can be introduced with artificial illumination. It is not essential but can sometimes be valuable. Backlighting with a slave flash will lighten the background and model the subject. Electronic flash slave units are available for firing remotely. In addition, it is possible to connect two regular units with a "Y" cord for direct synchronization.

CLOSE-UP FLASH EXPOSURES FOR ASA 64 FILM

| Type of Flash (with one layer of handkerchief) | Lens Opening* | |
	Subject Distance 10–20 inches	Subject Distance 30 inches
Flashbulbs		
Flashcube or magicube	f/16	f/11
AG-1B, shallow cylindrical reflector	f/16	f/11
AG-1B, polished bowl reflector	f/22	f/16
M2B, polished bowl reflector	f/22	f/16
M3B, 5B, or 25B, polished bowl reflector	f/22 with two layers of handkerchief	f/22
Electronic Flash		
Guide Numbers		
45–55 (700–1000 BCPS)	f/16	f/8
65–80 (1400–2000 BCPS)	f/16	f/11
95–110 (2800–4000 BCPS)	f/22	f/16
130–160 (5600–8000 BCPS)	f/22 with two layers of handkerchief	f/22

*For very light subjects, use one stop less exposure or place two layers of handkerchief over the flash reflector.

In photo at left, background is too dark and flower is insufficiently modeled. At right, a flash slave unit lightened the background and modeled the flower.

Basically, one light is sufficient for most close-ups. However, useful refinements are possible by an experienced photographer with a little ingenuity.

Basic Lighting Arrangement. There are three elements in good lighting:

1. The main light, which models the shape of the specimen or reveals its texture.
2. The fill-in illumination, which throws light into the dense shadows so that the film can record detail there, too.
3. The accent illumination, which serves either to separate the specimen from its surroundings or to lighten localized areas for tone contrast.

Mirrors or matte reflectors are usually best for supplying the first two elements. Using them pre-vents multiple shadows that usually occur when more than one lamp is employed. However, the use of two lamps can often result in the good delineation of symmetrical subjects.

The formula for good lighting is a simple one: move the main light around until the key details are visible from the camera viewpoint; use fill-in or accent illumination only when necessary.

Lighting Angles. The main illumination outdoors, and also in sets simulating outdoor scenes, should yield a natural effect. Usually, the light should come from the camera side of the subject. Animals should face in the general direction of the main light. Plants, even when taken indoors for photography, should be lighted from an angle above the lens.

Indoor lighting, which is logically unnatural or artificial, can come from almost any direction. In

As a general rule, some modification of architectural lighting furnishes good modeling. A light close to the front plane of the subject produces glancing illumination for a good rendition of surface texture. Photo by Bill Pinch.

general, it should be from above the lens, and the effect should make the front of the object brighter than the rear. Strong, dramatic lightings are permissible indoors.

Architectural Lighting. Architectural lighting comes from an angle 45° to the front and 45° above the subject. As a general rule, some modification of this furnishes good modeling. A light close to the front plane of the subject produces glancing illumination for a good rendition of surface texture.

Axial Lighting. Axial lighting comes from very close to the subject-lens axis. A ring light (a flash that encircles the lens) yields such illumination. It is almost shadowless but does produce some modeling in surfaces closely parallel to the axis. Flat surfaces perpendicular to the axis may reflect light directly back into the lens. The ring light is useful for photographing details in depressions or crevices that are difficult to reach or illuminate with other types of lamps.

Coins, cameos, and inscriptions can often be recorded by axial lighting. A clean, thin sheet of glass is placed in front of the camera between the subject and the lens and at 45° to the subject-lens axis. Illumination is beamed toward the subject side of the glass at 90° to this axis. The photographs are made through the glass. (See the accompanying diagram.)

Transmission Lighting. This type of lighting is produced by reflecting or focusing a beam of light through the back of a specimen. It is chiefly a photomacrographic technique but can be used for any semi-transparent or translucent objects. In close-up photography, the specimen is usually placed on a piece of transilluminated opal glass, or on clear glass through which a spotlight is focused. It is important to provide a black paper mask up to the edges of the camera field in order to preclude flare from stray light.

Lighting Contrast. The ratio of the brightness from the main light (plus any spilled light) to that of the fill-in illumination is called the lighting contrast. The close-up photographer should learn to gauge this ratio visually, because it is difficult to calculate or measure reflected intensities from small subjects.

Axial lighting for small subjects.

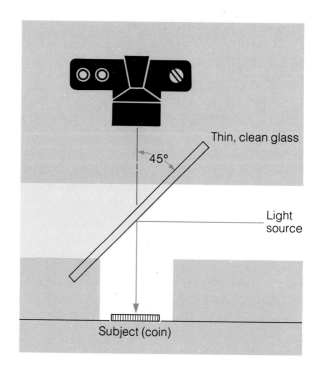

Thin, clean glass

45°

Light source

Subject (coin)

Close-Up Photography

1:1

1:2

1:3

1:4

This cuneiform tablet was lighted with two lamps so that the lighting ratio of main light to fill light could be accurately determined. The ratios are given with each example, and the result enables the reader to gauge the effects of lighting contrasts.

When two equivalent lamps are used at different distances, their intensities follow the inverse square law closely enough for practical purposes. In essence, the law says that the illumination ratio varies with the *square* of the distance ratio. For example, with lamps of equal intensity at 8 and 16 inches, the distance ratio is 8:16, which reduces to 1:2, or ½. Square the distance ratio: $(½)^2 = ¼$. The more distant lamp producess ¼ as much illumination at the subject as the closer lamp. Similarly, with lamps at 5 and 15 inches, the distance ratio is 1:3, and the illumination ratio is $(⅓)^2 = ⅑$, or 1:9—the close

This collage is a combination of two photographs cut up and combined to give the effect of an image produced by a fish-eye lens. Photo by Stanley W. Cowan.

lamp is effectively nine times brighter than the distant lamp.

For practical purposes, spilled light can be neglected in establishing a lighting ratio by measuring lamp distances. The accompanying illustrations were prepared with two lamps for illustrating lighting contrasts. The ratios are given under each picture. As a general rule, a 3:1 ratio is suitable for black-and-white photography, and 2:1 for color photography.

• *See also:* BELLOWS; BELLOWS EXTENSION; LENSES; OPTICS; PHOTOMACROGRAPHY; SUPPLEMENTARY LENSES.

Further Reading: Croy, Otto R. *Camera Close Up.* Garden City, NY: Amphoto, 1970;———*Croy's Creative Photomicrography.* Garden City, NY: Amphoto, 1968; Eastman Kodak Co., ed. *Close-up Photography and Photomacrography.* Rochester, NY: Eastman Kodak Co., 1977; Owens, William, ed. *Close-Up Photography.* Los Angeles, CA: Petersen Publishing Co., 1975; Simmons, Robert. *Close-Up Photography and Copying.* Garden City, NY: Amphoto, 1961.

Collage

Along with assemblage, montage, and photomontage, collage is one of the most widely used methods of physically altering and constructing photographic images, as distinguished from chemical and optical methods of alteration. The terms are taken from painting and sculpture; they may refer to the act or process of creating an image, or to the end result itself. Although strict definitions are not possible, the following distinctions are commonly made in reference to photography.

Collage

The art of collage refers to cutting one or more photographs into many pieces and reassembling all or some of the pieces to form a new image. The cut-and-assembled result is presented as an object in itself—no attempt is made to conceal the technique used. In fact, the shapes and spacing of the cut pieces may be intended to contribute to the visual impact. The final image may emphasize some aspect of the original subject; it may completely change its character; or it may create a completely new subject.

Basic collage approaches include cutting the image into regular or varied pieces, shifting the spacing or arrangement, or eliminating some elements of the total image. More than one original image is often used. The aim is to increase the expressiveness of the final result, not to create a puzzle or sheer graphic effect.

Assemblage

Assemblage consists of combining photographic elements with objects and bits and pieces of other materials—both two- and three-dimensional. The total universe of reproduced images and physical objects provides raw material for assemblage—torn cloth, paper, pebbles, matchboxes, bottle caps, paintings, photos. The list is endless. The composite result may be mounted on a flat surface like a low relief, or may form a three-dimensional sculpture piece.

Montage

Montage refers to the combining of various two-dimensional image-elements to form a single, unified image. The elements are used for their visual and graphic content, and may be the products of other media (drawing, painting, graphic arts processes, etc.) as well as photography.

428

Photomontage

The term photomontage is sometimes used to identify a composite in which all elements are photographic. Usually the edges of the individual pieces are shaped, painted over, or made as nearly invisible as possible. The result is then rephotographed so that examination of the final image will not reveal how it was constructed. Some photomontages are not collages—they are produced on one sheet of paper from a number of negatives. The junctures between the images may be sharp (created by masks on the surface of the paper), or they may blend into each other (by masking done on the negative).

All three methods of construction are primarily used for artistic purposes. Photomontage also has technical applications, as in the pasting and blending together of many separate aerial photographs to form a single image of an area being surveyed or mapped by photography.

• *See also:* COMBINATION PRINTING; MONTAGE; SPECIAL EFFECTS.

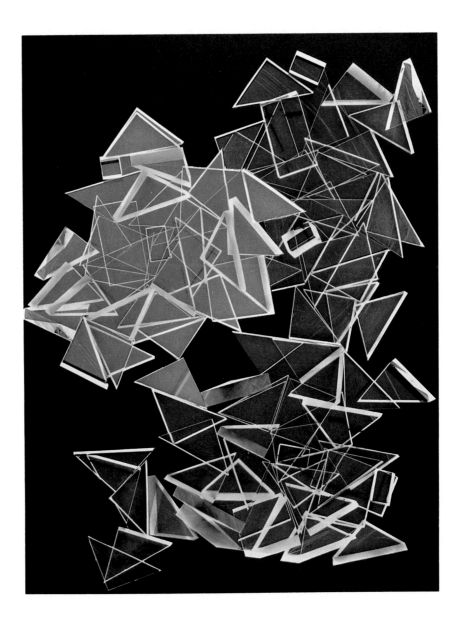

This is a collage of three photograms printed on color paper. The photograms were made by placing glass crystal ornaments directly on the paper and exposing through colored filters. Then the prints were cut up and combined in the design shown here, and copied to produce a slide. Photo by Frederick C. Enrich.

Collage

Collage

The photographs on these pages demonstrate the basic approach to collage, which involves cutting the image into regular or varied pieces and shifting the spacing or arrangement. More complex collages might be created by combining two or more photographs and/or by eliminating some elements of the total image. The aim is to increase the expressiveness of the final result, not to create a puzzle or a purely graphic effect.

Collage

Collodion

A solution of pyroxylin (gun cotton) in a mixture of ethyl alcohol and ether. Collodion was used in certain photographic processes as a carrier for sensitive silver salts, both in the wet form (wet collodion process) and in the dry form (collodion emulsion). The latter was used until fairly recently in the manufacture of printing-out papers; the wet collodion process was used in recent years only by photoengravers but is now totally obsolete.

Formula: Variable, mainly dinitrocellulose
Molecular Weight: Variable

Thick, syrupy liquid, colorless or faintly yellow. The solvents evaporate very rapidly when exposed to air, leaving a tough, colorless film.

DANGER: Collodion is very volatile and very flammable, and in some cases explosive. Keep tightly closed, away from flame, and in a cool place.

• *See also:* AMBROTYPE; ARCHER, FREDERICK SCOTT; FERROTYPE; WET COLLODION PROCESS.

"Camp of the 5th Dragoon Guards," by Roger Fenton. Published January 1, 1856, this is a classic example of one of the many photographs Fenton took on wet collodion plates during the Crimean War—one of the first major uses of the collodion wet photo process under field conditions. Photo courtesy International Museum of Photography at George Eastman House.

Collodion

Collotype

 **Colorama**

The collotype, or photogelatin graphic arts process, is a lithographic method of printing used to reproduce continuous-tone images. Unlike the regularly spaced dot pattern of a halftone screen, the image on the collotype plate is broken up into a completely random pattern. The collotype pattern will not combine with any regular patterns in the image being reproduced, such as a brick wall, to create the interference pattern called moiré. This makes excellent reproductions with virtually no visible grain.

The collotype is made on a glass plate coated with gelatin containing a bichromate. The plate is baked so that the gelatin reticulates, or breaks up into a pattern of almost microscopic cracks. This coating is then exposed by contact with a continuous-tone negative. Light passing through the negative causes the gelatin to harden in proportion to the intensity of light. The plate is then washed to remove the bichromate and is treated with a glycerine solution. The less hardened portions of the gelatin corresponding to the lighter tones of the subject become moist during this treatment. These areas will repel the greasy lithographic ink proportionately when the ink is applied to the plate. The hardened portions of the gelatin will readily accept ink into the microscopic reticulation cracks. When the paper is pressed against the plate, the ink image is transferred to the paper.

Because of the delicate nature of the gelatin surface, the image begins to deteriorate noticeably after about 1000 copies are made from the plate. This makes the process unsuitable for long printing runs and, therefore, expensive. In spite of this limitation, the results can be so beautiful that the collotype is still used for short runs of fine art prints or illustrations for special or limited editions of books.

In halftone color reproductions, four plates are generally used to print four colors of ink. In collotype reproductions of fine art originals, many more plates and inks may be used to achieve very accurate renditions of all colors.

• *See also:* PHOTOMECHANICAL REPRODUCTION METHODS.

A Kodak colorama is a large mural color transparency. The most famous colorama is displayed high over the vast interior of Grand Central Terminal in New York City. The first colorama was displayed on May 15, 1950, and nearly 400 different coloramas have been exhibited in the first 27 years of the display's existence. Currently, ten new colorama pictures are displayed each year. Each transparency has an area larger than that of over 100,000 35 mm slides, and is illuminated by mercury-vapor-type, metal arc lights. Originally, cold-cathode tube lighting was used; the change (1973) resulted in a reduction of nearly one-third in the amount of electricity used, with a slight increase in brightness.

Many of the pictures taken for the colorama are taken by professional photographers who work in Kodak's Photo Illustration Department. They have had to solve nearly every photographic problem imaginable for this project over the past quarter century. The pictures are generally taken on a

This was a colorama display high over the interior of New York's Grand Central Station. Smaller coloramas are displayed at Monroe County Airport in Rochester, N.Y., at Hollywood Lab in California, and at the Eastman Kodak Oak Brook, Ill., headquarters. Colorama photo by Ralph J. Amdursky.

This mountain view in Peru, displayed in Grand Central Station, was timed to coincide with a photo show on Peru at the Kodak Gallery in New York City.

Kodak color negative film, and enlarged onto color print film. A few coloramas have been enlarged from color transparencies. Because conventional-size negatives would not produce sharp enlargements 60 feet long at the time the colorama was started, a camera adapted to using 8″ × 20″ sheets of Kodak Ektacolor professional film was especially made to expose negatives for the colorama. Various lenses were used, from 14 inches to over 36 inches in focal length. Depth-of-focus problems with such lenses have often been severe; scenes that could be photographed with relative ease using smaller cameras

This is a black-and-white reproduction of the first colorama made. It was mounted in Grand Central Station in New York City on May 15, 1950. Entitled "Keep the Childhood Story in Snapshots," it is the first example of a theme that was, until recently, common to all coloramas: a picture-taking situation in a striking setting. This colorama is arranged as a triptych—a large central photograph flanked by two smaller ones.

become much more difficult with such a heavy, cumbersome camera.

In recent years, as Kodak color negative films have been improved in sharpness and fine-grain characteristics, the use of smaller negatives has become possible without lowering the quality level of the colorama transparencies. Currently, many of the negatives are being made with special roll-film cameras that make negatives about 2⅛″ × 6¾″ using 2¼″-wide Kodak Vericolor and Kodacolor films. This has made it much easier for the photographers —not only in reducing depth-of-field problems, but in making pictures possible that could not be taken with the original, cumbersome cameras.

Several coloramas have been made in the last several years from 35 mm Kodachrome slide originals. Enlarged internegatives are made from the slides and then enlarged to colorama size. This represents a total enlargement of over 500×.

A special enlarger has been made that projects the negatives onto a Kodak color print film. Since the whole colorama is much too large to make in one piece (no film in the world is made 18 feet wide), it is made of forty vertical strips 18 feet long and 19 inches wide. The strips are carefully registered, spliced together with transparent tape, and rolled onto an 18-foot-long spool. The spool, with the transparency rolled up on it, is placed in a special packing box and shipped from Rochester to New York City.

Four specialists in Grand Central Terminal remove the old transparency and hoist the new one on its spool to a platform on the smallest "railway car" in Grand Central. The bottom end of the spool rides a small truck down a tiny railway, unwinding the transparency as it goes. The colorama transparency

In recent years, several coloramas have been made from 35 mm Kodachrome slide originals. Enlarged internegatives made from the slides are then further enlarged to colorama size. This African scene was one of the earliest 35 mm coloramas. Photo by Ernst Haas.

itself is held tightly by springs attached to the huge steel supporting frame. The change is made in the early hours of the morning, and the lights go on behind the newly hung transparency in time for the 8 a.m. Monday opening. The whole cycle is repeated every five weeks.

Photographing a Colorama

Photographer Bob Phillips received the assignment to photograph the Rockettes, the internationally famous precision dance team at the Radio City Music Hall in Manhattan.

Weeks of careful planning preceded the day when the picture was made. It was obviously impractical to shoot the carefully planned scene during an actual show, so it had to be done early in the morning. When the theater closed at midnight following the last show, the 36 Rockettes who would be in the picture slept in their Radio City dormitory so they would be on hand for an early-morning set call.

During the night, three tons of equipment were moved into Radio City, including 88 professional electronic-flash condenser units—the greatest con-

In the past, coloramas of spectacular picture-taking situations were often used. More recently, the trend has been to feature only the scenic views or timely special events.

Colorama

One of the most spectacular of the colorama pictures, Bob Phillips's photograph of the Rockettes chorus line, required weeks of preplanning as well as last-minute improvisation.

centration of such lighting ever assembled for a single picture at that time. Each of the dozens of flash heads had to be carefully positioned, wired to its power supply, and test-fired. Every piece of equipment down to the last connecting cord and piece of tape had to be in the right place at the right time.

While electricians rigged the lighting units, stagehands shifted 55' × 90' drops into place. A blue nylon reflector curtain was rigged to bounce the lights. Window mannequins from 5th Avenue stores were dressed in Rockette costumes and placed on the stage for test exposures. Stagehands locked arms and "stood in" for the Rockettes for some of the tests. The actual dancers would occupy a 72-foot length of stage. By adjusting swings and tilts, the photographer was able to get everything in focus with a 16-inch lens set at $f/20$.

By 4:30 in the morning, the test shots were completed and rushed to a lab for processing, to make sure lighting, model positioning, and exposure were satisfactory.

When the girls appeared a few hours later, they had to change their usual order. Normally, the taller girls stand in the center of the stage to give the audience the appearance of a straight, even line. To produce the desired perspective in the picture,
though, the tallest girls had to be placed farthest from the camera.

With girls, lights, camera, and background all in order and ready to shoot, the photographer noticed a distracting light bouncing from the orchestra pit. He tore up a sheet of black paper and suspended a piece of it from tape stuck *inside* the camera bellows. According to the ground-glass image, the problem was solved.

The result was one of the most spectacular of the colorama pictures. It was used not only in Grand Central Station but also on the front and back covers of a record album featuring Radio City talent.

An Exterior Colorama

Kodak photographer Lee Howick encountered a number of problems in trying to photograph Hong Kong Harbor at dusk. After much searching, he found the right spot for his camera—at the end of a steep, rugged, rocky road that led to a cliff high over Victoria.

It was so windy on the cliff that a makeshift windscreen made out of focusing cloths was needed to prevent the big camera from moving during the time exposure that would be necessary for the dusk shot.

High winds and poor light presented special problems for Lee Howick's photograph of Hong Kong Harbor at dusk. This exposure was based on experience—it was too dark to read the meter.

One of the best times to take "night" pictures is after the sun has gone down but before the sky has turned completely black. When the light level was about the same in the sky and in the lights of the city, it was too dark to even see the numbers on the exposure meter. The exposure was estimated from experience at 60 seconds, with a 14-inch lens set at $f/16$. A few streaks of lights from moving boats show on the water, but the big boats at anchor are tack-sharp.

These are just two examples. Colorama pictures have been taken from helicopters and airplanes, under water, in snowy mountains, as well as inside locations all over the world; each has presented new problems to be solved.

• *See also:* LARGE COLOR PRINTS AND TRANSPARENCIES; MURALS.

Color Film Processing

Most color films can be processed in individual darkrooms with excellent results. (The major exception is Kodachrome film, which requires complex processing that can only be successfully achieved by automatic equipment in a laboratory.) Although there are a great number of color films available, there are just a few processing methods with which most manufacturers make their films compatible. The major requirements for color film processing are the necessary solutions—which are readily available—and a means of controlling solution temperature accurately. Beyond that, color film processing is simply a matter of following instructions exactly, working in standardized, repeatable ways, and avoiding careless errors.

How a Color Film Process Works

Color films are made up of several emulsion layers, each of which is sensitive to a particular color of light. In general, three layers are used: one sensitive to blue light, one sensitive to green light, and one sensitive to red light. After exposure, development of a negative film produces a negative silver image in each emulsion layer. At the same time, color dyes are formed along with the silver images. The dyes are complementary colors to the layer sensitivities: yellow in the blue-sensitive layer, magenta in the green-sensitive layer, and cyan in the red-sensitive layer. The dyes will remain in the film to form the final image. The silver image is bleached, and then removed by a fixing solution. After washing and drying, the negatives are ready for printing.

Color Negative Film

Red-sensitive layers of film contain silver halide crystals (triangles) and colorless globules (circles) of dye-forming substances called couplers. Green- and blue-sensitive layers are similarly composed. In addition to the colorless dye image-forming couplers, the red- and green-sensitive layers contain lightly colored coupler globules that form positive color-correcting masks during processing, which gives improved color reproductions in the prints made from the negatives. These statements refer to Kodak color negative films. Those made by other manufacturers may differ.

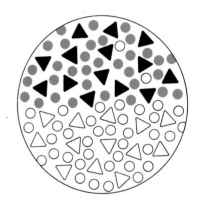

When the exposed silver image is developed, cyan dye is simultaneously formed in direct proportion to the amount of silver developed. Both silver and dye images are negative. At the same time, magenta dye forms with the silver image developed in the green-sensitive layer; yellow dye forms with the silver developed in the blue-sensitive layer.

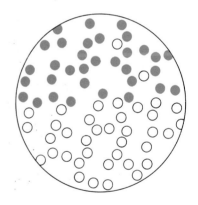

Silver is bleached, then all silver is removed by fixer. The dye image remains, along with some residual color couplers that compensate for variations in the printing characteristics of the image dyes. Residual couplers give a color negative an overall orange-brown cast.

Color positive films require reversal processing to produce transparencies or slides. During the first development, only a silver image, without dyes, is produced. The developed image is negative; the undeveloped silver remaining in each emulsion layer corresponds to a positive image. The undeveloped silver is sensitized (made developable) either by exposure to light or by chemical means. Then it is developed, and dyes are simultaneously formed.

This silver image and the corresponding dye image are both positives. All the silver is then bleached and fixed away, and the film is washed and dried.

Color film processes involve a few more chemicals and a bit more time than black-and-white film developing processes, but they are only somewhat more difficult to carry out. A major process used for color negative films is process C-41. The most modern process for developing color positive films is

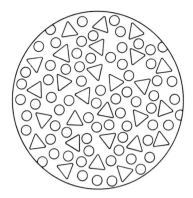

The red-sensitive layer of film contains silver halide crystals and color-forming globules of coupler. Other layers have similar composition.

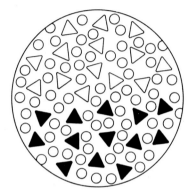

First developer reduces exposed halides to metallic silver, forming a black-and-white negative image. Unexposed halides are then sensitized chemically or by exposure to white light. In modern color processes, this takes place in a fogging color developer.

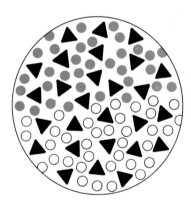

The color developer reduces the remaining halides to silver and forms corresponding amounts of cyan dye. The image produced is positive. In other layers, magenta and yellow dyes are formed in proportion to the silver being developed there in this step. The coupler globules that are not converted to dye remain colorless in the emulsion.

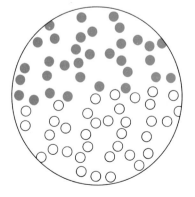

All silver is bleached and fixed away. Dyes remaining in the emulsion layers change white light used for viewing or projection to produce a full-color positive image of the original subject.

process E-6. For purposes of comparison, the steps in these processes are listed in the accompanying table, along with the steps of process K-14 used by laboratories for Kodachrome film processing. The procedures for carrying out the C-41 and E-6 processes are given later in this article, after a discussion of equipment and general color film processing considerations.

Processing Equipment

Although it is not practical for individuals to process Kodachrome films, the processes for Kodak Ektachrome, Vericolor II, Kodacolor II, and similar films are not difficult to accomplish. Prepared Kodak color film processing chemicals are readily available, and no special equipment is required. The instruction sheets packaged with the chemicals contain the detailed processing steps, and strict adherence to them is necessary if repeatable good results are to be obtained.

There are various kinds of automatic and semiautomatic color-film processing machines avail-

able from photographic-equipment manufacturers. But for the individual, sink-line equipment is both practical and affordable for medium- and small-scale processing.

For processing in a sink-line procedure, the sheets of film are placed in film hangers. It is advisable to use separators to space the hangers for improved processing uniformity. When 4″ × 5″ or 5″ × 7″ films are processed in 3½-gallon tanks, multiple hangers are often used. If some multiple hangers are used along with single-sheet hangers, they should be interspaced with a dummy single sheet (sheet of acetate cut to size) in a hanger to avoid uneven processing of the single sheet due to currents caused by the multiple-hanger frame.

Color roll films can be processed on stainless steel reels in small tanks. A number of reels can also be loaded in the processing rack that fits into a 3½-gallon processing tank. The processing rack accommodates up to 30 reels of 126-, 135-, or 828-size film; or up to 24 reels of 127-size film; or up to 18 reels of 120- or 620-size film. Reel sizes can be intermixed as necessary.

Processing hangers, reels, and tanks are made of corrosion-resistant materials, usually stainless steel.

COMPARISON OF STANDARD COLOR FILM PROCESSES

Negative Process C-41	Positive Processes	
	E-6	K-14 *(Kodachrome)*
Developer	Developer	Rem-Jet (black backing removal)
Bleach	Wash	Rinse
Wash	Reversal Bath	First Developer
Fixer	Color Developer	Wash
Wash	Conditioner	Red Re-exposure
Stabilizer	Bleach	Cyan Developer
Dry	Fixer	Wash
	Wash	Blue Re-exposure
	Stabilizer	Yellow Developer
	Dry	Wash
		Magenta Fogging Developer
		Wash
		Bleach
		Fixer
		Wash
		Dry

sult the instructions packaged with the color-processing kit or chemicals being used.

Simple and uniform agitation for sheet film can be provided by using bursts of nitrogen gas bubbles that work their way up through the processing solutions. Equipment available for this purpose includes the Kodak intermittent gaseous burst valve, model 90B. To distribute the gas supplied by the valve evenly over the bottom of the tank, a gas distributor for an 8″ × 10″ hard rubber tank is needed, unless provision for gas distribution is made by the tank itself, as in the case of the Kodak No. 3FD processing tank. Nitrogen is available in compressed form in cylindrical tanks. To complete the gaseous-burst agitation system, a pressure-reducing valve and interconnecting pipe and tubing are used.

Since there is no oxidation problem with solutions other than developers, oil-free compressed air can be used instead of nitrogen with these solutions. In process E-6, nitrogen must not be used for agitation in the bleach; this solution requires air for regeneration.

After processing, the reels and film hangers should be washed thoroughly and dried completely before they are used again. Processing tanks made of hard rubber or polypropylene are satisfactory for every processing solution. Stainless steel tanks are satisfactory if the joints are welded with other than tin solder. The stainless steel tank used for the bleach solution should be lined with tested plastic or other inert material if the bleach is to remain in the tank for long periods. If the bleach solution is transferred to a storage bottle immediately following the process, an unlined stainless steel tank can be used for the bleach.

Agitation

Proper agitation is important throughout color processing, but it is especially critical during the initial development step. Depending on the processing equipment and the particular color process, the recommended agitation techniques will vary. Con-

Hard rubber tank, 8″ × 10″ (3½ gallons), and lid.

Color Film Processing

It is not essential to have gas- or air-burst agitation for color film processing. Excellent results can be obtained with manual agitation of sheet film hangers. Roll films and 35 mm films on stainless steel and similar reels should not receive gaseous burst agitation because the film surfaces are too closely spaced for the even flow of solutions with this method of agitation. Manual agitation methods are used instead.

Replenishment

As processing solutions are used, either additional development time and other adjustments are required or the solutions must be replenished. For occasional and small-scale processing, time adjustments are most convenient. But when a photographer finds that film-processing volume necessitates replacing solutions more often than once each week, he or she should consider replenishment as a more economical and controllable system. Proper use of replenishers increases the capacity of the working solutions to a maximum and increases their life considerably. There is also a saving of mixing time. Also, improved control of color balance and speed is obtained by making gradual chemical compensation for the use and aging of the solutions.

Washing

Adequate washing facilities are important. Preferably, the rate of water flow should be about 0.4 gallon per minute per square foot of film processed; 0.3 is considered minimum. That is, satisfactory washing is achieved under average processing conditions by a complete change of water about every minute. When separate wash tanks are provided, each should have a minimum flow rate providing a complete change of water every 3 minutes or, for the final wash, two full changes every 3 minutes. To help prevent processing solutions from contaminating each other, use wash tanks that allow the top bars of the film hangers to be submerged. A complete change of water means that the flow should provide a volume of water equal to the tank capacity during the specified time.

Temperature Control

Temperature tolerances, particularly those for the developers, are critical, and appreciable deviation from them may result in speed and color-balance changes. In addition, physical defects such as reticulation of the emulsion or frilling along the edge of the film are apt to occur if the temperatures of the solutions are too high or if there is a big change of temperature from one solution to another.

Never should the temperature of the first developer be allowed to vary more than ½ F (¼ F for process C-41) from the recommended temperature. Use of an accurate thermometer is recommended.

It is important to control the temperature of the wash water. With process E-6, it is desirable that the temperature of the rinsing and washing operations be within the range of 33.5 to 39 C (92 to 102 F). With process C-41, the range is 24 to 40.5 C (75 to

105 F). Washing tends to become less efficient as the water temperature is reduced. Film-laden processing racks that have been placed in wash water of lower-than-normal temperature may cool the following chemical solutions excessively.

When color films are used only in small quantities, it is possible to get along with manual adjustment of temperature. For example, the drain of the darkroom sink can be fitted with a standpipe, and water from an ordinary mixing faucet can be allowed to overflow from the washing tank and surround the processing tanks to the level of the standpipe. With such an arrangement, a thermometer placed in the water flow and near the developer must be watched constantly to make sure that varying loads on the water-supply lines do not change the temperature of the mixture.

When color films must be processed on a production basis, a more accurate and dependable temperature-control system is almost a necessity in preventing mistakes and delays. One such system uses a thermostatic water mixer. For a single 3½-gallon processing line, the mixer should have a capacity of at least 3 gallons per minute, should normally control the water temperature within plus or minus ½ F or less, and should recover quickly from pressure variations in the hot- and cold-water lines.

With a thermostatic mixing valve, the temperature of the existing cold-water supply in the summer months must, of course, be at least as low as, and preferably lower than, the temperature required of the mixture. In areas where the cold water is warmer than the temperature required of the mixture, an auxiliary cooling system is necessary. This in turn necessitates a few additional fittings to permit switching the unit from the normal use of existing hot- and cold-water supplies to the use of cold and artificially cooled water. Also, some communities have codes requiring that check valves, such as those on the Kodak thermostatic mixing valve unit, be installed in mixing-valve supply lines.

Preparing Solutions

It is desirable to mix the solutions in a mixing container, such as a stainless steel pail or a large plastic container, rather than in the processing tanks themselves. This procedure is a safeguard against leaving any undissolved chemical particles in the corners of processing tanks. A propeller-type electric mixer is helpful for rapid, yet thorough, mixing of large volumes of solutions. However, avoid using the shaft at an angle that whips an excessive amount of air into the solution. The mixing pail and all other items contacting the solutions should be thoroughly rinsed before each solution is prepared.

To help avoid contamination, mix color-film processing solutions in the order in which they are used in processing. Do not mix more than one solution at a time in a single area. Carefully follow the mixing instructions given with each chemical preparation. Improper mixing can cause off-color results, and may also impair the keeping qualities of the solutions. The best way to avoid contamination is to have a separate mixing vessel for each solution. It is particularly important to start mixing in the specified volume of water. Clean, sediment-free tap water should be used for mixing all solutions; if necessary, it should be filtered. Nominally priced filters are available for attachment to water taps; larger units can be installed in water-supply lines.

When solutions are left in processing tanks, use floating lids and dust covers to prevent contamination and to minimize aerial oxidation. Check the temperatures of all solutions, particularly the developers, just before use.

For maximum life, unused or partially used developers or developer replenishers should be stored in full, stoppered glass bottles. In tanks with floating lids, the developer life is significantly reduced. Other processing solutions will last 8 to 12 weeks, depending on the particular processing solution. Each process instruction sheet states the recommended storage times for the chemicals used. Processing solutions should be prepared in quantities that will allow their full utilization before the storage time is exhausted.

Precautions in Mixing Developers. When mixing developers for color processes, be sure to follow the mixing instructions and place the designated volume of water in the mixing tank before adding any chemicals. If specified, small bottles containing liquid chemicals should be rinsed carefully with solution from the mixing vessel so that all of the concentrated liquid is transferred to the solution. Some liquid chemicals do not mix readily with water; it is a good idea to use a propeller-type electric mixer and to stir for a few minutes after the liquid has seemingly dissolved. The liquid is not completely dissolved if oil-like particles or droplets are floating on the surface. After a homogeneous solution has been obtained by mixing, add the remainder of the chemicals slowly, stirring them until they are completely dissolved. Avoid excessive mixing, however.

Viewing Wet Transparencies

Color transparencies of satisfactory density and color balance often appear somewhat opaque and too warm in color balance while they are still wet. When it is necessary to evaluate transparencies without waiting for them to dry, the opalescence that causes these effects can be eliminated temporarily by bathing the transparencies in Kodak rapid fixer concentrate (undiluted Solution A only—do not add Solution B). Immerse the transparencies in the concentrate for 1 minute after fixing; after viewing them, continue normally with the wash following the fixing step.

Viewing Negatives

Ektacolor, Vericolor, and Kodacolor negatives have an overall orange to light reddish-tan cast because colored couplers are left in the film to provide color-correction masks. This color, which appears as a minimum density even in the unexposed edges of the film, is normal and should be disregarded in appraising a negative. The effective printing colors of the negative are complementary to those of the original subject.

It is difficult to judge either the individual colors or the general color balance in a color negative. Saturated colors are distinguishable; for example, yellow is reproduced as purple, red as green, and so forth; but pastel tints, cool colors, and near-neutral colors are difficult to distinguish in the negative. However, the relationships among the three negative records may vary slightly from one subject or processing to another and still be well within the range of adjustment during printing.

Judging Negative Exposure. Generally, the same criteria can be used for judging color negatives as are used for judging black-and-white negatives: The highlights should not be blocked up, and there should be sufficient detail in the shadow areas.

To help evaluate the exposure of a color negative, a side-by-side comparison can be made between the color negative and an ordinary black-and-white negative of the same subject. To simulate the overall appearance of the color negative, an unexposed but processed piece of the color negative film being evaluated can be placed over the black-and-white negative. In addition, the negatives can be viewed through a green separation filter such as the Kodak Wratten filter No. 61, or the equivalent, which will further reduce color differences. Minor color differences will remain, but in areas such as the forehead of a portrait subject, it will be easy to compare densities.

A more precise check on exposure level can be made with a Kodak color densitometer or a suitable electronic densitometer equipped with a filter such as a Kodak Wratten filter No. 92 or a Kodak densitometer filter set MM (Certified). Depending somewhat on the nature of the subject and lighting, a normally exposed Vericolor II or Kodacolor II negative read through the red filter should have approximately the densities shown in the accompanying table. (The densities for Ektacolor negatives are about 0.05 to 0.10 higher than those given.) All values apply for exposures with recommended light sources and assume correct processing of the negatives.

Negatives having densities much below those listed will be underexposed and will not yield prints of satisfactory shadow gradation. The exposure latitude of Kodacolor II, Vericolor II, and Ektacolor films allows densities above those listed. Satisfactory

NEGATIVE DENSITIES	
Reference Area	**Red Filter Density**
The gray side of the Kodak neutral test card receiving the same illumination as the subject	0.70 to 0.90
The lightest step (the darkest in the negative) of a Kodak paper gray scale receiving the same illumination as the subject	1.15 to 1.35
The highest diffuse density in a normally lighted forehead—	
light complexion	1.00 to 1.30
dark complexion	0.70 to 1.10
Because of the extreme range in normal skin color, the red density values given for a normally lighted forehead should be used only as a guide. For greatest likelihood of normal exposure, the use of a Kodak neutral test card (gray side), or the equivalent is recommended.	

prints can be made from negatives that have densities resulting from an exposure of about 1 stop more than is required to obtain the densities listed.

The recommended developing time should not be changed in an attempt to alter the contrast of certain subjects. Overdevelopment does not increase contrast appreciably, but it may cause unequal increases in fog and graininess in all three emulsion layers.

Processing Faults

Reversal Films. Properly handled, Ekachrome films give results of outstanding quality. It is possible through errors in processing, however, to upset the normal color balance with consequent off-color results. The list in the following section will help you to recognize faults that may occur in using the E-6 process.

Color Negative Films. Since it is difficult to appraise color negatives, certain processing defects may not be evident until the negatives are printed. One of these is an overall reddish fog. Such fog is objectionable because it imparts a greenish cast to the shadows of the print. If present, this defect may have been caused by any of the following:

1. Overdevelopment caused by a higher-than-normal temperature or a prolonged developing time.
2. Handling the film under a green safelight. Process color negative film in complete darkness, and load sheet film in complete darkness.
3. Contamination of the developer by fixer.
4. Omitting the hardener and fixer, or shortening the time of any of the steps between the developer and the bleach. Actually, these errors impart a reddish stain to the negative, rather than a true fog, but the stain and fog appear alike.

It may be helpful to keep on hand an unexposed but normally processed sheet or roll of the color negative film you use regularly. The minimum density of any negative suspected of fog or stain can then be checked against this standard.

Reversal Color Processing—Process E-6

Compared to other color reversal film processes, process E-6 offers decreased processing time, greater

SUMMARY OF STEPS FOR PROCESS E-6 SINK LINE

Solution or Procedure	Remarks	Temperature C	Temperature F	Time in Minutes*	Total Time End of Step
1. First Developer	First three	38 ± 0.3	100.4 ± 0.5	6†	6
2. First Wash‡	steps in	33 to 39	92 to 102	2	8
3. Reversal Bath	total darkness	33 to 39	92 to 102	2	10
Remaining steps can be done in normal room light.					
4. Color Developer	—	38 ± 0.6	100.4 ± 1.1	6	16
5. Conditioner	—	33 to 39	92 to 102	2	18
6. Bleach	—	33 to 39	92 to 102	6	24
7. Fixer	—	33 to 39	92 to 102	4	28
8. Final Wash‡	Two tanks;	33 to 39	92 to 102	2	30
	Counterflow	33 to 39	92 to 102	2	32
9. Stabilizer	—	Ambient		½	32½
10. Dry	Remove films from hangers or reels before drying	Not over 60	Not over 140		

*Include drain time of 10 seconds in each step.

†Time for nitrogen agitation for sheet films. Increase time by 15 seconds when only manual agitation is used. Manual agitation must be used for roll films in reels.

‡For flowing water washes. Nonflowing water washes can be used as follows: for the first wash, use a single tank filled with water at 25 to 39 C (77 to 102 F). Replace this wash after two processing runs, regardless of the quantity of film processed. For the final wash, use three tanks filled with water at 20 to 39 C (68 to 102 F) for two minutes each. Replace the water in all three tanks after four processing runs, regardless of the total quantity of film processed. Do not use any final wash tank for a first wash tank. All wash tanks should be drained at the end of each day and left empty overnight.

process stability, and conservation of water and energy when operated to capacity. The seven chemical solutions are supplied as liquid concentrates, and there are only nine wet steps in all.

Processing Steps. The following are the steps for process E-6:

1. *First Developer*: This solution converts the silver halides exposed in the camera to metallic silver. The temperature is more critical here than it is for the other solutions and washes—38.0 $\pm$ 0.3 C (100.4 $\pm$ 0.5 F). As with process E-3, nitrogen-burst agitation is recommended with sheet films, but not with roll films on reels.

2. *First Wash:* This wash stops the action of the first developer and washes out chemicals from it to avoid contamination of the reversal bath. Water flowing at 7.6 litres (2 gallons) per minute is recommended for this and the final wash, but nonflowing washes can be used to conserve water and energy.

3. *Reversal Bath:* This bath fogs the remaining silver halides that were not converted to metallic silver in the first developer. Reversal exposure by light is not required as it was in some other reversal processes. After the film has been in this bath for 1 minute, the remainder of the process can be conducted in normal room light.

4. *Color Developer:* In this solution, the silver halides fogged in the reversal bath are developed to positive silver images. As the developing agent reduces the silver halides to metallic silver, it is converted to an oxidized form that reacts with dye couplers incorporated in the film emulsion layers. In this way, cyan, magenta, and yellow dye images are formed in the bottom, middle, and top emulsion layers, respectively.

   As with the first developer, nitrogen-burst agitation can be used with sheet films only, not with roll films on reels.

5. *Conditioner:* This solution prepares the metallic silver formed in the first and color developers for oxidation to silver halide in the following bleach step. It also helps protect the acidity of the bleach solution by reducing carry-over of the alkaline color developer into the bleach.

6. *Bleach:* This nonferricyanide solution oxidizes all the metallic silver formed during the first and color developing steps. Both the negative and positive silver images are converted to silver salts.

   In the bleach and the following fixer step, oil-free compressed air, either continuous or in bursts, is recommended. Nitrogen agitation must not be substituted. Note that air is needed to regenerate the bleach; in processing with manual agitation, sufficient aeration is provided by the lift and reimmersion cycles.

7. *Fixer:* This solution converts the silver salts formed in the bleach to water-soluble silver thiosulfates. Note that there is no rinse between the bleach and fixer; silver removal is more efficient without it.

8. *Final Wash:* This wash removes dissolved silver salts and processing chemicals, to prevent them from affecting the processed film adversely. Again, water flowing at 7.6 litres (2 gallons) per minute is recommended, but nonflowing washes can be used to conserve water and energy.

9. *Stabilizer:* This solution is necessary for optimum dye stability. It contains a wetting agent for spot-free drying.

Replenishment of Solutions. With proper replenishment and care to avoid dirt and oxidation of the developers, reversal bath, and conditioner, the processing solutions can be used for extended periods of time. For small-scale users, adjustments of the time in the first developer enable it to be used to a capacity of 0.44 square metre per litre (18 square feet per gallon). Other solutions have greater capacity.

PROCESS E-6—VISUAL EXAMINATION OF PROCESSED FILM

Appearance of Film	Probable Fault
Very High Maximum Density (no image apparent)	First developer and color developer reversed. First developer omitted.
Dark Overall	Inadequate time or low temperature in first developer. First developer diluted, exhausted, or underreplenished. Color developer starter added to first developer.
Very Dark (overall or in random areas)	Bleach or fixer (or both) omitted, reversed, diluted, exhausted, or underreplenished.
Light Overall	Excessive time or high temperature in first developer. Film fogged by light prior to processing. First developer too concentrated. First developer overreplenished or starter omitted in preparation of working (tank) solution. First developer contaminated with color developer.
Light Overall, Blue Color Balance	First developer contaminated with fixer.
Overall Density Variation from Batch to Batch	Inconsistencies in time, temperature, agitation, or replenishment of first developer.
Blue	Reversal bath too concentrated. Color developer alkalinity too low. Excessive color developer starter used in preparing tank solution. Color developer replenisher mixed.
Cyan	First and color developers underreplenished.
Yellow	Color developer alkalinity too high. Color developer starter added to first developer. Color developer replenisher mixed with only Part A.
Low Densities Blue-Green, High Densities Yellow	Color developer contaminated with first developer. Color developer contaminated with fixer.
Blue-Red with High Maximum Density	Color developer replenisher too dilute.
Green	Reversal bath exhausted, diluted, or underreplenished. Film fogged by green safelight. Wash used between reversal bath and color developer.
Very Yellow	Film exposed through base. Film fogged by room lights during first developer step.
Cross-Width Bar Marks (When using stainless steel reels)	Gaseous burst agitation used in first developer.
Scum and Dirt*	Stabilizer requires replacement. (Replace once a week.) Filters in recirculating systems require replacement. (Change once a week.) Air filters in dryer need changing. Dirt in other solutions. Use floating covers on tanks and replenisher solutions whenever possible. Stabilizer too concentrated.

*Foreign particles may be due to buildup of fungus or algae in processing solutions or wash tanks. To minimize this buildup, drain water wash tanks when not in use. When the processing equipment will be out of use for more than 6 weeks, drain and rinse the reversal bath tank and replenisher storage tanks. To remove fungus or algae, scrub the tanks with a stiff bristle brush and a sodium hypochlorite solution (1 part household bleach to 9 parts water). Rinse the tank thoroughly with water to remove the last traces of sodium hypochlorite solution. Use a 50-micrometer (or finer) filter in the water supply.

Process Adjustments for Increased Speed. Each of the process E-6 Ektachrome films should be exposed at the exposure index for which it was designed. When a film is underexposed and then over-developed, there is a loss in the maximum density, a decrease in exposure latitude, a color balance shift, and a significant increase in contrast. Overexposed film that is underdeveloped gives low toe (highlight) contrast and a color balance shift. If these sacrifices in quality can be tolerated, compensation for use of an exposure index differing from normal can be made simply by adjusting the first development time.

Film Exposure	First Development Time
One stop under	Approx. 8 minutes
(Normal)	(6 minutes)
One stop over	Approx. 4 minutes

Negative Color Processing—Process C-41

Kodak Flexicolor chemicals for process C-41, or the equivalent, are used to process Kodak Vericolor II professional films and Kodacolor II films. Some color negative films of other manufacturers are also designed for C-41 processing. Ektacolor and Vericolor films must not be processed in C-41 solutions or their emulsions will come off the film base.

Process C-41 operates at 37.8 C (100 F). There are six wet steps, and wet process time varies with the equipment used. Films may be processed in small and large tanks, in dip-and-dunk processors, and in continuous processing machines. The accom-

DEVELOPER CAPACITY—PROCESS

	Developer Capacity Rolls or Sheets per	
Film Size	Gallon	3½ Gallons
110–12	24	84
110–20	24	84
126–12	16	56
126–20	16	56
135–20	16	56
135–36	16	56
828	16	56
127	16	56
120, 620	16	56
116, 616	8	28
220	8	28
4″ × 5″	32	112
5″ × 7″	16	56
8″ × 10″	8	28

panying table lists the steps and times for processing with tanks in a sink line.

Capacity of Solutions. If not replenished, the Flexicolor developer for process C-41 can be used to process the number of rolls or sheets of film shown in the following table. The bleach, fixer, and stabilizer solutions have *twice* the capacities shown.

• *See also:* BLEACH-FIX; CHEMISTRY OF PHOTOGRAPHY; COLOR FILMS; DIRECT POSITIVE PROCESSING; SALVAGING COLOR FILMS PROCESSED AS BLACK-AND-WHITE.

Further Reading: Carroll, John S. *Amphoto Color Film and Processing Data Book,* rev. ed. Garden City, NY: Amphoto, 1975; Clerc, L. *Colour Processes.* Englewood Cliffs, NJ: Prentice-Hall, Inc., 1974; Current, Ira B. *How to Process Color Films at Home,* 2nd ed. Garden City, NY: Amphoto, 1968.

PROCESS C-41, SINK LINE, SUMMARY OF STEPS

Solution or Procedure	Remarks	Temperature C	F	Time in Min*	Total Min at End of Step
1. Developer	Total darkness	37.8 ± 0.15	100 ± ¼	3¼†	3¼
2. Bleach	Total darkness	24–41	75–105	6½	9¾
	Remaining steps can be done in normal room light.				
3. Wash	Running Water	24–41	75–105	3¼	13
4. Fixer		24–41	75–105	6½	19½
5. Wash	Running Water	24–41	75–105	3¼	22¾
6. Stabilizer		24–41	75–105	1½	24¼
7. Dry	Remove film from reels or hangers	24–43	75–110	10–20	

*Include a 10-second drain time in each step.
†For a replenished process.

Color Films

Films for color photography are of two types, negative and reversal. Reversal films produce positive transparencies when processed; negative films produce images from which paper or film prints must be made in order to obtain positive representations of the subject. Most color films are intended to produce a visually correct representation of subject colors. Therefore, they are sensitized, or given a *color balance* which will produce the desired results when used with illumination of a specified color temperature. A *daylight* type emulsion is balanced for 5500 K illumination. Films for use with tungsten illumination are designated either *type A,* for 3400 K light, or *type B* for 3200 K illumination. Most tungsten-balanced color films have type B emulsions.

Exposing a color film by illumination that is too high in color temperature produces an image that has too great a proportion of cool (bluish) colors and lacks a proper proportion of warm (red and yellowish) colors. Exposing a film to illumination that is too low in color temperature produces the opposite result—too much red and yellow, not enough blue. A film may be exposed by light of a different color temperature if appropriate filters are used to change the light entering the lens to match the color balance of the emulsion. Filters may be used in front of the lens or over the light sources. Depending upon their strength and color composition, they may make either major or minor changes in the spectral composition of the light. The camera use of filters with color film is discussed in the article COLOR PHOTOGRAPHY.

Color films are far more sensitive to variations in exposure than black-and-white films. A color negative film has an exposure latitude of only about one stop underexposure and a few stops overexposure; this degree of variation can be compensated for in the printing process in most cases. A color transparency film has an exposure latitude of only about one-half stop over- or underexposure before noticeable highlight or shadow loss occurs, with a possible color shift in the image. Most color films also exhibit reciprocity failure long before a black-and-white film would do so. Many color films will begin to exhibit reciprocity effects with exposures slower than one-tenth of a second. Some films are designed especially for use with slow speeds, from about one-tenth of a second to sixty seconds, with controllable reciprocity effect.

There are a number of special-purpose color films. Those designed for making duplicate negatives, duplicate transparencies, or internegatives (for prints from transparencies or other positive images) have lower contrast characteristics than camera-type films. This is to avoid loss of shadow or highlight detail in the duplicate or copy image. Films for photomicrography have increased contrast to make small variations in subject color more clearly visible. False-color films are sensitized so that infrared wavelengths outside the visible spectrum will affect the film. The final image does not reproduce normal subject colors, but rather produces colors that also represent the amount of invisible energy emitted or reflected by various parts of the subject.

Color Film Composition

The eye can be made to see almost any color by stimulating it with various proportions of red, green,

Films with daylight type emulsion are balanced for 5500 K illumination, and are intended for use where the main source of light is the sun plus open skylight. When adding artificial light, be sure to use electronic flash or blue flashbulbs or cubes, which are balanced for daylight. Daylight type films may also be used indoors with electronic flash, blue bulbs, or blue flashcubes.

and blue light. A color film analyzes the subject in terms of these three colors; it makes a record of the proportion of red, green, and blue in each area of the subject. In order to do this, most color films are designed with three basic emulsion layers. In conventional color films, the top layer of emulsion is sensitive to blue light, the middle layer to green light, and the bottom layer to red light. In actual film manufacture, each of these emulsion layers may be divided into two or more emulsion layers. For example, there may be both high-speed and low-speed green-sensitive layers in the middle of the film, and high-speed and low-speed red-sensitive layers at the bottom of the film. All of the layers are silver halide emulsions. Because it is not possible to completely eliminate the blue sensitivity of the green- and red-

Films designed for use with tungsten illumination are balanced for either 3400 K or 3200 K light. Clear flashbulbs or cubes must be used in situations requiring additional light sources, as in photo at left. Tungsten film may be exposed under daylight conditions if a suitable conversion filter is used to change the light entering the lens to match the color balance of the emulsion.

Color Films

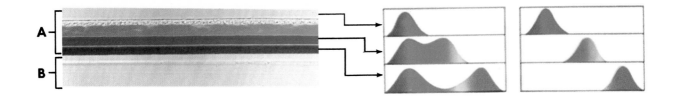

Color film composition. (Left) A cross section of fully exposed, processed (Kodak Ektachrome) color transparency film, magnified 1000X, shows blue-, green-, and red-sensitive layers (A) in which complementary yellow, magenta, and cyan dyes have formed during processing. Sublayer (B) adheres emulsions to the film base . Antihalation dye may be in the sublayer or on the back of the film base; it is removed during processing. (Center) Inherent color sensitivities of the three emulsion layers. (Right) Effective color separation obtained in the three layers when the yellow filter layer is included just below the blue-sensitive emulsion. The filter layer is removed during processing. Color negative films have essentially the same composition.

sensitive emulsions, a yellow filter layer is located just below the blue-sensitive emulsion. The yellow filter prevents any blue light from reaching the lower emulsion layers; it is removed during processing so that its color is not present to affect the appearance of the final image.

Color Image Formation

The first image produced upon development of a reversal color film is a silver negative image of the subject, just as produced by black-and-white films. The color in a film image results from dyes that are formed by color couplers activated by the products of the silver image development. (A color coupler is a chemical that combines with oxidized color developer to form a dye.) When a color negative film is processed, the color dyes are produced at the same time the negative silver image is developed. The silver image is then bleached away to leave only a negative color image of the subject. Most color negative films also have residual color couplers that give an overall orange-brown appearance to the image. This coloration helps improve the printing characteristics of the negative.

Essential Color Film Processing Steps
Negative film
1. Color developer
2. Bleach*
3. Fixer
Reversal film
1. Black-and-white developer

2. Fogging color developer
3. Bleach*
4. Fixer

With a transparency film, the first processing steps are essentially the same as those for black-and-white reversal processing. That is, a negative silver image is developed and bleached, the remaining silver halide is exposed to white light or chemically sensitized, and then it is developed to produce a positive silver image. The dyes of the color transparency image are formed along with the development of the positive silver image. Finally, the silver image is bleached away, leaving only the color dye image in the film. The amount of dye formed in each area of each layer is proportional to the density of the silver image in that part of the layer.

Color Couplers and Dyes

Dye-forming color couplers are incorporated in the emulsion layers of color negative films and in virtually all color transparency films. They are usually colorless until activated by the by-products of development. The one notable exception to this arrangement is Kodachrome film, for which color couplers are included in the color developers. In the color development stages of the Kodachrome film process, a separate color developer is used for each layer. Because of the complexity of the process and the need for extreme control throughout, this film

---

*The bleach and fixer steps may be combined.

Color Films

Image Formation in Color Negative Film

Original subject, represented schematically by color patches.

Cross section of color negative film. Silver halide grains exposed in the camera have been developed to produce negative silver images. Simultaneously, dyes are formed with color couplers in each emulsion layer.

Cross section of color negative film after the silver grains have been bleached.
* Residual color couplers.

Color negative.

Residual color couplers removed to illustrate that colors formed in the negative are complements of the original subject colors.

must be processed by a machine specifically designed for the purpose. Almost all other color films may be processed by the photographer in his own darkroom. Aside from the use of the proper solutions for a given emulsion, the primary concern in processing color film is to maintain the developer temperature with strict accuracy. A temperature variation of as little as one-half degree can cause a noticeable shift in the color balance of the final image. Although color shifts may be corrected in negative-positive printing, they cannot be corrected in transparencies. As with black-and-white films, some reversal color films can be push-processed by extending the time in the first developer to compensate for exposures made at higher-than-normal exposure indexes.

The dye color formed in each emulsion layer is complementary to the color sensitivity of that layer. Yellow dye is formed in the blue-sensitive layer; magenta dye in the green-sensitive layer; and cyan dye in the red-sensitive layer. These colors act subtractively when white light is shown through a negative for printing or through a transparency for viewing. The density of a dye determines what proportion of a single component of white light—red, green, or blue—is allowed to pass.

The yellow dye controls the blue component of the light. As the dye density increases, the amount of blue light transmitted decreases, and the visual effect of the red and green components increases proportionately. The eye interprets the red-green mix as yellow if their effects are equal, or as various oranges or lime greens if other dyes in the film change the red-green balance.

Image Formation in Color Reversal Film

Original subject, represented schematically by color patches.

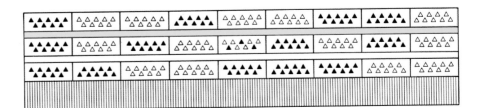

Cross section of color material after silver halide grains exposed to the subject have been developed to produce negative silver images.

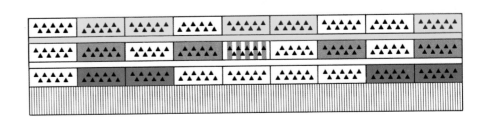

Cross section of color material after the remaining silver halide grains have been exposed to light (or subjected to chemical reversal) and developed to produce positive silver and dye images.

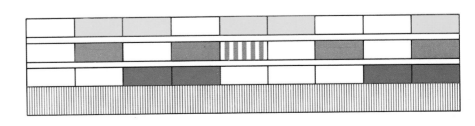

Cross section of color material after both negative and positive silver images have been removed, leaving only the positive dye images.

Dye images as they appear after processing is complete.

The magenta dye absorbs green light and lets proportionately more blue and red light pass. A maximum density of magenta dye absorbs almost all the green light; thus only red and blue light reach the eye, which "sees" a maximum intensity magenta as a result.

The cyan dye absorbs red light, letting blue and green light pass.

When two dyes are present in the same image area, only one color of light can pass. For example, maximum cyan density removes all red light; when maximum magenta density, removing all green light, is also present, only blue light reaches the eye. If the two dyes are in unequal proportions, the blue will either have some red mixed with it (less cyan dye), or some green mixed with it (less magenta dye). Any color of blue can be produced, depending on the cyan-magenta dye ratio.

Reds are produced by various proportions of magenta and yellow dyes, because they absorb green and blue light. Greens result from cyan and yellow dyes absorbing red and blue light. In this way the proper mixture of blue, green, and red is allowed to pass to the printing paper, or to the screen or eye in the case of viewing a positive image. The final result is an image in which all the original subject colors can be seen. For further explanation see the articles COLOR THEORY and VISION.

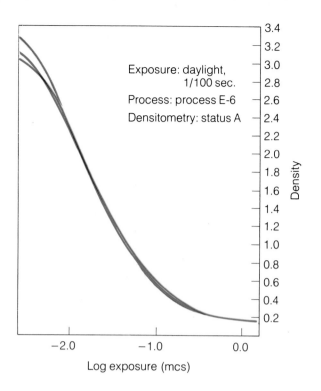

Exposure: daylight,
1/100 sec.

Process: process E-6

Densitometry: status A

Log exposure (mcs)

*The characteristic curves of a color transparency film (above)
and a color negative film (below). The densities of red- ,
green- , and blue-sensitive layers are measured and graphed
separately. The red layer contains various amounts of red-
absorbing cyan dye in proportion to the exposure received.*

Instant Print Films. Self-processing, color instant print films are similar to conventional films in that they contain three silver halide emulsion layers of blue-, green-, and red-sensitivity. Each layer has associated color couplers, or color-forming components. As the silver image in each layer is developed, the proper amount of color for a positive image is simultaneously formed. The dyes move by diffusion into an adjacent receiving layer where they form the final image. (*See:* DIFFUSION TRANSFER PROCESS.)

Other Characteristics of Color Films

For illustrative, artistic, and most practical photography, it is seldom necessary to obtain sensitometric and image-structure data for a color film. It is usually sufficient to know the color balance and ASA speed of a film, and to make some test shots to adjust exposure and filtration for a given subject, equipment, and processing procedure. However, there are some kinds of scientific and technical photography in which the photographer must know precisely the color response of a film and its ability to record detail. Some major manufacturers supply data sheets upon request, which give sensitometric and image-structure data for their color films. The kinds of data are discussed here.

Characteristic Curves. As with black-and-white films, the response of a color film emulsion to variations in exposure or processing can be graphed.

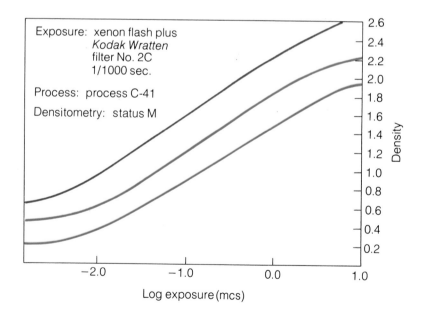

Exposure: xenon flash plus
Kodak Wratten
filter No. 2C
1/1000 sec.

Process: process C-41

Densitometry: status M

Log exposure (mcs)

Measurements are made through the red status filter on a color densitometer; increased amount of dye removes more red light, which is effectively greater density. The blue status filter is used to measure yellow dye densities in the blue-sensitive emulsion layer, while the green filter is used to measure magenta dye densities in the green-sensitive layer.

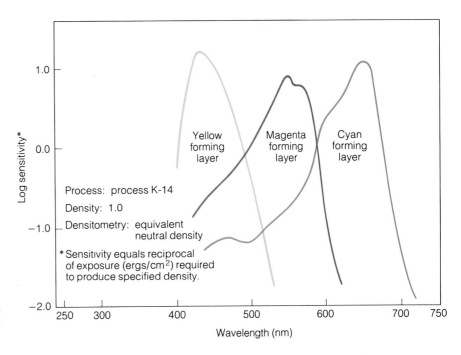

Spectral sensitivity curves of the emulsion layers of a color transparency film.

When a controlled series of increasing exposures is given with a specified illumination, the resulting graph is a characteristic curve of the film's response with the stated processing. Because color films have individual blue-, green-, and red-sensitive layers, there are actually three curves on the graph, one for each layer.

The curves are produced by making density readings through blue, green, and red *status filters*. When used with a densitometer that has proper unfiltered spectral response, status A filters adjust the illumination for reading the densities of color positive emulsions, such as slide films and transparency films. Status M filters adjust the densitometer for reading densities in color negative emulsions. All readings must be taken from an area of constant tonality. This is automatically provided when test strips are exposed in a sensitometer. When comparisons of films used under typical conditions are made, it is common either to include a neutral gray test card to provide a constant area for density readings, or to be sure that a key color area such as a subject's face is identically illuminated in all the test exposures.

As with characteristic curves for black-and-white emulsions, the slope of the straight line portion of the curve indicates the relative contrast characteristics of a film; the steeper the slope, the greater the inherent contrast of the film. The curve for a transparency film is high at the left and descends to the right with increasing exposure; the densest parts of the positive image correspond to the areas of the subject that gave the least exposure. Ideally, the red, green, and blue curves would lie exactly together. In actuality, they coincide at some points and separate at others. The useful exposure range of the film lies on the straight line and toe portions of the composite curve, where the three lines are most closely spaced.

The graph for a negative film is low on the left —the least exposure produces the least density in a negative—and rises to the right with exposure increase. The individual red, green, and blue curves are distinctly separated. This reflects two factors. First, for proper printing balance of a neutral tone, different densities of cyan, magenta, and yellow dyes are required. Second, the residual color couplers in a processed color negative affect the density readings to differing degrees, depending on whether the red, green, or blue filter is being used; this effect is constant regardless of the amount of exposure a particular area of the emulsion receives. In a properly exposed and processed color negative film, the lines

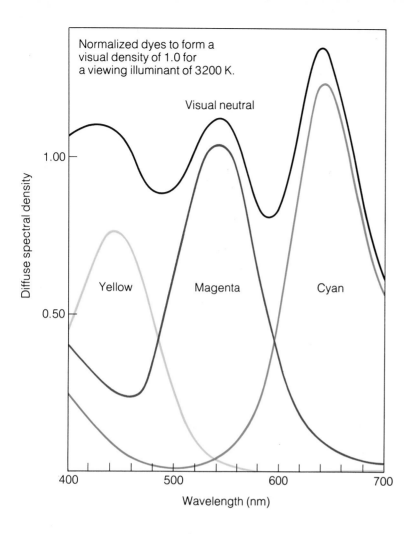

Diffuse spectral density

Normalized dyes to form a
visual density of 1.0 for
a viewing illuminant of 3200 K.

Visual neutral

Yellow   Magenta   Cyan

1.00

0.50

400   500   600   700

Wavelength (nm)

Spectral dye density curves of a color trans-
parency film.

retain their proportional spacing and remain parallel through that portion of the graph which indicates the useful exposure range of the film.

Spectral Sensitivity Curves. In a color film data sheet, spectral sensitivity curves show the response of each emulsion layer to a series of exposures throughout the visible spectrum. Each exposure is to a single wavelength of light, every 10 nanometres throughout the visible spectrum (i.e., 450, 460, 470, etc. nm). The response of each layer is expressed as "log sensitivity." Mathematically, sensitivity equals the reciprocal of the exposure that would be required to produce an equivalent neutral density of 1.0.

Spectral Dye Density Curves. For positive-image films, these curves represent the dye densities required to achieve a visual neutral density of 1.0 for exposures to various wavelength bands. The viewing illuminant must be specified for the curves to be meaningful. Reversal sheet films are measured with a 5000 K illuminant because they are most often viewed on illuminators. Reversal roll films and slide films, which are generally viewed by projection, are measured with a 3200 K illuminant.

Spectral dye density curves for negative films represent typical densities for a mid-scale neutral subject and for minimum density.

Resolving Power. The ability of a film to record fine detail distinguishably is its resolving power, or resolution. Resolving power is determined by photographing targets composed of groups of bars and spaces of equal width. Test charts contain many groups of targets of successively narrower bar widths, expressed as so many lines per millimetre. The processed film is examined with a microscope; the greatest number of lines per millimetre that can be distinguished is the resolving power of the film. Usually, a film is tested with both low-contrast and high-contrast targets. The contrast ratio for either of the test charts is the ratio of the luminance of the bars of each test pattern to the luminance of the surround. A standard low-contrast bar-to-surround ratio is 1.6:1; a high-contrast ratio is 1000:1. With high-contrast resolution figures, various descriptive adjectives can be used to classify a film's resolving power.

Lines per mm Resolved with 1000:1 Target Contrast	Resolving Power Classification
50 or below	Low
63, 80	Medium
100, 125	High
160, 200	Very High
250, 320, 400, 500	Extremely High
630 or above	Ultra High

Modulation Transfer Function. As subject details of a given contrast become finer and more closely spaced, they are recorded with progressively less contrast. In part this is due to light scattering within the emulsion; dark areas receive additional exposure from light scattered in adjacent light areas. This raises the density of the dark area and lowers the density of the light area, so the difference between the two is reduced; visually the result is lowered contrast between the two.

Modulation transfer function is a measurement method used to describe the ability of films (and other elements in any photographic system) to reproduce the detail contained in an object. The limits of film to form a perfect reproduction are caused by diffusion of light within the film emulsion layers. To obtain modulation transfer function (MTF) data, patterns having a sinusoidal variation in illuminance in one direction are exposed onto the film. The modulation of each pattern, M_o, can be expressed mathematically in terms of exposure. After processing, the photographic image is scaled in a microdensitometer, the densities of the trace are interpreted in terms of exposure, and the effective modulation of the image, M_i, is calculated. The modulation trans-

fer factor is the ratio of the modulation of the developed image to the modulation of the exposing pattern, $\frac{M_i}{M_o}$. The modulation transfer curve shows a plot of these factors (usually on a logarithmic scale) versus the corresponding spatial frequency of each pattern in cycles per millimetre. Usually the modulation transfer factor is expressed as a percent response as in the accompanying illustration.

For all films over most of the line-space frequencies, as the line width and spacing gets smaller, the density differences between them decrease, and thus the contrast decreases. Because the distinguishability of fine detail requires contrast, the data thus developed can be used to predict final image-detail characteristics.

It would be expected that the maximum response would be 100 percent, but because of development effects, the actual response is often slightly greater than 100 percent at low spatial frequencies usually between one and fifteen sine wave lines per millimetre.

Graininess; Granularity. A color photographic image is made up of specks of dye formed around developing silver halide crystals. As the image is enlarged, these specks become apparent—instead of a smooth, textureless appearance, the additive effect of the soft-edged dye particles causes a colored salt-and-pepper appearance. This visual appearance is called graininess. A specific measure of graininess is called granularity.

To measure granularity, a section of film is measured by a scanning microdensitometer through a very small circular aperture. The variations in density plot as a series of sharp-peaked, irregular waves. The degree of difference of the density variations from a reference value is calculated by a statistical method known as taking the root mean square (RMS). The correlation between these RMS values and classification adjectives is as follows:

Diffuse RMS Granularity Value	Graininess Classification
45, 50, 55	Very Coarse
33, 36, 39, 42	Coarse
26, 28, 30	Moderately Coarse
21, 22, 24	Medium
16, 17, 18, 19, 20	Fine
11, 12, 13, 14, 15	Very Fine
6, 7, 8, 9, 10	Extremely Fine
less than 5, 5	Micro Fine

As with black-and-white films, fast color films are usually grainier than slow films. Also, there is not an exact correlation between the granularity ratings and the graininess visible in different types of films. For example, a color reversal film and a color negative film may have the same granularity rating, but the color negative film may exhibit more graininess than the reversal film.

Storage and Care of Color Films

Photographic films are perishable products subject to damage by high temperatures, high relative humidities, and harmful gases. Unprocessed color films are more seriously affected than black-and-white films, since adverse storage conditions usually affect the three emulsion layers to different degrees, causing a change in speed, color balance, and contrast. Adverse storage conditions usually cause much larger changes in the color quality and speed of the film than does any permissible variation in manufacturing. Moisture at any temperature may also cause various physical effects such as mottle, abrasions, and static patterns. To prevent detrimental effects on unprocessed film, proper storage is necessary both before and after exposure.

Processed films also require proper storage and care to increase their longevity. It must be emphasized, however, that the quality of film processing plays an important part in the longevity of a transparency or negative. Film processing recommendations should be followed very closely.

Storage of Unprocessed Films. Follow the film storage recommendations printed on the original package. "Protect from heat" is the recommendation for Kodak color films intended mainly for nonprofessional use. These films do not require refrigeration, but they must be protected from heat. Keep them away from direct sun, steam pipes, and so forth. If desired, you may refrigerate them. Kodak professional color films should always be stored under refrigeration at 13 C (55 F) or lower. Some special-purpose color films should be stored at −18 to −23 C (0 to −10 F). Always follow the recommendations on the package.

Since high relative humidities are usually more harmful than high temperatures, protection from moisture is essential. To provide this protection, Kodak color films are sold in heat-sealed foil pouches, snap-cover plastic cans, and taped metal or

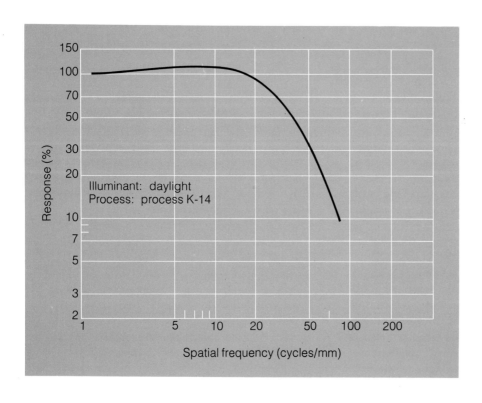

Modulation transfer curve of a color transparency film. Image contrast rises slightly, then decreases rapidly as the lines of the test target become narrower and more closely spaced (spatial frequency increases).

plastic cans. Original packages, therefore, should not be opened until the film is to be used. The foil pouches containing sheet film are vapor-tight but not necessarily 100 percent lighttight and, therefore, should not be subjected to normal room light.

Continue to protect all color films from excessive heat after they have been removed from the recommended storage condition. When color films are carried in a car, put them in an insulated picnic bag or chest, and place it behind the front seat. The temperature in a closed automobile parked in the sun for several hours can reach 71 C (160 F) and can seriously affect the quality of the film. Dry ice or other cold packs should be added to the container to keep Kodak professional color films cool.

CAUTION: Moisture may condense on film surfaces if boxes of refrigerated film are opened too soon. To avoid possible damage to the film, packages removed from cold storage should be allowed to reach approximate room temperature before they are opened. The times suggested in the accompanying table are for single packages, standing on end or on edge. Cold packages stacked flat on top of each other require much longer times to warm up.

WARM-UP TIMES FOR COLOR FILMS

Type of Color Film Package	Warm-Up Times (hours)	
	For 11 C (20 F) Rise	For 42 C (75 F) Rise
Roll film, including 828	½	1
135 magazines; 110 and 126 cartridges	1	1½
10-sheet box	1	1½
50-sheet box	2	3
35 mm, any length	3	5

After the film is removed from refrigeration, remember to protect it from adverse temperature and humidity conditions before exposure and processing; such conditions may cause unsatisfactory results in spite of the low-temperature storage.

Use Prior to "Process Before" Date. Storage of color films at −18 to −23 C in a freezer will retard changes in film characteristics for long periods of time. For best results, however, the film should be exposed and processed prior to the date stamped on the film package. Films kept past this date may be unsatisfactory, possibly showing undesirable changes in speed, contrast, stain, and color reproduction. The magnitude of changes in the film is largely dependent on the conditions of storage. Proper storage conditions decrease the rate of the inherent changes in sensitized products, but they do not eliminate them.

Protection from X-rays. In hospitals, industrial plants, and laboratories, all films, regardless of the type of packaging, must be protected from x-rays, radium, and other radioactive materials. In the U.S.A., airline passenger carry-on luggage is subject to inspection by low-dosage x-ray devices. Two or three of these inspections may not cause visible effects when the film is processed. If you anticipate multiple inspections or if you do not wish to have your films subjected to x-ray inspections, you can request a hand-inspection by security officials. It is also advisable to label packages of unprocessed films to be mailed across international borders "Contents: Unprocessed Photographic Film. Please Do Not X-ray." Commercial film processing mailers are generally recognized by customs and postal inspectors and are not x-rayed.

Process without Delay. Color films that are to be processed by a commercial processing laboratory should be shipped to the laboratory as soon as possible after exposure. In hot and humid weather, dispatch the film by airmail or air express.

Special provision must be made for keeping exposed films cool and dry if adverse climatic conditions (temperature above 24 C or relative humidity above 60 percent) are to be expected before processing. In warm weather, exposed films, whether dried or not, should be stored in a refrigerator (if available) until they can be processed or shipped to a processing laboratory. For a day or so, the films need not be sealed, but unsealed films should be placed as far as possible from the cooling coils.

Care of Processed Films

It is well established that over a period of time all dyes undergo hue and saturation changes to some extent. The dyes used in Kodak color films are as stable as is consistent with the optical and chemical requirements of color processes. The primary factors affecting the permanency of the dyes in a color image are light, moisture, and heat. It should be noted also that faulty processing (such as deviations from recommended procedures including improper processing times, temperature, agitation, washing, and replenishment) can hasten deterioration of dye images. To delay dye image changes in properly processed films, store films in a dark, dry, and cool place.

Protection from Light. The projection life of a color slide depends upon the amount of light and heat from the projection lamp falling on the slide and upon the total projection time. Prolonged projection with high-wattage lamps or arc lamps will shorten the life of, and may even physically distort, the transparencies. Avoid projection times longer than 1 minute. If long projection times are unavoidable, make duplicate slides of the original and use them for projection purposes. Never remove the heat-absorbing glass or use a lamp of higher wattage than that recommended for the projector. Do not obstruct the air intake for cooling the projector. When glass-bound slides are used in high-wattage projectors, moisture may condense on the inside of the glass. This difficulty can usually be eliminated by storing slides with activated silica gel.

Original and duplicate slides made on Kodak color films can be projected many times before changes in the dye are noticeable. Color negatives should not be subjected to light other than the normal exposure received during printing and enlarging operations. Do not allow negatives to remain on lighted illuminators for long intervals.

Protection from Heat and Humidity. Processed films should be stored on the main floors of buildings, never in basements, which may be damp, or in attics, which may be hot. A relative humidity (RH) between 15 and 40 percent and a temperature of 21 C (70 F) or less are recommended.

It must be emphasized that *high relative humidities are dangerous* because of the possibility of fungus growth. In localities where inside relative humidities of 60 percent or higher prevail, it may be advisable to build a moistureproof box in which to store a film collection with silica gel. Remember that silica gel needs to be replaced or rejuvenated occasionally to maintain its effectiveness. Make the box of metal or of wood lined with metal, sealing all joints with solder or another moistureproof and durable sealant. Provide a rubber gasket to make a tight-closing lid, and arrange the films to permit adequate circulation of air within the box.

A relative humidity under 15 percent should be avoided because excessive brittleness may result. Color films should never be humidified purposely, except under carefully controlled conditions.

Protection from Physical Damage. Color transparencies and negatives should be kept as clean and dust-free as possible. They should never be touched with the fingers except at the edges. Sheet- and roll-film originals should be kept in transparent sleeves for protection against dirt and finger marks. At relative humidities above 60 percent (not a recommended condition), shiny spots may occur on the emulsion surface of an original stored in contact with a sleeve or, in fact, any smooth surface. These spots, as well as dirt and fingerprints, can be reduced by washing and drying the original. Use water between 18 and 24 C (65 and 75 F) and limit the washing time to a few minutes. Bathe the film for about 30 seconds in Kodak Photo-Flo solution (diluted as directed on the bottle), or the equivalent, and hang it up to dry.

If sleeves are not used, roll-film originals are best stored in envelopes with side seams. The paper and adhesive should meet the requirements of American National Standard PH4.20–1958. A variety of containers for 2" × 2" slides is offered by photo dealers.

Carpet beetles and other insects that frequently inhabit old carpets, books, and stuffed furniture will damage film if it is stored near them. Such insects feast on the emulsion, and if hungry enough, will eat the base also. If you suspect that your slides have been damaged in this way, you can prevent further damage by removing and discarding the slide mounts. Clean the slides with Kodak film cleaner, or the equivalent. Remount the slides in new mounts and place them in an uncontaminated slide box. Do not store film in the presence of moth-preventive chemicals such as paradichlorobenzene crystals. Such chemicals tend to crystallize on the film and damage adhesives used in mounts. Gases such as nitrous oxide, hydrogen sulfide, and sulfur dioxide may cause slow dye fading.

Keep films away from chemical dusts; alkaline dust particles and hypo particles on the emulsion may cause dye fading after a prolonged storage period. Slide mounting glass should be cleaned to remove contaminants before the slides are mounted.

Most original color slides made on Kodak camera films should retain satisfactory image quality for many years, provided they have received high-quality processing; have been treated with care in respect to heat, light, humidity, and the other hazards discussed in this section; and have been stored in the dark at a temperature of 21 C (70 F) or less and a relative humidity between 15 and 40 percent. Under these conditions, original and duplicate color slides made on Kodachrome film have the best dark-storage dye-stability characteristics of any current Kodak color film. No significant dye fading is normally to be anticipated on Kodachrome slides for 50 years or longer. Perceptible dye fading may be noticed on original Ektachrome slides and duplicate slides made on Ektachrome slide duplicating film after a period of 10 to 20 years. Color negatives processed and kept under similar circumstances are capable of making satisfactory prints for a period of at least 2 to 5 years.* Longer periods are possible for both slides (transparencies) and negatives if processed films are stored at refrigerated temperatures.

Long-Term Keeping. Any color transparency or color negative image that is intended for posterity should be separated into its three color-component parts. Three color-separation negatives (or positives) should be made on black-and-white film. The silver density images in properly processed black-and-white negatives have an estimated stable life of hundreds of years when stored under optimum conditions. Thus, these silver images can be used to produce good color images at any future time.

The best method for delaying changes in color images of transparencies or negatives is storage at refrigerated temperatures. Kodak color negatives that are stored in a refrigerator at 1.5 C (35 F) can be expected to retain satisfactory reprinting characteristics at least ten times longer (20 to 50 years) than those stored at room temperature. Storage of negatives in a freezer at −18 to −23 C should provide maximum stability of the dye images, enabling

*These time periods are estimates based on accelerated testing procedures. Manufacturers are working to improve the keeping characteristics of dyes. These figures are representative of keeping characteristics at the time of publication.

properly processed negatives to print satisfactorily after very long, indefinite periods of time. When stored at these low temperatures, the negatives must be protected to maintain proper moisture content.

Suitable moistureproof packaging material consists of aluminum foil (such as three wraps of household heavy-duty aluminum foil) with folds and seams sealed with moistureproof tape (such as plastic electrical tape). Kodak storage envelopes for processed film, 4″ × 5″ and 8″ × 10″, made of polycoated aluminum paper material, and heat-sealable, can be purchased for storing processed films at refrigerated temperatures. These envelopes are similar to those used to package several types of unexposed Kodak film. Each envelope will accommodate about 50 sheets of noninterleaved negatives or a lesser number if the negatives are placed in sleeves or other inert enclosures. You should limit the number of negatives and enclosures in one storage envelope to a total thickness of ½ inch or less. Use enclosures that meet the specifications of American National Standards PH4.20–1958 and PH1.43–1971. Kodak sleeves, or equivalent sleeves made of cellulose acetate, virgin polyethylene, or uncoated polyester (polyethylene terephthalate), are recommended to protect negatives from scratches and finger marks.

Separated negatives, enclosures, and storage envelopes should be preconditioned for at least an hour in a small, air-conditioned room at a temperature of 21 C (70 F) or lower, and a relative humidity between 25 and 30 percent. (One or more refrigeration-type dehumidifiers controlled by a humidistat may be necessary to achieve the desired humidity. Use a hygrometer or psychrometer to measure the relative humidity.) Insert negatives in individual enclosures or groups of negatives into a common enclosure. Carry out the negative insertion and heat-sealing of the storage envelopes in the same air-conditioned room.

After inserting the negatives, smooth out, with light pressure, as much air as possible. Seal the opening with either a commercial heat-sealing unit or an electric (dry) flatiron at a temperature between 120 and 150 C (about 250 and 300 F). The "Cotton" setting on most modern irons will approximate the required temperature. When making the seal, be careful that the hot iron does not get close to the negatives. For maximum protection from moisture, seal one sealed storage envelope within another. The sealed envelope can now be stored at refrigerator or freezer temperatures. Avoid excessive pressure on the sealed films during storage periods.

The preconditioning and sealing of negatives you wish to store at refrigerated temperatures can be done periodically; every three months is a good time interval.

Warm-Up Time. To prevent moisture condensation on material taken from a freezer, the package must be allowed to reach equilibrium with the room temperature before being opened. The warm-up time required depends on the temperature differential between the film and the ambient air, the dew point of the air, the quantity of film, and the size and insulation properties of the packaging.

Since warm-up time recommendations cannot be given for all the different conditions that might be encountered, a practical test should be made for the particular conditions. Moisture condensation is not only harmful in itself but also might lead to subsequent return of the film to storage in a high-moisture condition. Bear in mind that film should be resealed in equilibrium with low relative humidity before it is returned to cold storage.

Cleaning Transparencies and Negatives. Light dust can be removed from color films with a clean, dry, camel's-hair brush. Light fingerprints or oily smudges can be removed by applying Kodak film cleaner, or the equivalent, sparingly on a plush pad or wad of cotton.

Kodak processing laboratories stopped lacquering Kodachrome slides and Kodacolor negatives in 1970. If you feel that your color films need protection from fingerprints, light scratches, and fungus growth, apply Kodak film lacquer, or the equivalent, as directed on the label. A lacquered surface is more readily cleaned, and in cases of minor damage, it is possible to restore the surface by removing the old lacquer and applying new. Most lacquers can be removed by either of the following methods. (If there is fungus growth on the film, use the second method.)

Method No. 1—Sodium Bicarbonate Solution. Dissolve a level tablespoon of sodium bicarbonate (baking soda) in 240 ml (about 8 fluid ounces) of room-temperature water. (If used for Kodachrome slides, add 15 ml [½ fluid ounce] of formaldehyde, 37 percent solution.) Agitate a transparency for 1

minute, or a color negative for 4 minutes. Rinse for 1 minute in room-temperature water. Bathe the film for about 30 seconds in Kodak Photo-Flo solution (diluted as stated on the bottle), or the equivalent, and hang it up to dry in a dust-free place. When the film is completely dry it can be relacquered. Apply Kodak film lacquer, or the equivalent, as directed on the label.

Method No. 2—Ammonia-Alcohol Solution. Add 15 ml (about a tablespoon) of nondetergent household ammonia to 240 ml (about 8 fluid ounces) of denatured alcohol. Use shellac-thinning alcohol. Agitate the film in the solution for no longer than 2 minutes at room temperature. Longer times may change the color in areas of minimum density. Hang the film up to dry.

How to Treat Water-Soaked Films. Water from floods, fire-fighting, burst pipes, leaky roofs, and so forth, can inflict serious damage on stored negatives and transparencies. You can keep the damage to a minimum if you act quickly to salvage the films.

The first thing to remember is to keep the water-soaked films and their enclosures (mounts, envelopes, sleeves, and so on) wet. Do not allow them to dry. Immerse them completely in plastic containers of cold water, below 18 C (65 F), containing about 15 ml of 37 percent formaldehyde solution (formalin) per litre of water. The cold water and the formaldehyde will help prevent the swelling and softening of the gelatin emulsion, which are the major causes of damage and the growth of bacteria.

As soon as possible, carefully separate the films from their enclosures and wash the films for 10 to 15 minutes in water at 18 C (65 F) or lower. If necessary, the films can be swabbed, but extreme care should be taken because the wet emulsion is very susceptible to physical damage. Avoid any sudden temperature changes in the wash waters. Rinse negatives and Kodachrome slides for 1 minute in diluted Kodak Photo-Flo solution, or the equivalent. Rinse Ektachrome slides for 1 minute in a working solution of Kodak stabilizer, Processes E-3 and E-4, or the equivalent. Dry in a dust-free area. Movie films, after drying, should be treated with a cleaner such as Kodak movie film cleaner (with lubricant), or the equivalent.

Exposed water-soaked film should be kept wet and should be processed as soon as possible.

• *See also:* CHARACTERISTIC CURVE; COLOR FILM PROCESSING; COLOR PHOTOGRAPHY; COLOR PRINTING FROM NEGATIVES; COLOR PRINTING FROM TRANSPARENCIES; COLOR SEPARATION PHOTOGRAPHY; COLOR TEMPERATURE; COLOR THEORY; DENSITOMETRY; DIFFUSION TRANSFER PROCESS; EMULSIONS; FILMS AND PLATES; RESOLVING POWER; VISION.

Further Reading: Carroll, John S. *Amphoto Color Film and Processing Data Book,* rev. ed. Garden City, NY: Amphoto, 1975; Eastman Kodak Co. *KODAK Color Films.* Rochester, NY: Eastman Kodak Co., 1975; —— *KODAK Films for the Amateur.* Rochester, NY: Eastman Kodak Co., 1974; Editors of Time-Life Books. *Light and Film.* New York, NY: Time-Life Books, 1971.

Color Photography

A great number of factors can affect results in photographing subjects in color. These factors include the following:

1. Color qualities of the subject and the illumination.
2. Differences among types of color films, and manufacturing variations in the production of each type.
3. Storage and handling of materials before exposure and processing.
4. Sensitivity differences related to illumination level and length of exposure (reciprocity).
5. Variations in equipment (lenses, shutters, exposure meters, etc.).
6. Nonstandard processing.
7. Characteristics of print materials.
8. Viewing conditions and illumination.
9. Subjective factors in the perception of color that vary from one individual to another.

This article discusses techniques for controlling those factors that are directly related to taking color pictures. Important additional information is included in the articles COLOR FILMS, COLOR TEMPERATURE, and COLOR THEORY, as well as in the other entries listed at the end of this article.

Basic Controls

Color films can nearly always produce outstanding results in the realistic rendition of a subject, and in the creative, interpretive use of color. But they have significant limitations in comparison to some characteristics of black-and-white films. Color films have far less exposure latitude, and their processing is largely inflexible. It is generally not possible to "expose for the shadows and develop for the highlights," for example. You cannot choose among a number of developers for different effects, nor change developing time to raise or lower contrast significantly. Any departure from specified and recommended procedures changes the color rendition and is likely to produce unacceptable results.

Because of these inherent limitations, the primary controls in color photography are utilized when the exposure is made in the camera. The first control is accurately evaluating the characteristics of the subject and the illumination in terms of how a particular color film will respond, rather than in terms of how they appear—or seem to appear—to the eye. A second control is selecting a film appropriate to the conditions. A third is adjusting the level and ratio of the illumination to bring it within the range of the film. And a fourth—the most versatile control—is using filters to change the quality of the illumination falling on the subject, or the quality of the light as it enters the lens.

Color Quality of Illumination

Most experienced color workers are well aware that the films they use are balanced in manufacture for exposure to light of a certain color quality. Color negative materials have considerable latitude in this respect, depending on how they are printed. With a transparency material, however, compensation must be made by use of a filter whenever the light source differs in color quality from that for which the film is balanced. Photographers sometimes fail to realize that light may be changed appreciably in color quality as it passes from source to subject to film. Discolored or dirty reflectors, discolored plastic flash shields, greenish condenser lenses, and camera lenses that are tinted yellow or some other hue are all potential causes of off-color results. Also, the color quality of tungsten and fluorescent lamps usually changes with age and voltage fluctuations.

The color quality of the light source is an all-important consideration in color photography. Essentially, the problem in color work arises from the fact that a color film does not always "see" colors as the human eye sees them. For example, if the cover of a book appears green in daylight, that is, in illumination that is a combination of sunlight and skylight, it is thought of as having the same color in tungsten light. Although the difference in the quality of the illumination actually affects the quality of the light reaching the eye, our vision automatically compensates for the change. A color film, having no such automatic compensation, reproduces color approximately as the eye sees it only when the illumination is the same as that for which the film is balanced.

Thus, the book cover will be reproduced as green by daylight-type film exposed in daylight, or by artificial-light film exposed in tungsten light. If daylight-type film were to be exposed without a compensating filter in tungsten light, it would reproduce the book as yellowish-green. Similarly, artificial-light film exposed without a filter in daylight would reproduce the book as bluish-green.

Except for special effects, light sources that are appreciably different in spectral-energy distribution cannot be mixed for any one exposure. In viewing an original scene lighted by two different light sources, the eye adapts to an intermediate color quality, thus tending to minimize the visual effects of the color differences between the two sources. The film, however, has no power of adaptation and will show the full color difference in parts of the subject illuminated by a light source differing in quality from that for which the film is balanced.

Film manufacturers have been working to lessen these differences. For example, early color films had extended ultraviolet sensitivity. When exposed in light that contained a high degree of ultraviolet radiation, pictures became bluer in cast than when there was little or no ultraviolet radiation in the light. Today's films have effectively much less ultraviolet sensitivity, making them change less in hue as the ultraviolet content of the illumination changes. Some very fast, modern color negative films have been made with sensitivity that lessens the hue differences when the film is exposed to artificial light and daylight, so that pictures can be made without the extreme hue differences that formerly were reproduced.

Subject Contrast

At first glance, subject contrast might be considered as a property of the physical subject matter before the camera lens. Suppose that the subject is a man wearing a white shirt and a dark suit. If the shirt reflects eight times as much light as the suit, and these are the lightest and darkest objects in which detail must be reproduced, it might be assumed that the subject contrast ratio is 8 to 1. Actually, 8 to 1 is the reflectance ratio. From the point of view of the film, subject contrast involves an additional and very important factor which is *lighting contrast.*

Lighting contrast can be defined as the ratio between the highest and lowest amounts of illumination falling on the principal subject. Subject contrast can be described in terms of the brightness range the film must reproduce. The two are closely related.

With a lighting ratio of 3 to 1, an area of the subject's white shirt that is fully illuminated will be eight times as bright as a corresponding fully illuminated area of his suit and twenty-four times as bright as an area of his suit that is illuminated only by the fill-in light. The overall subject contrast is the product of the reflectance ratio of the subject (8 to 1) and the lighting contrast ratio (3 to 1). In this case, the product is 24 to 1. Since the reflectance ratio is established by the nature of the subject itself, it is apparent that the lighting offers the only practical method of contrast control.

Since reversal color materials like Kodachrome film and Kodak Ektachrome films are processed to positives by standardized techniques that do not allow the selective control possible in developing and printing black-and-white negatives, softer basic lighting is necessary. Light-colored and dark-colored objects cannot be reproduced successfully in the same transparency unless the lighting is adjusted to offset the more extreme differences in tone. Otherwise, dark areas will be much too dark and off-color, while light areas will be "burned out," lacking color and detail. In general, the lighting ratio should not be greater than about 3 to 1. The use of higher lighting ratios for special effects should be undertaken only after the photographer has gained considerable experience with relatively soft lighting.

If the reflectance range of the subject is low, a correspondingly higher lighting ratio, perhaps 4 to 1, can be used without exceeding the overall subject-contrast range that the particular reproduction process is capable of handling. In a color picture, however, color contrast accomplishes a part of the subject delineation that must be secured through tonal contrast alone in black-and-white work. Thus in color photography, high-contrast lighting is seldom necessary for brilliant results.

Color negative materials like Kodacolor films and Kodak Vericolor films allow little more leeway in the matter of lighting contrast than the reversal films, because the range of tone values that can be reproduced satisfactorily in a color print—either photographic or photomechanical—is more limited than that reproducible in either a color negative or a color transparency. If excessive lighting contrast is permitted to introduce errors in tone rendering and color rendering, the prints will not be acceptable. In the case of positive transparencies intended only for projection, however, higher lighting contrast is possible because the projected image can retain a much greater range of tonal values than any type of print that is viewed by reflected light.

This discussion has been principally in terms of indoor work, which allows control of lighting contrast by variations in the placement of the lights. In outdoor work, the sun can be considered as the main light, and the sky as the fill-in light. On a clear day, the ratio of sunlight to skylight is frequently too high for satisfactory detail in both shadows and highlights, especially with nearby, side-, or back-lighted subjects. In such cases, the lighting contrast can be reduced by supplementing the natural skylight illumination of the shadow areas, either with electronic flash or blue flash lamps (which approximately match daylight in color quality), or with reflectors to direct sunlight into the shadows. On a hazy day, the natural lighting is softer, and supplementary lighting is seldom necessary. Soft lighting on a bright, clear day can be obtained by moving the subject into open shade—an area illuminated by no direct sunlight, but ample scattered and reflected light. Professional photographers often use "scrims" (large diffusers) to soften the contrast of the light falling on a brightly sunlit subject.

The effects of the flare level of the camera lens must also be considered. Modern, multi-coated, prime camera lenses have a very low flare level, under one percent, while old, uncoated lenses may have a flare level of over ten percent, as may a zoom lens with many glass-air surfaces. Since the optical image is formed by the camera lens, not the original subject, it is the flare level of the lens together with the flare conditions around the subject that affects the contrast of the final color image.

Color films are essentially made to reproduce a normal luminance-range subject (about 7 stops from diffuse highlight to detailed shadow) when imaged with a moderate flare-level lens (1.5 to 4.5 percent) under typical outdoor, front-sunlit conditions. A high flare-level lens can be used to lower the luminance range of a contrasty (high luminance range) subject, while a low flare-level lens can be used to increase the contrast of a flat (low luminance range) subject. Aiming the camera toward the light source increases the flare level and covers the contrast. The use of effective lens hoods helps to lower the amount of flare.

Exposure Accuracy

Reversal color films have little exposure latitude: There is a relatively small difference between the greatest and least amounts of exposure that will produce satisfactory results. Lens settings must therefore be determined with a correspondingly greater degree of accuracy.

The reason for the limited latitude of reversal color films is clear if it is remembered that to be certain of proper color balance, the films must be processed by standardized techniques. There is no separate printing stage, as in the case of a negative-positive process, at which compensation for over- or underexposure in the camera can be introduced.

Color negative materials have somewhat more latitude than reversal films, particularly on the overexposure side. For best results, however, they must be exposed with considerably more care than black-and-white films. Color printing materials, too, have limited exposure latitude, and a color print tends to be judged more critically than a black-and-white print. Therefore, every phase of color photography requires careful determination of exposure, and attention to this factor is a prerequisite for success with any color process.

In the determination of camera settings, an exposure meter can be of real assistance, especially under unusual lighting conditions and with complex studio lighting arrangements. However, the meter must be properly calibrated, and it should be used in accordance with instructions. Furthermore, the photographer must be fully aware of the characteristics and limitations of his or her meter if he or she is to obtain consistently reliable exposure indications. For the most critical work, an actual photographic exposure test is recommended.

Daylight lighting conditions such as clear sun and hazy sun are constant enough so that it is practical to give fixed exposure recommendations in the form of tables, guides, and built-in camera computers. These recommendations give excellent results under the specified conditions. Similar exposure aids are supplied for use with simple arrangements of artificial lights.

Electronic Flash Guide Numbers. The accompanying table can be used as a starting point in determining the correct guide number for your equipment with different-speed daylight films. Divide the indicated guide number by the flash-to-subject distance to determine the f-number for average subjects. Adjust the number to fit your requirements.

Existing-Light Pictures. Match the type of film to the illumination. Some photographers, however, prefer the warm balance that a daylight-type film renders in a tungsten-lighted outdoor scene. If you can't take a reading with a light meter, then use the settings in the accompanying table as guides, bracketing them by the equivalent of one or two stops.

Illumination Level and Exposure Time

Although it might reasonably be supposed that 1 unit of illumination falling on a film for 100 seconds would produce the same effect as 100 units of illumination for 1 second, this is not necessarily the case. As a practical matter, the effective sensitivity of a photographic emulsion varies with the illumination level and exposure time. This phenomenon is sometimes referred to as the "reciprocity effect."

At some particular illumination level, the effective sensitivity is at a maximum. A much lower illumination level has less effect, even though compensated by a corresponding increase in the exposure time. Similarly, a much higher illumination level also shows less effect, even though compensated by a correspondingly short exposure time.

With black-and-white films, the tendency toward loss of speed at abnormally low or high illumination levels is somewhat less important, because of wide exposure latitude. With reversal color films, the situation is entirely different. Allowance must be made not only for the overall loss of speed but also, by means of filters, for the change in color balance caused by differences in the amount of the speed change in the three emulsion layers.

Determining Exposure Time. Frequently, long exposure times are necessary when a small lens opening is used to get the required depth of field. In such a situation, the lens cannot be opened up to compensate for the loss of film sensitivity at the low level of illumination falling on the film. Therefore,

GUIDE NUMBERS FOR ELECTRONIC FLASH

Film Speed	Output of Unit (BCPS)		350	500	700	1000	1400	2000	2800	4000	5600	8000
ASA 50	Guide Number	Feet	30	35	40	50	60	70	85	100	120	140
	for Trial	Metres	9	11	12	15	18	21	26	30	36	42
ASA 64	Guide Number	Feet	32	40	45	55	65	80	95	110	130	160
	for Trial	Metres	10	12	14	17	20	24	29	33	40	50
ASA 80	Guide Number	Feet	35	45	55	65	75	90	110	130	150	180
	for Trial	Metres	11	14	17	20	22	27	33	40	46	55
ASA 160	Guide Number	Feet	55	65	75	90	110	130	150	180	210	250
	for Trial	Metres	17	20	22	27	33	40	46	55	65	75
ASA 200	Guide Number	Feet	60	70	85	100	120	140	170	200	240	280
	for Trial	Metres	18	21	26	30	36	42	50	60	70	85
ASA 250	Guide Number	Feet	65	80	95	110	130	160	190	220	260	320
	for Trial	Metres	20	24	29	33	40	50	60	65	80	95
ASA 400	Guide Number	Feet	85	100	120	140	170	200	240	280	340	400
	for Trial	Metres	26	30	36	42	52	60	73	85	103	121

SETTINGS FOR EXISTING-LIGHT PICTURES

PICTURE SUBJECT

	Shutter Speed (sec.)	Suggested Starting Aperture for either ASA 125, 160, or 200 Speed Film
Interiors, Night:		
Bright tungsten lights	1/30	f/2.0
Average tungsten lights	1/15	f/2.0
Bright fluorescent lamps	1/30	f/4.0
Candlelighted close-ups	1/8	f/2.0
Stage shows, circuses (flood lights)	1/30	f/2.8
Ice shows, bright arc lights	1/125	f/2.8
Swimming pool, tungsten lights	1/30	f/2.0
Church or school stage and auditorium	1/15	f/2.0
Exteriors, Night:		
Fairs, amusement parks	1/30	f/2.0
Brightly lighted street scenes	1/30	f/2.8
Brightly lighted theater districts like Las Vegas	1/30	f/4.0
Illuminated store windows	1/30	f/4.0
Baseball, football games, etc.	1/60	f/2.8
Floodlighted monuments, fountains, etc.	1/2	f/4.0
City skyline (buildings lighted at night)	1	f/2.0
Aerial fireworks display (Keep shutter open for several bursts.)	Time or Bulb	f/11

the exposure time must be lengthened. Some film instruction sheets provide effective film speeds that take into account the loss of speed at low illumination levels. Corrective filtration is also given, if required. With a little experience, it is easy to estimate the time range into which the final exposure will fall. Calculating the proper exposure time at the desired lens opening is done by setting the exposure-meter calculator at the effective film speed for the approximate exposure time selected.

If the camera-to-subject distance is less than eight times the focal length of the lens, it may be necessary to make an additional exposure calculation. This additional step is *not* necessary when metering is done through the lens or when a positive supplementary lens is used with a fixed-back camera. However, when the close focusing is accomplished with lens extension—by use of either a bellows or an extension tube—the *f*-number shown by the lens-opening pointer no longer indicates the effective aperture. If this factor is ignored, an exposure error is introduced; for example, if the bellows is extended to produce 1:1 magnification, the underexposure will be equivalent to 2 full stops. (*See:* CLOSE-UP PHOTOGRAPHY.)

At very low illumination levels, the effective contrast of some photographic emulsions increases appreciably. For this reason, it is usually desirable to keep the lighting contrast as low as possible.

Filters for Color Photography Control

Under certain circumstances filters are required for making pictures on color films. For example, filters are needed in order to expose a film by a light source for which the film is not balanced, or to obtain a bluer or yellower color rendering, or to change the overall color balance of color reversal films.

Filters used in exposing color films can be divided into three groups:

1. *Color compensating filters* (CC filters) change the overall color balance of photographic results obtained with color films; they also compensate for deficiencies in the quality of the light by which color films must sometimes be exposed. They are available in several densities in each of six colors (red, green, blue, cyan, magenta, yellow). The red, green, and blue filters each absorb two-thirds of the visible spectrum; the cyan, magenta, and yellow filters each absorb one-third of the spectrum.

2. *Light balancing filters* change the color quality of the illumination so that you can obtain cooler (bluer) or warmer (yellower) color rendering. Unlike CC filters, which absorb a specific portion

FLUORESCENT LIGHT STARTING FILTER CORRECTION TABLE

Kodak Film Type	Type of Fluorescent Light					
	Warm White Deluxe	Warm White	White	Cool White Deluxe	Cool White	Daylight
	Filter and Exposure Adjustment in Stops (S)					
Daylight*	60C + 30M	40C + 40M	20C + 30M	30C + 20M	30M	40M + 30Y
	+1⅔S	+1⅓S	+1S	+1S	+⅔S	+1S
Type A (3400 K)	None	30M + 10Y	40M + 30Y	10M + 20Y	50M + 50Y	85 + 30M + 10Y
	—	+1S	+1S	+⅔S	+1⅓S	+1⅔S
Type B Tungsten (3200 K)	+10Y	30M + 20Y	40M + 40Y	10M + 30Y	50M + 60Y	85B + 30M + 10Y
	+⅓S	+1S	+1S	+⅔S	+1⅓S	+1⅔S

*Includes Kodak Type S films and Kodacolor films, except Kodacolor 400 film, which needs no filter correction.

NOTE: Increase the meter-calculated exposure by the amount indicated in the table. If the exposure times require, make the necessary additional corrections for reciprocity effect, both in exposure and filtration. With transparency films, run a test filter series up to ±CC20 from the given values (usually in the M⟷G and Y⟷B directions) under each lighting condition.

Filters specified above are Kodak color compensating filters and Kodak Wratten filters. Exposure increases or filters with the same designations from other manufacturers may differ.

of the visible spectrum, light balancing filters provide an adjustment throughout the spectrum so that the energy distribution of a tungsten light source is changed from one color temperature to another.

3. *Conversion filters* change the color quality of various light sources so that you can use these illuminants with specific types of color films.

Color Compensating Filters. You can use these filters singly or in combination in order to introduce almost any desired color correction. Such corrections are often required, for example, when color films are exposed with different types of fluorescent lamps (see Fluorescent Light Starting Filter Correction Table). Color compensating filters are also used in critical color work to correct for minor variations in color balance caused by normal manufacturing variations or by causes beyond manufacturing control.

If you use several filters together over a camera or enlarger lens, you may adversely affect definition and contrast by scattering the light. Try to use the minimum number of filters that will produce the desired correction. Generally, the number should not exceed three, if definition is of major importance. Of course, definition is also affected by the condition of the filters. Keep the filters clean and free from scratches or other defects.

The density of each color compensating filter is indicated by the numbers in the filter designation, and the color is indicated by the final letter. In a typical filter designation, CC20Y, "CC" stands for "Color Compensating," "20" for a density of 0.20, and "Y" for "Yellow."

The densities of CC filters are measured at the wavelength of maximum absorption. That is the reason the term *peak density* is used in the table of color compensating filters. Thus, for example, the density of a yellow filter is given for blue light. But the density values do not include the density of the gelatin in which the filter dye is coated, nor do they include the density of the glass in which a filter may be mounted. In critical work, the density of the gelatin or glass support may become significant. On a suitable densitometer, the exact density of the filter

Color Photography

plus the gelatin and any glass support can generally be measured.

The standardized density spacing of these filter series (5, 10, 20, 30, 40, 50, in each color) helps in predicting the photographic effects of filter combinations. In the red, green, and blue series, each filter contains the same dyes in approximately the same amounts as the two corresponding yellow and magenta, yellow and cyan, or magenta and cyan filters. Therefore, the following substitutions, for example, can be made: a 10R for a 10Y + 10M; a 30G for a 30Y + 30C; or a 20B for a 20M + 20C. (See the following section.)

Combining Color Compensating Filters. A common source of difficulty in the exposure of color films is uncertainty as to how the various color compensating filters should be added and subtracted to arrive at the simplest combination. There are two reasons why the number of separate filters used together should always be held to the minimum:

1. To prevent scattering of light from impairing the definition and contrast of the pictures.
2. To eliminate neutral density, which serves only to increase the exposure without accomplishing any color correction.

If the color balance of a test transparency is not satisfactory, the extent of the filtering required to correct the color balance can be estimated by viewing the transparency through color compensating filters. These filters are available in six colors: yellow, magenta, cyan, red, green, and blue. (Two series of cyan filters are available.) Each color is available in six densities: .05, .10, .20, .30, .40, and .50.

KODAK COLOR COMPENSATING FILTERS

Peak Density	Yellow (Absorbs Blue)	Exposure Increase in Stops*	Magenta (Absorbs Green)	Exposure Increase in Stops*	Cyan† (Absorbs Red)	Exposure Increase in Stops*
.025	CC025Y	—	CC025M	—	CC025C	—
.05	CC05Y‡	—	CC05M‡	⅓	CC05C‡	⅓
.10	CC10Y‡	⅓	CC10M‡	⅓	CC10C‡	⅓
.20	CC20Y‡	⅓	CC20M‡	⅓	CC20C‡	⅓
.30	CC30Y	⅓	CC30M	⅔	CC30C	⅔
.40	CC40Y‡	⅓	CC40M‡	⅔	CC40C‡	⅔
.50	CC50Y	⅔	CC50M	⅔	CC50C	1

Peak Density	Red (Absorbs Blue and Green)	Exposure Increase in Stops*	Green (Absorbs Blue and Red)	Exposure Increase in Stops*	Blue (Absorbs Red and Green)	Exposure Increase in Stops*
.025	CC025R	—	—	—	—	—
.05	CC05R‡	⅓	CC05G	⅓	CC05B	⅓
.10	CC10R‡	⅓	CC10G	⅓	CC10B	⅓
.20	CC20R‡	⅓	CC20G	⅓	CC20B	⅔
.30	CC30R	⅔	CC30G	⅔	CC30B	⅔
.40	CC40R‡	⅔	CC40G	⅔	CC40B	1
.50	CC50R	1	CC50G	1	CC50B	1⅓

*These values are approximate. For critical work, they should be checked by practical test, especially if more than one filter is used.
†Another series of cyan color compensating filters with more absorption in the far-red and infrared portions of the spectrum is available in the listed densities. These filters are designated with the suffix "-2" (i.e., CC025C-2) and should be used in preference to other cyan filters when required in filter packs for printing Kodak Ektacolor and Ektachrome papers. Similar Kodak color printing filters (acetate) are available in .025, .05, .10, .20, and .40 cyan densities.
‡Similar Kodak color printing filters (acetate) are available.

472

Too much cyan; use CC20R filtration.

Too much magenta; use CC20G filtration.

Too much yellow; use CC20B filtration.

Too much red; use CC20C filtration.

Too much green; use CC20M filtration.

Too much blue; use CC20Y filtration.

(Left) Picture with normal color balance. Each of the smaller pictures (above) shows a color imbalance that could be corrected by filtration of CC20 density. Although a negative could be corrected during printing, it is better to achieve balanced results at the time of shooting—and it is essential to do so with slides or transparencies intended for projection or direct viewing. Correction is made by using filtration of the opposite (complementary) color in front of the camera lens.

Color Photography

The cyan, yellow, magenta, and red filters are also available in a density of .025.

The determination of filter combinations can usually be simplified by thinking of all the filters in terms of the subtractive colors. Bear in mind these relationships:

Red (absorbs blue and green)=
yellow (absorbs blue)+
magenta (absorbs green)
Green (absorbs blue and red)=
yellow (absorbs blue)+
cyan (absorbs red)
Blue (absorbs green and red)=
magenta (absorbs green) +
cyan (absorbs red)

The following method of calculation is recommended:

1. Convert the filters to their equivalents in the subtractive colors—cyan, magenta, and yellow—if they are not already of these colors. For example,
   20R = 20M + 20Y
2. Add like filters together. For example,
   20M + 10M = 30M
3. If the resulting filter combination contains all three subtractive colors, cancel out the neutral density by removing an equal amount of each. For example, 10C + 20M + 20Y = 10M + 10Y + 0.10 ND (neutral density, which can be eliminated).

4. If the filter combination contains two different filters of equal density, substitute the equivalent single red, green, or blue filter. For example,
   10M + 10C = 10B

Example: Suppose a test transparency was exposed with a CC10R filter over the lens. On a standard illuminator, however, the test transparency is distinctly magenta in color balance. When viewed through a CC10G filter, the transparency appears satisfactory in color balance. The problem, then, is to combine a CC10R and a CC10G.

Proceed as outlined above. First, convert the filters to subtractive terms:

CC10R is equivalent to CC10Y + CC10M
CC10G is equivalent to CC10C + CC10Y
The sum of the filters is:
CC10Y + CC10M + CC10C + CC10Y

The presence of yellow, magenta, and cyan filters in the total means absorption of blue, green, and red, or in other words, neutral density. Since these filters are all the same strength, they can simply be cancelled out, leaving only CC10Y. This is the filter that should be used in exposing the film for the final transparencies.

Of course, many determinations do not resolve themselves so easily, and the final combination may include two or even three filters. However, the four-step procedure given above is always applicable. Following it carefully will prevent the use of the wrong filters or a combination of filters heavier than necessary in order to obtain the desired color-balance adjustment.

Filter calculations can also be carried out conveniently with the CC filter computer, a dial-type calculator in the KODAK Color DATAGUIDE, Kodak publication No. R-19, sold by photo dealers.

Exposure Increases for Filters. When the final transparencies are exposed, allowance must be made for any change in illumination caused by a change in the filters used. The exposure increases for Kodak CC filters (see the table "*Kodak* Color Compensating Filters") provide a rough guide to the exposure adjustments required for a single filter. The exposure increase for two or more filters of different colors is best determined by practical test, using initially the sum of the increases suggested for the individual filters.

Conversion Filters. The accompanying table indicates the Kodak filter to be used when converting the color quality of the exposing light source to the light source for which the film is balanced. For example, if tungsten light is used with daylight-type film, a filter of the No. 80 series is required. If daylight illumination is used with tungsten-type film, a filter of the No. 85 series is required. Conversion filters are similar to light balancing filters, but stronger, so that they provide a greater change in color temperature. For further data on conversion filters see COLOR TEMPERATURE.

Light Balancing Filters. There are two series of Kodak light balancing filters: the No. 82 (bluish)

CONVERSION FILTERS FOR *KODAK* COLOR FILMS
(See film instructions for current recommendations and corresponding speed values.)

Light Source	*Kodak* Film Type			
	Daylight	Type A	Type B or Tungsten	Type L
Daylight	None*	No. 85	No. 85B	No. 85B
Electronic Flash	None†	No. 85	Not recommended	Not recommended
Blue Flashbulbs	None	No. 85	Not recommended	Not recommended
Clear Flashbulbs	No. 80C or 80D§	No. 81C	No. 81C	Not recommended
Photolamps (3400 K)	No. 80B	None	No. 81A	No. 81A
Tungsten (3200 K)	No. 80A	No. 82A	None	None

*With reversal color films, a skylight filter (Kodak Wratten filter no. 1A) can be used to reduce excessive bluishness of pictures made in open shade or on overcast days, or of pictures of distant scenes, such as mountain and aerial views.
†If results are consistently bluish, use a CC05Y, CC10Y, or 81B filter.
§Use a No. 80D filter with zirconium-filled clear flashbulbs, such as AG-1 and M3.

series and the No. 81 (yellowish) series. Using filters in the bluish series is equivalent to raising the color temperature of the light, to produce pictures with a colder appearance. Using filters in the yellowish series is equivalent to lowering the color temperature of the light, to yield pictures with warmer color balance.

The term "color temperature" is usually associated with the Kelvin color temperature scale, and values such as 3200 K and 5500 K are used in connection with light sources. Such numbers refer to the radiation of "black-body" sources at that temperature, measured in absolute degrees. In its use in color photography, color temperature works very well for some sources and not at all for other sources that do not fit into the black-body category. It works quite well for incandescent sources and for most electronic flash sources and daylight conditions; however, it does not work well for fluorescent lights.

Color temperature meters are of two types. One is a two-color (red-blue) meter that works well only for sources that come close to black-body conditions. The other type measures the content of the three primary colors of light: red, green, and blue. This type can be used with all types of sources.

Only light balancing and conversion filters are required to match the color temperature to a film balance when the light approaches black-body conditions. Color compensating filters are required in addition when the source departs from black-body conditions.

Light balancing filters provide relatively small shifts in color temperature, while conversion filters provide greater shifts. The two types are often required in combination.

The conversion effect of a light balancing filter can be expressed in terms of the color temperature of the light source and the desired color temperature. These color temperatures can also be expressed in microreciprocal degrees, or mireds, obtained by dividing the color-temperature value into 1,000,000. The conversion effect of the filter can then be expressed as a Mired Shift Value. The Decamired, another unit often used, equals ten Mireds. (See COLOR TEMPERATURE for data on light balancing filters.)

Reciprocity Effect. At exposure times longer or shorter than those for which a color film is designed, light balancing filters may not produce exactly the results expected. At such short or long exposures, color films may change in relative sensitivity (reciprocity effect) and thus require adjustments with CC filters, as well as a change in film speed. A typical table showing reciprocity compensation for Kodak Ektachrome films is included here.

Polarizing Filters. The use of yellow, green, or red filters to darken the sky and make clouds stand out (as is done in black-and-white photography) cannot be carried over into color photography because the pictures take on the color of the filter. However, in many cases, polarizing filters can be

Light balancing filters provide relatively small shifts in color temperature. Such shifts may be required to match the color temperature to a film balance in those circumstances where the light approaches black-body conditions. (Left) This outdoor portrait was taken on daylight film in the late afternoon. No filter was used, and the face appears too reddish. (Right) Use of a No. 82C filter enabled the photographer to render the face in normal-appearing skin tones and the sweater as its true white. Photos by Andreas Feininger.

EXPOSURE AND FILTER COMPENSATION FOR RECIPROCITY EFFECT OF FILMS

Kodak Film	Exposure Time (Seconds)					
	1/1000	1/100	1/10	1	10	100
Ektachrome 64 (Daylight)	None No Filter	None No Filter		+½ stop CC10B	+1 stop CC15B	Not Rec.
Ektachrome 200 (Daylight)	None No Filter	None No Filter		+½ stop CC10R	Not Recommended	
Ektachrome 160 (Tungsten)		None No Filter		+½ stop CC10R	+1 stop CC15R	Not Rec.

used to accomplish these effects. Since such filters are practically neutral in color, they can be used with all color films.

The blue sky is naturally partially polarized; the polarization is strongest in the region at right angles to a line extending from the sun to the camera. A polarizing filter, rotated so that its polarizing angle is opposite to the direction of polarization of the sky, will darken the sky more than it darkens clouds and terrestrial objects.

Specular reflections from non-metallic surfaces are partially polarized. Outdoors, much of the

Color Photography

specular reflection on object surfaces is from the sky. This reflection tends to lower the color saturation of such surfaces. Use of a polarizing filter will cut down the specular reflections and let the diffuse color of the surfaces photograph without dilution, increasing the color saturation. Looking through the filter while rotating it helps find the best angle for maximum effect.

When photographing through glass or water, objects are often obscured by reflections. Since these reflections are partially polarized, they can be reduced in intensity by use of a polarizing filter.

Glare and reflection from light on glass, water, and other shiny surfaces can result in loss of detail and color saturation. In this photograph of a lake in the woods, note sky reflections in water and glare on the leaves.

Use of a polarizer eliminates glare on water and leaves and improves color saturation. Photos by Andreas Feininger.

Color Photography

The filter factor commonly used is 2.5, which is equivalent to an increase in exposure of 1⅓ stops.

Skylight Filters. The Kodak skylight filter No. 1A reduces the bluishness of scenes made in open shade or on heavily overcast days. Distant mountain and aerial scenes are also improved through the use of this filter. No exposure increase is necessary. The filter should be used only with daylight-type films. In open shade, a light balancing filter such as the 81EF, or a conversion filter such as the 85C, can be used to provide a full correction of color temperature. The skylight filter tends to undercorrect in open shade.

Special Applications of Filters. In addition to the filter uses already described, other effects are possible with color compensating and light balancing filters, such as:

1. Introducing deliberate departures from normal color balance, either to enhance the mood of the picture or to satisfy your preference.
2. Correcting an undesirable overall tint of color in a transparency that is to be duplicated or printed in color.
3. Modifying the color balance of small transparencies that show overall tints of color in viewing or projection. This can be done by mounting pieces of gelatin filters in glass slides directly with the transparencies.

(Left) An outdoor portrait photographed on daylight film in the open shade. The model's face, illuminated by blue skylight only, appears bluish in color. (Right) Use of an 81G (reddish) filter enabled the photographer to render the face in more natural tones despite the strong blue tinge of the ambient light. Photos by Andreas Feininger.

Color Photography

4. Balancing light sources used for color printing and duplicating, controlling the color balance of the results.

5. Compensating for peculiar absorptions, such as when you take pictures under water or through tinted windows.

Supplementary Information

Some instruction sheets for professional color films contain supplementary data as the following:

SUPPLEMENTARY INFORMATION		
Emulsion Number		6116–97
Exposure Time	Effective Speed	Suggested *Kodak* Filter(s)
½ sec.	ASA 32	—
5 sec.	ASA 20	CC05R
30 sec.	ASA 12	CC10R

At a normal ½-second exposure time, the emulsion is rated at ASA 32. No filter is suggested at a ½-second exposure time because the film is within the manufacturing color-balance tolerances. For critical work, a practical exposure test is made using the ASA 32 speed at ½ second to determine what filter, if any, is necessary to obtain the best color balance.

Both effective speeds and suggested filters are specified for long exposure times of 5 and 30 seconds. These recommendations must be applied to the ½-second practical test-exposure result.

Suppose, for example, your ½-second practical exposure test indicated that a CC10R filter was required to obtain the best color balance, and your final exposure is to be about 30 seconds.

½-second test	= CC10R
30-second recommendation	= CC10R
(Addition)	CC20R
Filter to be used	= CC20R

Since the suggested effective speed is specified as ASA 12 for the CC10R filter and you will be using a CC20R filter, refer to the table "*Kodak* Color

Compensating Filters" to see how much additional exposure is required. The chart does not indicate any increase in exposure between a CC10R and CC20R, so you would use an effective speed value of ASA 12 for the 30-second exposure time.

As another example, suppose the ½-second practical exposure test indicated that a CC05C filter was required to obtain what you considered was the best color balance for the transparency. If the final exposure is to be about 5 seconds, you would add the CC05C to the CC05R filter suggested for the 5-second exposure. However, these filters cancel each other and you would use no filter. Following the method given previously for combining filters, here are the steps that lead you to this conclusion:

½-second test	= CC05C
5-second recommendation	= CC05R
(Addition)	CC05C + CC05R

CC05C =	CC05C
CC05R =	CC05M + CC05Y
(Addition)	CC05C + CC05M + CC05Y
(Subtract Neutral Density)	CC05C + CC05M + CC05Y
Filter to be used =	none

The suggested effective ASA speed is specified as ASA 20 for the CC05R filter, but since you will not be using it, you can reduce the exposure ⅓ stop by using ASA 25 for the 5-second exposure time.

• *See also:* CLOSE-UP PHOTOGRAPHY; COLOR FILM PROCESSING; COLOR FILMS; COLOR TEMPERATURE; COLOR THEORY; FILTERS; LIGHTING; VISION.

Further Reading: Bomback, Edward S. *Manual of Color Photography,* 2nd ed. Garden City, NY: Amphoto, 1972; Eastman Kodak Co. *Color as Seen and Photographed,* pub. No. E-74. Rochester, NY: Eastman Kodak Co., 1978.———. *Filter Data for KODAK Color Films*; pub. No. E-23. Rochester, NY: Eastman Kodak Co., 1972.———. *KODAK Color Films,* pub. No. E-77. Rochester, NY: Eastman Kodak Co., 1975.———. *KODAK EKTACHROME Professional Films, Process E-6,* pub. No. E-37. Rochester, NY: Eastman Kodak Co., 1977.———. *KODAK Professional Photoguide,* pub. No. R-28. Rochester, NY: Eastman Kodak Co., 1975. Editors of Time-Life Books. *Color.* New York, NY: Time-Life Books, 1970; Feininger, Andreas. *Basic Color Photography.* Englewood Cliffs, NJ: Prentice-Hall, Inc., 1972; Lewinski, Jorge, and Bob Clarke. *Colour in Focus.* Dobbs Ferry, NY: Morgan & Morgan, Inc., 1976; Mante, Harold. *Color Design in Photography.* Cincinnati, OH: Van Nostrand Reinhold Co., 1972; Skoglund, Gosta. *Color in Your Camera,* 6th ed. Garden City, NY: Amphoto, 1975; Spencer, D.A., et al., *Spencer's Colour Photography in Practice,* rev. ed. Garden City, NY: Amphoto, 1976.

Color Printing from Negatives

The color negative-positive system is a very versatile method of producing images in photography. From a color negative, you can make positive prints on paper in contact size, reduced, or enlarged to any size, including murals. You can use the negative to make slides or transparencies on film in any size. You can make dye-transfer prints, color separation prints, and even black-and-white prints that give a gray tone rendering on material such as Kodak Panalure or Panalure portrait paper.

Printing. The printing stage in negative-positive color photography is basically the same as in black-and-white. The one additional factor that must be considered in color negative printing is the required use of filters for obtaining the optimum color balance from each negative. Once the filter technique is understood, color printing is relatively easy. One color negative in the enlarger can produce many results. The print can be made lighter or darker by simply decreasing or increasing the printing exposure time. Overall color balance can be altered subtly or radically by changes in the filter pack. Dodging techniques are the same as in black-and-white printing, with an added twist: Color filters can be used as tools to affect both density and color balance.

Processing. There are more steps involved in color processing than in black-and-white processing, but not one of the steps is more difficult to accomplish than any black-and-white processing step except that temperature control is more critical. The time between placing the exposed sensitized material into the developer and hanging it up to dry is often shorter for color materials than for black-and-white. However, color print processing is not as flexible as black-and-white processing. Generally, you cannot alter solutions or procedures to control or modify the print to any significant degree. The primary control in color printing is in the exposure given, and in the use of filters to change the quality of the exposing light in order to change results in the print. This article deals with those controls in color printing. You can process a print easily and correctly simply by carefully following the instructions given with the print material and chemicals.

The major factor that differentiates color negative printing from black-and-white printing is the use of filters to obtain optimum color balance from each negative. Filters may be used not only for correction, but also to achieve the photographer's preferences in expressive qualities such as the warmth or coolness of the colors. Photo by Neil Montanus.

The negative-positive system provides maximum technical and expressive control in producing color photographs. This Zulu rickshaw man in Durban, South Africa, was photographed on Kodak Ektacolor negative film. Photo by Norman Kerr.

Color Printing from Negatives

The Color Negative-Positive Process

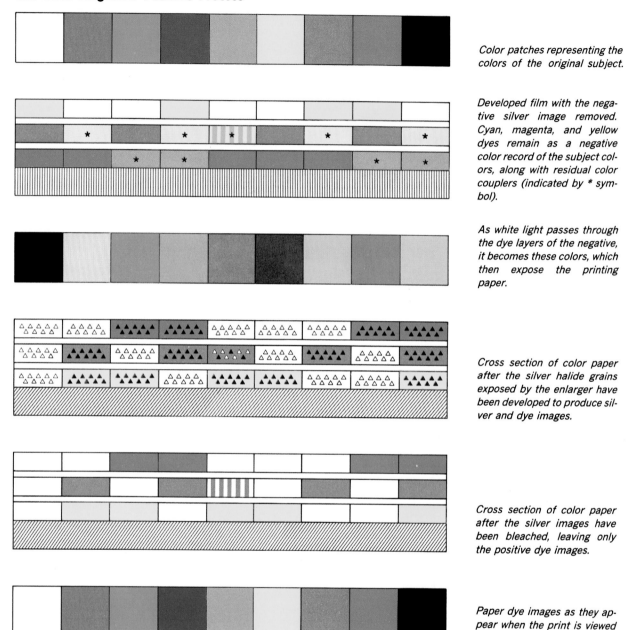

Color patches representing the colors of the original subject.

Developed film with the negative silver image removed. Cyan, magenta, and yellow dyes remain as a negative color record of the subject colors, along with residual color couplers (indicated by * symbol).

As white light passes through the dye layers of the negative, it becomes these colors, which then expose the printing paper.

Cross section of color paper after the silver halide grains exposed by the enlarger have been developed to produce silver and dye images.

Cross section of color paper after the silver images have been bleached, leaving only the positive dye images.

Paper dye images as they appear when the print is viewed by reflected light.

How the Negative-Positive System Works

A color negative film has three emulsion layers which are individually sensitive to red, green, or blue light. When exposed, each layer is affected by the amount of light of the color it is sensitive to that comes from each area of the subject. When the film is developed, a negative silver image and a corresponding dye image are produced in each layer. The dyes are the opposite, or complementary, colors of the emulsion sensitivities: yellow for blue, magenta for green, cyan for red. The negative silver image is bleached and fixed away, leaving the complementary color dye image of the subject. There are also masking colors in the film which give an overall orange-brown appearance to the image. These make it difficult to evaluate the colors by eye, but they improve the printing characteristics of the negative. (See the accompanying diagram on the color negative-positive process.)

Color printing paper also has three emulsion layers. It is essentially the same as the film, except that in printing paper, the red-sensitive layer is on the top and the blue-sensitive layer is on the bottom. This arrangement improves the visual quality of the final image.

The negative becomes the subject in the print exposure. White light passing through the negative takes on the colors there, and exposes the various layers of the print paper in proportion to the amount of red, green, and blue each color contains. When the paper is processed, a silver image and an accompanying dye image are formed in each layer. The same dyes—cyan, magenta, and yellow—are produced. After the silver image is bleached and fixed away, the dyes remain. They modulate white viewing light so that the eye sees a positive image of the original subject in its full colors.

Outline of Color Negative Printing

The basic equipment and procedures for making your first color print are outlined here. They are explained in greater detail in following sections.

Equipment Required. The following equipment is needed to make a print from a color negative.

Enlarger. Use heat-absorbing glass and a tungsten lamp (such as the photo enlarger lamp No. PH212 or PH302). A tungsten-halogen lamp is a suitable light source if it is used in an enlarger designed to dissipate the intense heat that is generated by this type of lamp. Do not use fluorescent lamps for color printing.

Paper. Use one of the Kodak Ektacolor RC papers or other standard color printing paper for printing color negatives.

Filters. Color printing filters (acetate): CP2B (always used), CP05M, CP10M, CP20M, CP40M, CP80M, CP05Y, CP10Y, CP20Y, CY40Y (2 of these), CC025M, and CC025Y. The CP filters must be used above the negative. If the enlarger has no provision for placing the filters between the light source and the negative plane, CC filters (color compensating) made of gelatin film may be placed below the lens.

Dichroic glass filters, in enlargers designed for their use, are suitable for color printing.

Safelight. Use a Kodak safelight filter No. 13 (amber) with a 15-watt bulb or Kodak safelight filter No. 10 (dark amber) with a 7½-watt bulb (for Ektacolor 37 RC paper—other papers may require different bulb sizes).

Procedure. The following procedure is used for making a print from a color negative.

1. Place the negative in the enlarger with the emulsion side toward the lens. Use 50M + 50Y filters (40M + 10M + 40Y + 10Y) or others specified in the paper instructions to make a test-strip series of four exposures at the same magnification that will be used for the final print. Expose one strip for 10 seconds at $f/4.5$; another for 10 seconds at $f/5.6$; another for 10 seconds at $f/8$; and a final one for 10 seconds at $f/11$. Do *not* vary the exposure time in this series.

2. Process the paper. Dry the print.

3. Judge the best exposed test strip for color balance. Look at sensitive areas, such as neutral midtones or flesh tones. Make two decisions:
   (a) What color is in excess?
   (b) How much is that color in excess? Slightly, considerably, or greatly?

4. Apply these decisions to selecting a filter pack that will control the color of the exposing light. Add to filter pack filters of the same color or colors as those in excess in the test. Add a 10 filter for a slight change, a 20 for a considerable change, and for a great change add a 30 filter (a 20 filter + a 10 filter). Some extreme color casts may require as much as a 50 filter addition to the pack.

5. Expose the print, using the estimated filter pack. You will need to adjust the exposure according to the composition of the filter pack.

6. With experience, the second print will be close to the proper balance but, without experience, a third or fourth test print may be necessary. Assess each print in the same way as you did the first test.

Reprint, making changes in the filter pack and exposure time, until the desired result is obtained.

The Enlarger and Light Source

Color prints may be made by contact printing or enlarging. Print paper can be exposed with almost any enlarger equipped with a tungsten lamp, an ultraviolet filter, and a heat-absorbing glass. Enlargers equipped with fluorescent lamps are not recommended. Fluorescent lamps that are deficient in red require heavy filtering; with such lamps, therefore, exposure times may be impractically long.

A tungsten enlarger must be equipped with a heat-absorbing glass; a tungsten-halogen enlarger must have forced-air cooling fans in addition to a heat-absorbing glass. For white-light exposures, an ultraviolet absorbing filter must be included, preferably above the negative.

It is desirable for the enlarger to have provision for placing the filter pack between the lamp and the negative. Color printing (CP) filters (acetate) are recommended for use in this position. If the filters are placed at the lens, color compensating (CC) filters (gelatin) are recommended.

A number of enlargers are available that have been specifically designed for printing color negatives. These have two advantages: a diffuse light source and dial-in filters in place of a filter drawer or other device for using separate filters.

A diffuse optical system has the advantage of minimizing the effects of any scratches or dirt that may be on the color negative. The use of a diffuse enlarger for color printing does not significantly reduce print contrast, because the translucent dyes that form the negative image do not scatter the light nearly so much as do silver grains.

Dial-in filters built into the enlarger head make selecting exactly the right filter combination considerably less difficult than with individual filters. The increased ease and speed of operation are particularly useful in using an on-easel color-analyzing photometer. Because the color of the light source is continuously variable, the color required to give a zero reading on the photometer dial is easily obtained.

Some dial-in filter enlargers use conventional subtractive cyan, magenta, and yellow filters in a wedge continuously graduated from 0 to 180 density. Other enlargers use dichroic interference filters. These filters show a much greater resistance to fading, an advantage where high intensity tungsten-halogen lamps are used and heat is difficult to dissipate. Tungsten-halogen lamps excel over ordinary tungsten lamps because they do not blacken with age. Thus, light output and color temperature remain constant throughout the life of the lamp.

The enlarger lens should be of sufficient focal length to cover the negative sharply to the edges. As a general rule, a suitable focal length is equal to the diagonal measurement of the negative. A lens of longer focal length can be used, but this will increase the lens-to-paper distance.

A good quality enlarger lens is indispensable to making good color enlargements; camera lenses are seldom suitable for this purpose. Coated color-corrected lenses will give prints showing better definition and greater freedom from color fringing than some older lenses intended only for black-and-white work. Whatever lens you use, make sure that it is clean and free from dust and fingerprints, because a good enlargement cannot be made with a dirty lens.

Voltage Control. Stable voltage is necessary for consistent results. Changes in the voltage applied to a tungsten lamp affect both the light output and the color quality of the light. In the normal operating range (100–125 volts), a 5-volt variation changes the output by about 15 percent and the color quality by about the magnitude of a CC10 filter. The effect is greatest with the blue component of tungsten light, and least with the red. Changes in the color quality and output of the illumination cause changes in the color balance and density of prints.

The effect of either slow or sudden changes in the line voltage can be eliminated by installation of appropriate equipment. There are two applicable forms of voltage controller on the market. The first type is the constant-voltage transformer, sometimes called "voltage stabilizer" or "voltage regulator." When this type of unit is placed in the line between the source of power and the enlarger lamp, it automatically smooths out any fluctuations in the voltage. Even though the input voltage varies anywhere between 95 and 130 volts, the output from the transformer will remain essentially constant at the rated value.

The other type of voltage controller consists of a manually adjustable variable transformer, or "autotransformer." This type does not automatically adjust the output voltage when the input changes, but the control knob allows manual adjustment back to the desired voltage. In general, this type of controller is cheaper than the constant-voltage type and allows voltages other than 110 or 115 to be used if desired. The major disadvantages are that it is not self-regulating, therefore requiring more time to be adjusted, and that it cannot be made to compensate for rapid fluctuations.

If a variable transformer is used to adjust the lamp voltage, a voltmeter must be provided (if one is not built into the controller) to allow checking and adjustment of the voltage before each exposure.

The controller may have more capacity than is needed. However, the lamp cannot have a higher wattage rating than the volt-ampere rating of the controller, or instability and failure of the unit will result.

Darkroom Ventilation

An important consideration in producing high-quality color prints is proper atmospheric conditioning of the darkroom. Printing and processing operations in color photography are accompanied by chemical fumes, high humidity from elevated temperatures of processing solutions, heat from electric motors and light sources, and dust from practically everywhere.

Much more than the comfort and efficiency of personnel is involved in the proper conditioning of darkroom atmosphere. The quality of every print can be adversely affected by the contaminants mentioned above. The remedy for excess heat and humidity is properly installed air conditioning that will maintain temperatures between 21 and 24 C (70 and 75 F) and relative humidity between 45 and 50 percent. Air-conditioning units that maintain a positive pressure in the darkroom in addition to filtering the incoming air will assist in keeping dust to a minimum. Good housekeeping, with frequent vacuuming, is essential for keeping dust under control.

Filters for Color Printing

White-Light Printing Filters. The basic difference between black-and-white printing and color printing is that black-and-white printing involves only one silver negative image and one light-sensitive emulsion, whereas in color printing, each of the three dye images in the negative must correctly control the exposure of each of the three light-sensitive emulsion layers of the printing material. The exposure of these three layers is manipulated both by the exposure time and by the color of the light reaching the paper. In white light printing, the color of the light is controlled by placing filters of various hues and saturations in the light beam of the enlarger. These filters act as densities to their respective complementary colors in the enlarger light source, thus modifying it to the specific requirements of the negative being printed.

Either color printing (CP) or color compensating (CC) filters can be used. In addition to a set of such filters, a Kodak Wratten filter No. 2B or a color printing filter CP2B is needed to absorb any ultraviolet radiation emitted by the enlarger light source.

In the typical filter designation CP20Y, "CP" stands for "Color Printing," "20" for a density of 0.20, and "Y" for "Yellow," the color of this filter. The density designation applies only for light of the color that the filter is designed to absorb (its complement); in this case, blue light. In other words, if a CP20Y filter is placed in a light beam, it reduces the blue-light exposure by 0.20 log exposure units or

CP FILTERS			
Red	**Cyan**	**Magenta**	**Yellow**
—	CP025C-2	—	—
CP05R	CP05C-2	CP05M	CP05Y
CP10R	CP10C-2	CP10M	CP10Y
CP20R	CP20C-2	CP20M	CP20Y
CP40R	CP40C-2	CP40M	CP40Y
CP80R		CP80M	—
CP2B (Equivalent to Kodak Wratten filter no. 2B)			

*The ultraviolet-absorbing CP2B filter should, if possible, be placed between the negative and the lamp. This position is advised even with enlargers that have no special provision for accepting filters above the negative because the CP2B stays in the system and is not involved in any adjustments in the filter pack. If placement of the ultraviolet absorber in the path of image-forming light cannot be avoided, the Kodak Wratten filter no. 2B can be located directly above the lens.

acts like 0.20 neutral density for the blue-light exposure. It does not affect appreciably the passage of red and green light.

Color Printing (CP) Filters. For use in enlargers that provide a convenient means for placing the filter pack between the light source and the negative, the acetate-film color printing filters are recommended. These filters are less expensive than gelatin-film filters, but they cannot be used below the lens because they would affect definition.

The CP filters are not supplied in green or blue, because the number of filters between the lamp and the negative is not important. Hence these colors can, if they are needed, be obtained by using the proper combinations of cyan, magenta, and yellow filters.

Color Compensating (CC) Filters. For use at the lens, gelatin-film filters are recommended. These are somewhat more expensive than the acetate filters, but they can be used in a much smaller size. In order to avoid flare and loss in definition, it is important to use the smallest possible number of filters at the lens. Color compensating filters are supplied in red, green, and blue in addition to cyan, magenta, and yellow, and in a more complete range of densities than color printing filters. With not more than three CC filters, it is therefore possible to obtain practically any color and density combination needed.

CC FILTERS

Red	Green	Blue
CC025R	—	—
CC05R	CC05G	CC05B
CC10R	CC10G	CC10B
CC20R	CC20G	CC20B
CC30R	CC30G	CC30B
CC40R	CC40G	CC40B
CC50R	CC50G	CC50B
Cyan*	**Magenta**	**Yellow**
CC025C-2	CC025M	CC025Y
CC05C-2	CC05M	CC05Y
CC10C-2	CC10M	CC10Y
CC20C-2	CC20M	CC20Y
CC30C-2	CC30M	CC30Y
CC40C-2	CC40M	CC40Y
CC50C-2	CC50M	CC50Y

*Another series of cyan filters is available in the listed densities. These filters do not have the suffix "-2" and are less suitable for color printing.

Whichever filters are used, *they must be free from dust, scratches, and finger marks.* The condition of filters should be checked regularly to prevent a gradual loss of definition from occurring in the color prints. Filters that have been damaged by careless handling should be replaced for printing purposes, though they can still be used for viewing test prints to help judge the color correction needed. Also, filters fade in time. Therefore, to maintain proper transmission characteristics, do not expose filters to daylight for prolonged periods of time. Avoid subjecting filters to extreme temperatures and high humidities. (To make certain a filter produces satisfactory results, test it photographically from time to time.)

Tricolor Printing Filters. Tricolor printing eliminates CP filter packs by exposing the layers of the paper one at a time through red, green, and blue separation filters. The primary recommendation for this type of printing is Kodak Wratten filters No. 25 (red), No. 99 (green), and No. 98 (blue) or equivalent. A heat-absorbing glass should be in place near the light source. This method requires a means of timing the three different exposures without disturbing the enlarger or paper easel. Assuming that a photo enlarger lamp No. 212 or No. 302 is used as the light source, typical exposure times at *f*/8 for a $3 \times$ enlargement from a normal color negative are: red— 4 seconds, green—15 seconds, and blue—5 seconds. Because color balance, as well as the density of the print, depends entirely upon the exposure times through these three filters, the use of electronic color densitometry is an essential part of tricolor printing involving any amount of production.

Tricolor printing techniques are not covered here. Instructions furnished by manufacturers of tricolor printing equipment should be followed.

Color Compensating by Filter Combinations. The CC filter combination to be placed in the exposing light beam should always be the simplest one possible—the combination that uses the fewest filters to produce the desired color correction. There are two reasons for keeping the number of filters to a minimum:

1. When prints are made by projection through the filters, definition may be impaired by scattered light unless the least number of filters is used.

Color Printing from Negatives

2. If filters of different colors are merely stacked together, the resulting combination may contain some neutral density, which will serve only to increase the exposure time. Unwanted neutral density is present when the filter pack contains all three subtractive colors—cyan, magenta, and yellow.

The determination of CC filter combinations can be simplified by thinking of all filters in terms of the subtractive colors (cyan, magenta, and yellow), as follows. Note, however, that a particular red, green, or blue filter may not give exactly the same color adjustment as the corresponding subtractive pair.

1. A red filter (absorbs blue and green) is equivalent to a yellow filter (absorbs blue) plus a magenta filter (absorbs green).
2. A green filter (absorbs blue and red) is equivalent to a yellow filter (absorbs blue) plus a cyan filter (absorbs red).
3. A blue filter (absorbs green and red) is equivalent to a magenta filter (absorbs green) plus a cyan filter (absorbs red).

The above relationships form the basis for the following operations in combining filters.

1. Convert the filters to their equivalents in the subtractive colors—cyan, magenta, and yellow—if not already of these colors (for example, 20R = 20M + 20Y).
2. Add the values for each color (for example, 20M + 10M = 30M).
3. If the resulting filter combination contains all three subtractive colors, take out the neutral density by removing an equal amount of each color (for example, 10C + 20M + 20Y = 10M + 10Y + 0.10 neutral density, which can be removed).

Exposure Adjustments for Filter Changes. An exposure time that produced a print of satisfactory density may not produce the same density when the printing filter pack is changed. The new trial exposure time can be found by either of two procedures, depending upon which of the following methods is used to judge color prints.

1. In printing color negatives, some workers think of exposure time as controlling density and of the filter combination as controlling color balance. They therefore judge the *overall* apparent density and color balance of a print. Whenever the filter pack is changed, allowance should be made for the change in exposure introduced by (a) the change in filtering action, and (b) the change, if any, in the number of filter surfaces. The accompanying table provides methods of determining such exposure adjustments. The filter factors include an allowance for the loss of light caused by reflections from the filter surfaces.

When the pack is changed, the filter factors provide a mathematical means of finding the new exposure. There are also published charts that give the necessary altering combinations.

2. If color prints are evaluated in terms of the three separate dye layers, the exposure change for a filter-pack change need allow only for the change in the number of filter surfaces.

If one filter is added to the pack, increase the exposure time by 10 percent; if two filters are added, increase the exposure by 20 percent; and so forth. If one filter is subtracted from the pack, decrease the

FACTORS FOR *KODAK* CC AND CP FILTERS

Filter	Factor	Filter	Factor
05Y	1.1	05R	1.2
10Y	1.1	10R	1.3
20Y	1.1	20R	1.5
30Y	1.1	30R	1.7
40Y	1.1	40R	1.9
50Y	1.1	50R	2.2
05M	1.2	05G	1.1
10M	1.3	10G	1.2
20M	1.5	20G	1.3
30M	1.7	30G	1.4
40M	1.9	40G	1.5
50M	2.1	50G	1.7
05C	1.1	05B	1.1
10C	1.2	10B	1.3
20C	1.3	20B	1.6
30C	1.4	30B	2.0
40C	1.5	40B	2.4
50C	1.6	50B	2.9

(Left) A five-step exposure series of a fire fighter. Exposure controls print density with very little latitude for most print subjects. This test strip method of exposure determination can be used for black-and-white as well as color printing. (Right) Consistent processing every time helps to ensure that the exposure chosen from the test strip will produce the best final print.

exposure time by 10 percent; if two filters are subtracted, decrease by 20 percent; and so on.

Dichroic Filters. Filter factors are not required for computing exposures when your enlarger is equipped with cyan, magenta, and yellow dichroic filters. No increase in exposure is necessary to compensate for changes in the number of filter surfaces. You will definitely see a difference in the density of a second print after a change in filtration, but it will be a color density difference, not an exposure difference. For example, if a first print appears to be plus magenta but of a good density, the proper amount of magenta filtration is added, and the second print will be neutral in color but light in density. This is because judgment was affected by the relative excess of magenta dye. When the amount of magenta dye is corrected, the print appears light. There may be an exposure change called for, particularly with gross filter changes, but the amount of change cannot be predicted on the basis of filter factors. Since individual dichroic filter sets have their own characteristics, use an on-easel color photometer or use experience to estimate exposure corrections.

A rule of thumb that many workers have found

useful is to change the exposure time by 1 percent for every unit CC value change in magenta filtration. For example, if the magenta filtration is increased by 20 CC, increase the exposure time by 20 percent. Usually no cyan filtration is necessary, and changes in yellow dichroic filtration do not usually result in any exposure changes.

The Test Print

For making the first print and as a basis for producing prints from negatives of unknown printing qualities, it is advisable to select a test negative that has been carefully exposed with a light source of normal color quality. The subject matter should be, as nearly as possible, typical of that to be printed in the future, and should contain some neutral areas (such as a reproduction of the gray side of a neutral test card). It may also be useful to have some evenly exposed skin tone. If you do not have a good standard negative you can purchase a variety of them from Eastman Kodak Company for the purpose of running tests.

Make sure the negative is free from dust and place it in the enlarger so that its emulsion side is

Color Printing from Negatives

toward the lens. (The emulsion side of Kodak color roll films is toward you when the edgeprinting appears reversed. In sheet films, the emulsion side is toward you when the code notch is at the top right-hand corner.) Elimination of stray light around the edges of the negative image is absolutely essential. Masks of black paper or black masking tape in the negative carrier will prevent stray light from fogging the paper.

Trial Exposure. Since enlarging equipment varies considerably, it is difficult to specify exact exposure times and filtration for a properly exposed print. The starting filter pack can be found by trial and error using a test negative. Suggested starting filter packs are provided with packages of Kodak Ektacolor RC papers, and other manufacturers make filter recommendations for printing various negatives on their papers.

NOTE: In making test exposures, the use of a Kodak projection print scale, as in black-and-white enlarging, is not recommended. Because of variations in sensitivity of the emulsion layers with illumination level and exposure time, a device like this is unlikely to lead to reliable exposure predictions.

Judging Test Prints

Viewing Conditions. The color quality of the viewing light source strongly influences the apparent color balance of the print. Ideally, the evaluation area should be illuminated by light of the same color quality and intensity as that under which the final print is to be viewed. From a practical standpoint, some average condition must be selected.

The intensity of the light source influences the amount of detail that can be seen in a print. For good viewing, a light source should provide an illuminance of 100 ± 50 footcandles. An illuminance of 50 footcandles should be considered a minimum level. The color temperature of the light source should be 4000 K $\pm$ 1000 K. A color temperature of 3800 to 4000 K serves well as an average of various viewing conditions.

A good quality of illumination for evaluating prints—one having a color temperature near 4000 K—is produced by fluorescent tubes (in fixtures), such as the Westinghouse Living White or the Deluxe Cool White tubes made by several manufacturers. Satisfactory lighting can also be obtained by using a mixture of incandescent and fluorescent light. For

each pair of 40-watt Deluxe Cool White fluorescent tubes, a 75-watt frosted tungsten bulb can be used. The two 40-watt fluorescent tubes and 75-watt tungsten bulbs placed at a distance of 4 feet from the center of the print-display area provide the minimum level of illumination recommended.

Print Examination. Study the color balance and density level of the test print. Look at the areas that should be reproduced as tones of gray and decide whether they have been affected by a variation from neutral color balance. In recognizing the variation from neutral color balance, think of it as an overexposure or underexposure of one or more of the paper emulsion layers. For example, if the grays appear greenish and light, the magenta dye layer has been underexposed. On the next printing of this negative, more light of the color to which this layer is sensitive (i.e., green light) must be allowed to strike the paper. If, on the other hand, the grays appear greenish and dark, the dye layers that combine to make the color green (cyan and yellow) have been overexposed and should be corrected on the next printing by shortening the red and blue exposure time. In both examples magenta filtration must be removed from the pack.

If the print appears magenta and dark, hold back green light on the next printing by adding magenta filtration to the pack.

Look at the reproduction of highlights and decide whether overexposure has caused them to be muddy or underexposure has caused them to lack detail.

Some changes in exposure conditions will probably be necessary. If the test print is far from the proper density or color balance, the changes required can probably be estimated only roughly. A second test will be necessary before the final print(s) can be made.

Use of a Ring-Around. Comparing the test print to a series of prints that vary in known amounts from a standard print of acceptable balance is a simple method of determining color and density correction, particularly on a test print that is far from correct. The test print is matched as closely as possible to one of the ring-around. The amount and color of filtration that should be added to the filter pack is the same as the designation of the ring-around. (If the color is cyan, green, or blue, subtract the complementary color.)

Color Ring-Around

The ring-around is used to compare the test print for acceptable color balance and density. The normal print is reproduced in the middle, the overexposed and underexposed prints above and below it. Three degrees of color-balance variation from normal are given for each of the six colors: red, green, blue, cyan, magenta, and yellow. The prints with the lesser degree of deviation from normal are ½ stop overexposed or ½ stop underexposed. The greater degree of deviation represents a full stop overexposure or a full stop underexposure. The prints deviate from normal color by CC10, CC20, and CC30. That is, if a filter of the amount in excess (say, CC10) were added to the printing filter pack, the "normal" color balance would be obtained in the next print.

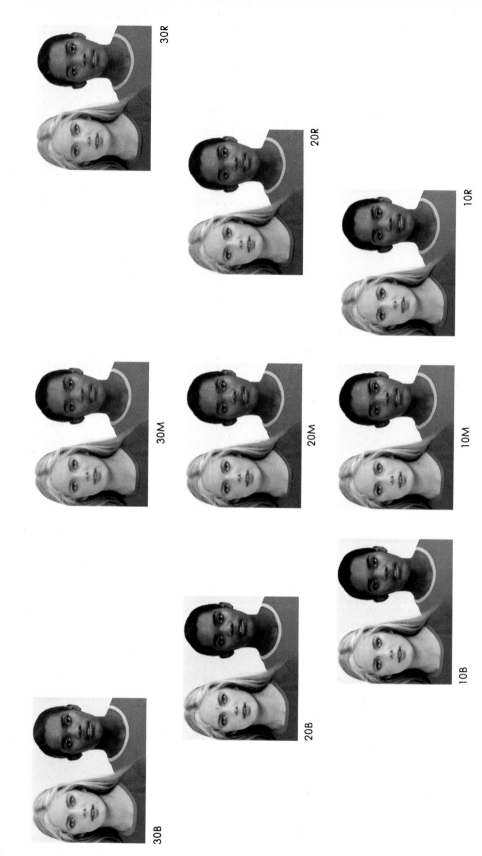

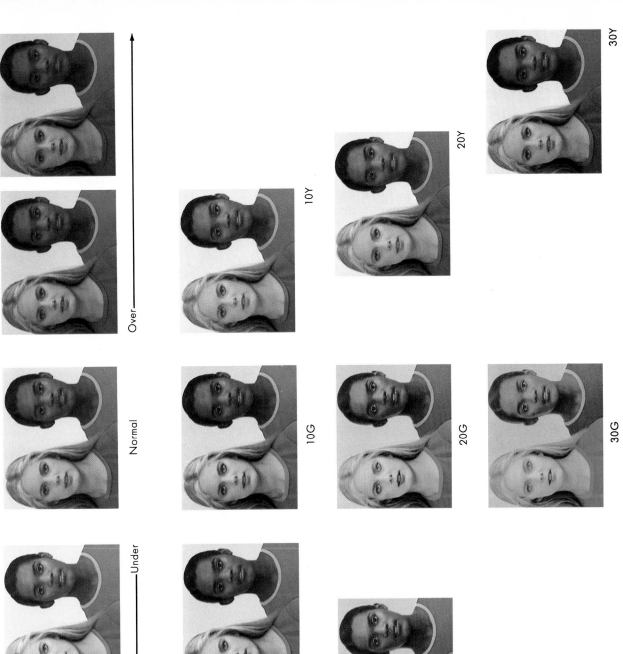

Over

Normal

Under

10Y

20Y

30Y

10G

20G

30G

10C

20C

30C

If the test print is reasonably close to being satisfactory, it should be possible to predict the final exposure conditions accurately. Once again, thinking of the test print in terms of the exposure of the three dye layers will simplify the choice of correcting filters.

Use of Viewing Filters. If a test print is reasonably close to desirable color balance, viewing it through CC or CP filters provides a means of determining accurately what color change is required. Since a filter used in this way tends to overcorrect the highlights and undercorrect the shadows, it should be selected on the basis of correcting the lighter middletones to the desired color balance. Be sure to view the print under the proper lighting conditions and to hold the filter neither so close to the print that the light falling on the print passes through the filter first, nor so close to the eyes that the filter influences general color adaptation. Do not stare through the filter at the print for an extended length of time, but rather flick the filter in front of the print and then away several times, observing the degree of correction it makes. Try several filters of different values and colors when evaluating a test print. If, for example, the print looks "cold" to you, evaluating it through a series of red, magenta, and

yellow filters will determine whether the offending balance is cyan, green, or blue. Similarly, viewing a "warm" print through cyan, green, and blue filters will determine if the offending balance is red, magenta, or yellow.

Since the contrast of the print material is fairly high, a filter used in exposing a print tends to produce a greater change in color balance than might be expected from the visual effect of a filter of the same strength used in viewing. In general, the filter added to the filter pack for white-light printing should be the complement and half the strength of the viewing filter that makes the lighter middletones of the test print appear best.

Suppose, again, that the test print is too green —that is, the magenta dye image is too light relative to the cyan and yellow dye images. The print will look best through a magenta filter, but getting relatively more exposure into the green-sensitive layer where the magenta dye is formed necessitates adding green filtration to the pack or removing magenta filtration. If a 20M filter was best for viewing, adding a 10G filter or, better, removing a 10M filter from the pack should accomplish the desired correction.

Modifying the Filter Pack. When it has been decided which color predominates in the test print,

Dodging and printing-in are important exposure controls in obtaining the highest quality prints. In this straight print, the center of the flower is too dark, and the highlight on the leaf is too bright.

Color Printing from Negatives

a filter of that same color can be *added* to the pack. However, it is more desirable to *subtract* a complementary filter, and this procedure should be adopted whenever possible.

The following table may be useful in determining what filter adjustment should be made.

FILTER ADJUSTMENTS

If the color balance is:	If possible, subtract these filters:	Or, add these filters:
Yellow	Magenta and Cyan (or Blue)	Yellow
Magenta	Cyan and Yellow (or Green)	Magenta
Cyan	Yellow and Magenta (or Red)	Cyan
Blue	Yellow	Magenta and Cyan (or Blue)
Green	Magenta	Cyan and Yellow (or Green)
Red	Cyan	Yellow and Magenta (or Red)

For example, if the print is too red, remove a cyan filter from the filter pack. If there is no cyan filter present in the filter pack, add yellow and magenta filters (or the equivalent red filter).

The following rough guide may also be helpful: When a slight shift in color balance is needed, use an 05 or 10 filter change; when a moderate shift is needed, use a 15 (05 plus 10) or 20 change; and when the shift required is too large to estimate, try a 30 change.

The effect of filter changes on exposure must be kept in mind. For example, if diffuse whites in a test print are reddish, it may work out well to add a 10R filter, or 10M plus 10Y, to the pack and to use the same exposure again. On the other hand, correcting the color balance by removing a 10C filter from the pack will definitely call for a decrease in exposure.

With experience, exposure adjustments can be estimated fairly accurately when the test print is close to the desired density and color balance.

Color Printing Controls

The same printing controls used in black-and-white enlarging can be used in color enlarging. An area can be held back to lighten it or printed-in to darken it. For example, a heavy shadow can be lightened by shading it during a portion of the exposure

This improved version was made by printing-in the leaf for an additional 15 seconds and dodging the center of the flower for 8 seconds during the initial exposure.

Color Printing from Negatives

CC filters cut to the proper shape add a valuable dimension to color-printing control. Bluish hair highlights were caused by blue skylight from a nearby window recorded in a rather slow available-light exposure.

time, or a sky area can be darkened by giving it more exposure time than the rest of the picture.

The basic tool for holding back is an opaque card of appropriate size and shape, fastened to the end of a stiff wire; for printing-in, it is a larger opaque card containing an opening of appropriate size and shape. In either case, the tool is held in the light beam, between lens and paper, and it is kept in motion to avoid producing a sharp line of demarcation in the print.

CC (*not* CP) filters cut to the proper shape add a valuable dimension to color-printing control. A common instance of their need is excessive blue in the shadow under a tree or along the side of a building. The remedy is to keep a blue filter in motion over that area during part of the print exposure. Similarly, a brick-red face tone can be corrected by use of a red filter. In general, a CC30 to CC50 density is suggested—a weaker filter may not have enough effect, and if the filter is too strong, it can simply be used for a smaller part of the exposure.

Filters are equally helpful in printing-in. For example, a white highlight might have a tendency to pick up too much color when darkened by extra exposure. Placing a filter of the same color over the hole in the card will restore the area to neutral.

There are numerous other situations in which local print control is desirable, not necessarily because of any fault in the color reproduction but perhaps to show a product to best advantage or to

Color Printing from Negatives

compensate for uneven lighting of the original scene. Then too, the colors of faces, dresses, buildings, and many other areas can be shifted, intensified, lightened, or darkened so easily that local control should often be considered simply to make the picture more pleasing.

Contrast Control. Occasionally, a negative requires more exposure adjustment than can be achieved by holding-back or printing-in. In such a case, a mask sandwiched with the negative during the print exposure can create a significant change in contrast. A mask is a black-and-white sheet film image made from the negative. A positive mask is used to reduce contrast. A negative mask, made from an interpositive of the color negative, is used to increase contrast. The techniques and procedures for making and using masks are explained in the article MASKING.

• *See also:* BLEACH-FIX; BURNING-IN; COLOR FILM PROCESSING; COLOR FILMS; COLOR PRINTING FROM TRANSPARENCIES; COLOR THEORY; COMBINATION PRINTING; CONTACT PRINTING; DENSITOMETRY; ENLARGERS AND ENLARGING; MASKING; PAPERS, PHOTOGRAPHIC; PRINTING, PHOTOGRAPHIC.

Further Reading: Borowsky, Irvin J. *Handbook for Color Printing.* Philadelphia, PA: North American Publishing Co., 1974; Coote, Jack H. *Colour Prints,* 4th ed. Garden City, NY: Amphoto, 1973; ———. *The Photoguide to Color Printing from Negatives and Slides.* Garden City, NY: Amphoto, 1976; Mitchell, Bob. *Color Printing.* Los Angeles, CA: Petersen Publishing Co., 1975; Vickers, John. *Making and Printing Colour Negatives.* London, England: Fountain Press, 1971.

Local dodging with a heavy blue filter throughout the entire print exposure, combined with additional blue-light exposure, brought the color to its normal yellow.

Color Printing from Negatives

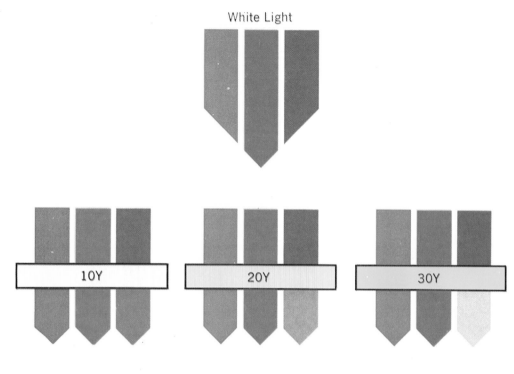

White Light

10Y 20Y 30Y

10C + 10M + 10Y = NEUTRAL

10R = 10M + 10Y

10G = 10C + 10Y

10B = 10C + 10M

10M + 20M = 30M

A combination of many filters, expressed in terms of the subtractive primaries, may reveal the absorption of all three components. This absorption is neutral density. Since it reduces the intensity of the light without giving any color correction, it should be removed.

To figure the neutral density of a filter system, reduce all filter colors to their equivalents in cyan, magenta, and yellow. Note that the color density remains the same in the division: 10R becomes 10M and 10Y, not 05M and 05Y. The converse is also true: 20C plus 20Y equals 20G. Similarly, 10C plus 10M plus 10Y equals 0.10 neutral density.

However, when filters of the same color are combined, the densities add normally. For example, 10M plus 20M equals 30M.

Filter Fundamentals

White light is made up of red, green, and blue components. When these components are absorbed differentially by filters, there is a change in both the color and intensity of the light. A yellow filter transmits almost all of the red and green components of white light, but absorbs or subtracts part of the blue component. The proportion of blue light that is sub-

tracted depends on the density of the yellow filter. The same principle applies to filters of the other two subtractive primary colors. A magenta filter transmits red and blue light, but subtracts green light. A cyan filter transmits green and blue light, but subtracts red light.

Color Printing from Negatives

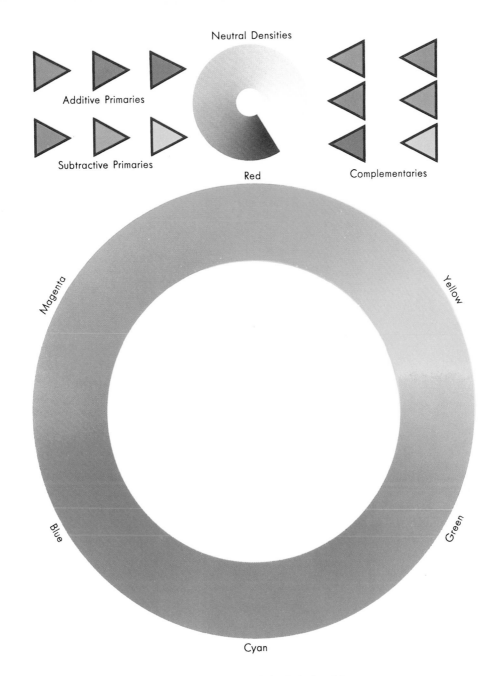

Neutral Densities

Additive Primaries

Subtractive Primaries

Red

Complementaries

Magenta

Yellow

Blue

Green

Cyan

Photographic Color-Light Relationships

This color circle represents the visible light spectrum. The six individual colors—red, green, blue, cyan, magenta, and yellow —are single points on this continuously changing band of light. However, they have special photographic relationships to each other. The additive primary colors (red, green, and blue) added together in approximately equal amounts, as with three projectors aimed at a screen, will produce white light. The subtractive primary colors (cyan, magenta, and yellow) added together in approximately equal amounts, as with three filters on a single light source, will absorb all color and produce black or shades of gray; that is, neutral density. Each primary color on the light-spectrum circle is composed of equal amounts of its adjacent colors, and is complementary to the color directly across the center of the circle. Complementary colors, added together, also form neutral densities. The interaction of the additive primary colors, in photographic light sources, and the subtractive primary colors, in the filters, form the controls necessary in color photography.

Color Printing from Transparencies

It is possible to copy a color slide or transparency on negative film in order to make positive prints on paper. However, to be able to reproduce the colors and densities of a transparency on paper without the trouble, time, and expense of making an internegative is an immense advantage. This can be achieved by the use of reversal color paper. Just as reversal film, when exposed to a subject, produces a positive image, so reversal paper produces a positive image when exposed to a positive original such as a slide or transparency. Modern papers and chemicals make it possible to obtain color prints from color transparencies in a darkroom equipped with conventional color printing equipment, and to process a print in less than 13 minutes.

How the Color Reversal Process Works

A normal black-and-white photographic film, exposed and developed in the usual manner, yields a negative image of its subject. The silver deposit is heaviest (darkest) in areas corresponding to the brightest areas of the subject and least (lightest) in areas corresponding to the darkest areas of the subject. From such a negative, it is simple to make positive black-and-white prints by repeating the process, using photographic printing paper.

When a positive transparency is the final goal, it is possible to process the original film in such a way that a positive is produced directly. This "reversal" processing is based on the fact that development of a negative image leaves in the emulsion a small amount of silver halide where the negative density is highest, and a large amount of silver halide where the negative density is the lowest. Thus the silver halide *not* used to form the negative has the gradations of a positive.

In processing color reversal films and papers, the technique employed produces positive color images. First, the exposed color material is developed in a black-and-white developer, which produces a negative silver image in each of the three emulsion layers. Then the emulsion is either reexposed in order to fog the remaining silver halide and render it developable, or it is subjected to chemical reversal in the color developer. This latent positive silver image is then processed by a method called "coupler development" to form three positive dye images: cyan, magenta, and yellow. After all silver is bleached and removed, the dyes remain. They alter the white light used to view a print so that the eye sees a positive, full-color image of the original subject. Coupler development forms the required amounts of the three dyes in the paper emulsion.

There is another way to produce a color print from a slide or transparency; it requires a printing paper in which all three dyes are present in full strength before exposure. After exposure, processing destroys the unneeded portion of each dye and leaves only the proportions of cyan, magenta, and yellow that are required to form the positive image. This method of color image formation is discussed in the article DYE DESTRUCTION COLOR PROCESS.

The principles of positive-to-positive color printing are the same whether coupler-development or dye-destruction print materials are used. The technique is simply to make a contact or enlarging exposure, using colored filters to adjust the printing light in order to obtain desired results, and to process the print material in the chemical solutions designed for it. Color print processing is essentially inflexible; it cannot be altered as black-and-white processing can to achieve significant changes in results. Therefore, the primary controls in color printing are making the exposure and using filters to adjust the color balance of the light that reaches the paper. This article deals with exposure and filtration in color printing. Proper processing can be achieved by strictly following the instructions for the print material used.

Equipment

Reversal color papers are typically exposed on printers and enlargers designed for color negative

Color reversal paper makes it possible to print directly from slides or transparencies without the need to make an internegative. With the right transparency and full utilization of relatively simple techniques, beautiful prints can be produced. Photo by John Stanton.

 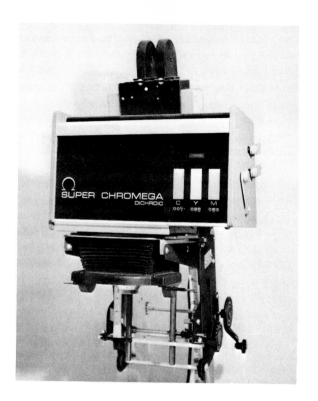

(Left) An enlarger modified for color printing. Color printing filters are assembled in a frame and inserted in the drawer below the lamphouse. This model is the Omega type DII. (Right) An enlarger designed for color printing. Internally contained dichroic filters are adjusted by controls under the right side of the lamphouse and the amount of filtration is indicated in .01 increments on color-coded digital readouts. This model is the Super Chromega Dichroic. Both enlargers are manufactured by Simmon Brothers Inc., a division of Berkey Photo Inc.

printing. The light source should be tungsten or tungsten-halogen with a color temperature of from 2950 K to 3200 K. The use of fluorescent lamps is *not* recommended. The enlarger should be equipped to hold color printing (CP) filters (acetate), color compensating (CC) filters (gelatin), or dichroic filters. Different reversal papers have different requirements for UV and IR cut-off filters. For example, Kodak Ektachrome RC paper, type 1993, requires the use of Kodak Wratten filter No. 2E for UV control and Kodak infrared cut-off filter No. 301A for IR control; along with a heat-absorbing glass, while Kodak Ektachrome RC paper, type 2203, requires a Kodak Wratten filter No. 2A for UV control, but does not require any filter for IR control. Other manufacturers' papers may have different UV and IR cut-off filter recommendations.

Correct positioning of the No. 301A filter is critical. Place the filter in a perpendicular position to the enlarger's optical axis, close to the light source in a specular, parallel part of the light beam. Tipping the filter or passing light through it at an angle changes the spectral quality of the filter.

The enlarger lens should have a focal length long enough to cover the transparency sharply to the corners, but short enough to provide ample magnification on the enlarger baseboard. It should be of good quality, color-corrected, and coated to reduce flare. Also, it must be clean and free of dust and fingerprints so that the print contrast will not be reduced by the flare caused by such dirt on the lens surfaces.

Voltage Control. As in printing from color negatives, stable voltage is necessary for consistent

Color Printing from Transparencies

results in printing from color transparencies, and fluctuations in line voltage are more common than is generally realized. Most color enlargers using tungsten-halogen lamps are equipped with step-down transformers which automatically act as voltage regulators. If your enlarger does not have this device, it is highly recommended that you install a voltage regulator for this work.

Filters for Printing

In order to make color prints from transparencies on reversal papers, it is necessary to have a method of controlling the color of the printing light source so that it will produce a balanced print on a particular emulsion of paper from a particular type of color transparency. Two methods of color control are available: The first method is the tricolor method, in which three additive color exposures, through red, green, and blue separation filters, such as Kodak Wratten filter Nos. 29, 61, and 47B, print the information contained in the cyan-, magenta-, and yellow-colored dye layers of the transparency onto the print material. The ratio of the exposure times controls color balance in the print. The second method is the white-light method, in which a single exposure is made by tungsten light. Subtractive filters—cyan, magenta, or yellow (or a combination of two colors)—modulate the quality of the printing light. Because it is the most commonly used, this discussion concentrates on the white-light method.

White-Light Printing Filters. Either color printing (CP) or color compensating (CC) filters can be used.

In the typical filter designation CP20Y, "CP" stands for "Color Printing," "20" for a density of "0.20," and "Y" for "Yellow," the color of this filter. The density designation applies only for light of the color that the filter is designed to absorb (its complement); in this case, blue light. In other words, if a CP20Y filter is placed in a light beam, it reduces the blue-light exposure by 0.20 log exposure units, or acts like 0.20 neutral density for the blue-light exposure. It does not affect appreciably the passage of red and green light.

Color Printing Filters. For use in enlargers that provide a convenient means for placing the filter pack between the light source and the transparency, acetate-film color printing filters are recommended. These filters are less expensive than gelatin-film

AVAILABLE CP FILTERS

Red	Cyan*	Magenta	Yellow
	CP025C		
CP05R	CP05C	CP05M	CP05Y
CP10R	CP10C	CP10M	CP10Y
CP20R	CP20C	CP20M	CP20Y
CP40R	CP40C	CP40M	CP40Y
CP80R	—	—	CP80Y

filters, but they cannot be used in the path of the image-forming light because they would affect definition.

The CP filters are not supplied in green or blue because the number of filters between the light source and the transparency is not important. Hence these colors can, if they are needed, be obtained by using the proper combinations of cyan, magenta, and yellow filters.

Color Compensating Filters. For use at the lens, gelatin-film filters are recommended. These are somewhat more expensive than acetate filters, but they can be used in much smaller sizes. In order to avoid flare and loss in definition, it is important to use the smallest possible number of filters at the lens. Color compensating filters are supplied in red, green, and blue, in addition to cyan, magenta, and yellow, and in a more complete range of densities than color printing filters. With not more than three CC filters, it is therefore possible to obtain practically any color and density combination needed.

CC FILTERS

Red	Green	Blue	Cyan*	Magenta	Yellow
CC025R	—	—	CC025C	CC025M	CC025Y
CC05R	CC05G	CC05B	CC05C	CC05M	CC05Y
CC10R	CC10G	CC10B	CC10C	CC10M	CC10Y
CC20R	CC20G	CC20B	CC20C	CC20M	CC20Y
CC30R	CC30G	CC30B	CC30C	CC30M	CC30Y
CC40R	CC40G	CC40B	CC40C	CC40M	CC40Y
CC50R	CC50G	CC50B	CC50C	CC50M	CC50Y

*Another series of cyan filters is available in the listed densities. These filters, having the suffix "-2," are not recommended for printing color transparencies.

Making the First Print

The basic goal in making a color print from a transparency is to make as faithful a reproduction as possible. Once a method of doing this is established, changes can be introduced in order to improve upon the original or to make color derivations and interpretations of the original.

The Standard Transparency. For making the first print, and as a basis for producing prints from other transparencies of unknown quality, it is advisable to select a test transparency that has been carefully exposed with a light source of correct color quality and the proper intensity. Use the type of film that you will be exposing regularly, or better still, make several standard transparencies on the various color materials you will be using. Retain these standard transparencies carefully and use them to establish standard filter packs for paper of unknown emulsion characteristics.

Trial Exposure. Make sure that the transparency is free from dust and place it in the enlarger so that its emulsion side is toward the lens. (In this position, the projected image will appear in the proper orientation on the easel.) Elimination of stray light around the edges of the transparency is absolutely essential. Use masks of black paper or black masking tape to prevent stray light from fogging the paper.

Since enlarging equipment varies considerably, it is difficult to specify exact exposure times and filtration for a properly exposed print on a particular paper. Therefore, the following procedure is recommended for determining your first printing filter pack and exposure time for a standard transparency:

1. Set up the enlarger with an ultraviolet absorber, such as the Kodak Wratten filter No. 2E (or No. 2B), or the equivalent, and heat-absorbing glass between the light source and the transparency.
2. Remove all color printing filters from the light beam, giving a printing pack designation of 0 cyan, 0 magenta, and 0 yellow.
3. With the enlarger positioned to make an 8″ × 10″ enlargement from a 35 mm transparency, make a series of exposures at 10, 20, and 40 seconds at f/5.6.
4. Process and dry the test print (prints on some papers have an opalescent bluish cast when wet which affects apparent color balance), and then evaluate the density and color balance as described in the next section.
5. Make the estimated filter pack additions and make another test print at the selected exposure time and f/stop. Once again, process, dry, and evaluate the test print.
6. When you are satisfied that the density and color balance are correct, record the filter pack and exposure information as your standard printing conditions *for the type of transparency used as the standard.* All other transparencies of that type should produce equally good prints when that standard printing condition is used (at the same diameters of enlargement and on the same batch of paper).

Use the standard printing condition that you have determined for one type of transparency as a starting filter pack for determining the standard printing condition for other types of transparencies, rather than returning to the 0 cyan, 0 magenta, and 0 yellow filter pack designation.

In making test exposures, the use of the Kodak projection print scale, as used in black-and-white enlarging, is not recommended. Because of variations in sensitivity of the emulsion layers with illumination level and exposure time, the use of a device of this type is not likely to lead to reliable exposure predictions.

Judging Test Prints. The color quality of the viewing light source strongly influences the apparent color balance of the print. Ideally, the evaluation area should be illuminated by light of the same color quality and intensity as that under which the final print is to be viewed.

The intensity of the light source influences the amount of detail that can be seen in the print. For good viewing, a light source should provide an illuminance of 100 ± 50 footcandles. An illuminance of 50 footcandles should be considered a minimum level. The color temperature of the light source should be 4000 K ± 1000 K. A color temperature of 3800 to 4000 K serves well as an average of various viewing conditions.

Light of good color quality and proper color temperature for judging prints is produced by several types of fluorescent lamps (in fixtures), such as General Electric Living White, General Electric Deluxe Cool White, Sylvania Deluxe Cool White, Westinghouse Deluxe Cool White, and Westinghouse Living White. Satisfactory results can also be obtained by using a mixture of incandescent and fluorescent lights. For each pair of 40-watt deluxe cool white fluorescent tubes, a 75-watt frosted tungsten bulb can be used.

When comparing a reversal paper print to its original color transparency for color balance, be sure that the transmission and the reflection light sources are equal in both color temperature and quality.

It is difficult to compare a print to a transparency for density correction. The density range of a reflection print is inherently much lower than that of a transparency viewed by a transmitted light. Therefore, prints on paper should be evaluated for density by examination of highlight and shadow detail, not by comparison with the original transparency. Remember, in making exposure corrections, that you are using a reversal paper. Therefore, add exposure time or intensity to make a lighter print; subtract exposure time or intensity to make a darker print.

The simplest method of evaluating the color balance of a print is to compare it to the original transparency. Examine the midtones to see if they vary in color from the midtones of the transparency. If it is difficult to decide what color is in excess, examine the print through filters, such as those contained in the *Kodak Color Print Viewing Filter Kit,* publication No. R-25, until the overall appearance of the print most nearly matches the transparency. The filter that makes the print appear most pleasing represents the correct color to add to the printing filter pack.

The following table will be helpful in determining the filter pack adjustment.

FILTER PACK ADJUSTMENTS

If the overall color balance is:	Subtract these filters:	or	Add these filters:
Yellow	Yellow		Magenta + Cyan
Magenta	Magenta		Yellow + Cyan
Cyan	Cyan		Yellow + Magenta
Blue	Magenta + Cyan		Yellow
Green	Yellow + Cyan		Magenta
Red	Yellow + Magenta		Cyan

When making filter corrections to the printing filter pack, remove filters from the pack whenever possible. For example, if a test print is reddish in balance, remove yellow and magenta filters rather than adding cyan filters.

(If you are accustomed to making color prints from color negatives, you may find that it takes a greater change in filter pack to accomplish the desired result with a reversal paper.)

The filter pack should not contain more than two colors of the subtractive filters (cyan, magenta, and yellow). The effect of all three is to form neutral density, which lengthens the exposure time without accomplishing any color correction. To eliminate neutral density, remove the filters of one color entirely, and remove the same density value of each of the other two colors.

When you have found a filter pack that makes balanced prints for one transparency, the same pack will generally print balanced prints from all other transparencies of the same film type as long as other conditions remain constant. Only if you want to change the balance of a given transparency will it generally be necessary to make a change.

Exposure Adjustment for Filters. Whenever the filter pack is changed, allowance should be made for the change in exposure introduced by (1) the change in filtering action and (2) the change, if any, in the number of filter surfaces. Otherwise, the density of the corrected print will differ from that of the test print.

Use of the appropriate filter factors in the following table will help in calculating the correct exposure. The color-printing computer in the *Kodak Color Dataguide,* publication No. R-19, can also be used to find exposure time changes.

FACTORS FOR *KODAK* CC AND CP FILTERS

Filter	Factor	Filter	Factor
05Y	1.1	05R	1.2
10Y	1.1	10R	1.3
20Y	1.1	20R	1.5
30Y	1.1	30R	1.7
40Y	1.1	40R	1.9
50Y	1.1	50R	2.2
05M	1.2	05G	1.1
10M	1.3	10G	1.2
20M	1.5	20G	1.3
30M	1.7	30G	1.4
40M	1.9	40G	1.5
50M	2.1	50G	1.7
05C	1.1	05B	1.1
10C	1.2	10B	1.3
20C	1.3	20B	1.6
30C	1.4	30B	2.0
40C	1.5	40B	2.4
50C	1.6	50B	2.9

Dichroic Filters. Filter factors are not required for computing exposures if the enlarger is equipped with cyan, magenta, and yellow dichroic filters. No increase in exposure is necessary to compensate for changes in the number of filter surfaces. With gross filter changes, exposure compensation for relative differences in print dye densities will be necessary, but the amount of change cannot be predicted on the basis of filter factors. Since individual dichroic filter sets have their own characteristics, use an on-easel color photometer, or draw on experience to estimate exposure corrections.

A useful rule of thumb is to change the exposure time by one percent for each CC unit change in magenta filtration and about eight percent for each CC change in cyan filtration. No change is needed for changes in yellow filtration.

Adjustment for Change of Emulsion Number. In multilayer color materials, there are unavoidable differences in color balance and speed from one emulsion number to another. The extent of these variations is noted in the form of "filter correction" values on the package label or the instruction sheet for the paper. After the material leaves the factory, further color-balance and speed variations are minimized by proper storage and processing.

Note that the filter correction may contain both + and − values. This information is helpful in changing from one emulsion number to another. Follow the procedure below to determine the new filter pack and exposure time when changing to a new emulsion.

Filter calculations are made easier by converting all filters to their equivalents in subtractive colors, if they are not already of the subtractive colors (for example, 20R = 20M + 20Y). Also, filters of like colors should be added together in the calculations (for example, 10M + 20M = 30M).

1. Determine the basic filter pack by *subtracting* the filter correction printed on the label for the old emulsion from the filter pack used for that emulsion.

Example:
Step 1: Suppose the filter pack required for the old emulsion was 10C + 05Y, and the filter correction printed on the package label of that emulsion was +10C − 25M − 05Y. Set up these values as follows:

Filter pack used for the old emulsion	+10C 0M	+05Y
(Subtract) old emulsion filter correction value	+10C −25M	−05Y

To simplify the subtraction of minus values, follow this rule: "Change all the signs of the values to be subtracted and proceed as in addition."

$$+10C \quad 0M \quad +05Y$$
$$-10C +25M \quad +05Y$$
$$\overline{\quad 0C +25M \quad +10Y}$$
(basic filter pack)

2. Determine the filter pack required for the new emulsion by *adding* the filter correction value printed on the label for the new emulsion to the basic filter pack.

Example:
Step 2: Suppose the filter correction value of the new emulsion is −05C + 25M − 20Y.

Basic filter pack	0C + 25M + 10Y
(Add) Filter Correction Value for new emulsion	−05C + 25M − 20Y
Preliminary filter pack	−05C + 50M − 10Y

3A. If negative filter values are present in the pack, add (by calculation) C, M, and Y "neutral density" equal to the largest negative filter. In this way, one of the three filters will become zero. Look up the neutral density factor in Section A of the accompanying table.

Example:

Step 3A: Since negative filter values are present in the pack, add 10 neutral density ($+10C + 10M$ and $+10Y$) to these values.

Preliminary filter pack	$-05C + 50M - 10Y$
(Add) neutral density	$+10C + 10M + 10Y$
Final filter pack for new emulsion	$+05C + 60M \quad 0Y$

Look up a 10 neutral density in Section A of the table below. The neutral density factor comes out to 1.3 in this case.

or

3B. If all the filter values are positive, subtract C, M, and Y "neutral density" equal to the smallest positive filter value. At least one of the three will now be zero. Look up the neutral density factor in Section B in the table.

or

3C. If the filter values are positive and at least one is zero, go to Step 4. Your neutral density factor is 1.0.

4. Calculate the new exposure time by the following formula:

$$\begin{array}{l} \text{Exposure} \\ \text{Time for} \\ \text{the New} \\ \text{Emulsion} \end{array} = \begin{array}{l} \text{Exposure} \\ \text{Time for} \\ \text{the Old} \\ \text{Emulsion} \end{array} \times (\text{Neutral Density Factor})$$

Example:

Step 4: Suppose the exposure time used for the old emulsion was 8.5 seconds and the neutral density factor was 1.3. Calculate the new exposure time by the formula:

$$\begin{array}{l} \text{Exposure} \\ \text{Time for} \\ \text{the New} \\ \text{Emulsion} \end{array} = \begin{array}{l} \text{Exposure} \\ \text{Time for} \\ \text{the Old} \\ \text{Emulsion} \end{array} \times (\text{Neutral Density Factor})$$

New Exposure Time = 8.5×1.3
                  = 11 seconds

This is the exposure time that should be tried for the new emulsion.

5. Use the new filter pack and the printing times calculated as a starting point for a series of test prints using a standard transparency.

Additional information about computing filter combinations is included in the article COLOR PRINTING FROM NEGATIVES. In reversal printing, you subtract filtration of the color you want to remove from a print; in negative printing, you add filtration (or subtract the complement) to achieve the same result. The other aspects of using filters are the same in the two methods of printing.

NEUTRAL DENSITY FACTORS

CC Neutral Density Added in Step 3A or Subtracted in Step 3B	Section A	Section B
5	1.1	.89
10	1.3	.77
15	1.4	.70
20	1.6	.62
25	1.8	.54
30	2.1	.48
35	2.3	.43
40	2.6	.38
45	3.0	.33
50	3.4	.29
55	4.5	.22
60	5.6	.18
65	7.0	.14
70	8.3	.12
75	9.5	.10
80	10.7	.093
85	11.7	.085

Color Printing Controls

The same printing controls used in black-and-white or color-negative enlarging can be used in making color prints on reversal paper with one big difference: *They work in the opposite direction.* An area can be held back to darken it or printed-in to lighten it. For example, a heavy shadow can be lightened by giving the area more exposure time than the rest of the picture, or a sky can be darkened by shading it during a portion of the exposure time.

The basic tool for dodging is an opaque card of appropriate size and shape fastened to the end of a stiff wire; for printing-in, it is a larger opaque card containing an opening of appropriate size and shape. (Do not use the commercially available tools made of red acetate.)

CC (not CP) filters cut to the proper shape add a valuable tool to color-printing control. A common instance of their need is excessive blue in the shadow under a tree or along the side of a building. The remedy is to keep a *yellow* filter in motion over that area during part of the print exposure. Similarly, a brick-red face tone can be corrected by using a *cyan* filter. In general, a CC30 to CC50 density is suggested. A weaker filter may not have enough effect, and if the filter is too strong, it can simply be used for a smaller part of the exposure. (If you are accustomed to making color prints from color negatives, you may find that it takes more color-dodging time to accomplish the desired result with reversal papers.) Since color dodging also affects print density, it may be necessary, at times, to burn-in the dodged area with the same color filter, in order to lighten it to its original density while maintaining the desired color correction. This is done by placing the dodging filter over the hole in the large, opaque burning-in card.

White Borders. In reversal printing, areas that receive the least exposure will be the darkest after processing. Therefore, borders of the paper covered by the retaining edges of a printing easel will be black. To obtain white borders, expose the border areas of a print while the picture area is protected by an opaque mask. When the enlarger is adjusted to make a normal print, an exposure from 1½ to 2 times the print exposure time will be required, with no transparency in the light beam. Do not remove the printing filters when flashing the border. A slight overlap of the print exposure and the border exposure is necessary to eliminate dark edges, so make the opaque mask a bit smaller than the exposed picture area.

Contrast Control

The most favorable condition under which a color picture can be viewed is by projection, in positive transparency form, in a dark room. The screen becomes an isolated patch of colors with a completely dark surround. Under these conditions, the eye adapts to the overall color balance and to the color saturation of the transparency, making the reproduction appear more nearly correct than it re-

ally is. To lesser degrees, this is true of a transparency viewed over an illuminator in a partially darkened room or in a well-illuminated room. Reflection color prints, however, are viewed in normal surroundings, usually under uniformly distributed illumination, and have all the visual effects working to make obvious any faults which the print may have, either in color balance or in contrast. Comparison of a print and a transparency of the same subject, therefore, is biased against the print.

Reversal print papers are matched to the normal contrast characteristics of most color transparency films. Occasionally, however, a subject is encountered that would reproduce better at a contrast level different from that afforded by straight transparency-to-paper printing. In such cases, there are two methods which can be used to modify the printing characteristics of the problem transparency: flashing and silver masking.

Flashing. The easiest way to reduce contrast is simply to flash the color paper after making the original exposure. Remove the transparency from the enlarger and add a neutral density filter of a 2.0 value to the filter pack. Try a test exposure equal in time and lens aperture to the original exposure. Vary the density of the neutral density filter or the exposure time to produce the desired result with your equipment. The additional exposure will have the greatest effect on those areas that received the least exposure previously. The flashing exposure will cause them to print somewhat lighter, thus reducing the overall contrast of the print. You may find that some correction of the color balance of maximum-density areas is possible with the flashing technique by changing the printing filter pack balance toward the desired color.

This technique is limited in the amount of contrast reduction possible. Overflashing will fog the shadows and middletones, giving a smoky effect, with no increase in visible detail.

Further information about this method of contrast control is contained in the article FLASHING.

Silver Masking. A more controllable and effective method of controlling contrast in reversal printing is to sandwich a black-and-white sheet film mask with the transparency to make the print exposure. A low-contrast negative made from the transparency is used as a mask to reduce contrast. A positive image, made from a black-and-white inter-

Reversal print papers are matched to the normal contrast characteristics of most color transparencies. Certain photographs, however, such as this one, could benefit by reproduction at a lower contrast level, achieved by either flashing or silver masking. Photo by Richard Faust.

negative of the transparency, is used as a mask to increase contrast. The preparation and use of silver masks is covered in the article MASKING.

Multiple-Image Printing. An excellent way of creating new compositions from existing color transparencies is to combine images into a single print.

Not only can multiple images be produced, but texture can be added to a print, clouds and color can be added to a bald sky, a foreground silhouette can be added to an overly two-dimensional composition, and many other creative combinations can be obtained.

Contrast reduction by flashing in color reversal printing. (Left) Print is unflashed. (Right) This print received a post-exposure flashing that was 2 percent of the original print exposure. This was achieved by removing the transparency from the enlarger and adding 1.70 neutral-density filtration to the pack used for the print; the second (flashing) exposure was equal to the original exposure time. Because the background appeared excessively reddish, a CC30 cyan filter was also added for the flash exposure.

There are two methods of printing multiple images—printing sandwiched transparencies and combination printing. The choice of method depends upon the effect you wish to create. If you want to put details from one scene into the *highlights or upper middletones* of another scene, you should print with sandwiched transparencies. If you want to put images from one scene into the *shadows* of another scene, you must make a combination print. Because your original subjects are on color transparency film, there are no superimposed colored coupler masks to contend with and, if the originals are on the same type of transparency material, no filter-pack changes to make. Multiple-image printing with color reversal materials is much easier than it is with color negatives.

Printing Sandwiched Transparencies. The simplest method of producing a multiple-image print is to select a transparency that has relatively large areas of highlight for use as a background, and a transparency in which the subject is fairly isolated in a high-key surround. Overlay the two unmounted transparencies, emulsion-to-emulsion, on a transilluminated viewer or light table. Arrange the composition so that the subject of one is located in the highlight area of the other. Use black masking tape to bind the two transparencies together in position, and as an opaque mask on all four sides to prevent unwanted areas from printing. Since the transparencies are bound with both emulsions facing in, position the sandwich in the enlarger carrier in whichever orientation makes the most pleasing

Color Printing from Transparencies

composition. If three transparencies are sandwiched, keep those with the most important details in the same focal plane by placing their emulsions together.

You may find that the basic filter pack will need adjustment and that the normal printing time will be extended. Remember that unwanted details can be subdued by holding back and that important areas can be lightened by burning-in, whenever necessary.

Combination Printing

This technique, often called double printing, consists of making multiple-image prints from two or more transparencies onto a single sheet of paper by means of separate exposures.

In color-reversal printing, the dark areas of a print are the relatively unexposed areas; therefore, it is possible to project a second image into the shadows of a first image. Proceed as follows:

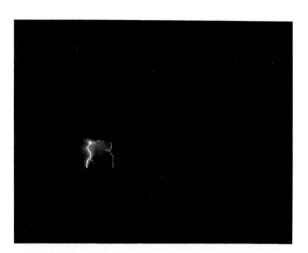

Drama was heightened in this imaginative reconstruction of Noah's Ark (right) by sandwiching the color transparency of the Ark and animals (above left) with a black-and-white transparency of the lightning (above right). Certain combinations, such as this one, may be planned in advance; others may occur to the photographer at a later occasion. For more information on this technique, see the article on Combination Printing. Photos by Norman Kerr.

Color Printing from Transparencies

1. Make a plan of the composition by projecting the transparencies, in turn, onto a sheet of thin, white paper taped in place on the easel. With a soft pencil, trace the main elements of the transparencies onto the paper.
2. Leaving the paper plan taped on the easel, make test prints of the component transparencies.
3. Evaluate the test prints and list the necessary changes.
4. Place a sheet of reversal paper on the easel and start the combination print with the exposure of the background transparency. If the test print showed any excess detail in the shadow area to be imprinted, dodge that area with an opaque card.
5. Remove the paper from the easel and place it in a dark drawer, first marking a corner for orientation reference. (Clip the corner with a pair of scissors, or if you are making a borderless print, attach a paper clip.)
6. Compose the second transparency, using the paper plan for position. Change the enlarger settings.
7. Replace the sheet of exposed print paper in the easel in the same orientation, and make the second exposure. Use an opaque card with a hole in it to prevent unwanted exposure in areas containing only background exposure.
8. Remove the exposed paper for processing.

Combination prints containing elements from many transparencies can be produced in this manner if care is taken to limit the imprint exposures to carefully planned areas and if all extraneous light is eliminated from the easel.

• *See also:* BLEACH FIX; BURNING-IN; COLOR FILM PROCESSING; COLOR FILMS; COLOR PRINTING FROM NEGATIVES; COLOR THEORY; COMBINATION PRINTING; CONTACT PRINTING; DIRECT POSITIVE PROCESSING; DYE DESTRUCTION COLOR PROCESS; ENLARGERS AND ENLARGING; FLASHING; MASKING; PAPERS, PHOTOGRAPHIC; PRINTING, PHOTOGRAPHIC.

Further Reading: Borowsky, Irvin J. *Handbook for Color Printing.* Philadelphia, PA: North American Publishing Co., 1974; Coote, Jack H. *The Photoguide to Color Printing from Negatives and Slides.* Garden City, NY: Amphoto, 1976; Engdahl, David A. *Color Printing.* Garden City, NY: Amphoto, 1970.

This multiple-image print was made by combining a high-contrast transparency of the boats with a background transparency that had large areas of highlight and that was sufficiently out-of-focus to lack distracting details.

C Color Separation Photography

In photography, a color record of a subject is made by analyzing it in terms of three primary colors: red, green, and blue. Color films do this by means of three silver halide emulsion layers; the film is made so that each layer records just one of the primary colors.

The same kind of color analysis can be made on three separate sheets of black-and-white film; however, emulsions that are individually sensitive to red, green, and blue are not available. To make color separations, panchromatic film, which is sensitive to all colors, is used with filters that control which primary color will expose each film.

A common set of filters used for this kind of color analysis directly from real subjects are Kodak Wratten filters No. 25 (red), No. 47 (blue), and No. 58 (green). With the red filter in place, practically no green or blue light can pass through to the film; only the red light from the subject exposes the film. Although made on panchromatic film, the resulting *red record* is the same as if it had been made on an emulsion having only red sensitivity.

Making color separation negatives. Each subject color reflects light composed of various proportions of the primaries, red, green, and blue. Separation filters absorb two primary colors and pass only light of their own color. The densities in each black-and-white separation negative represent the amount of one primary color present in each area of the subject. Only subject areas reflecting some blue light register on the blue record negative. The green and red records are similarly selective.

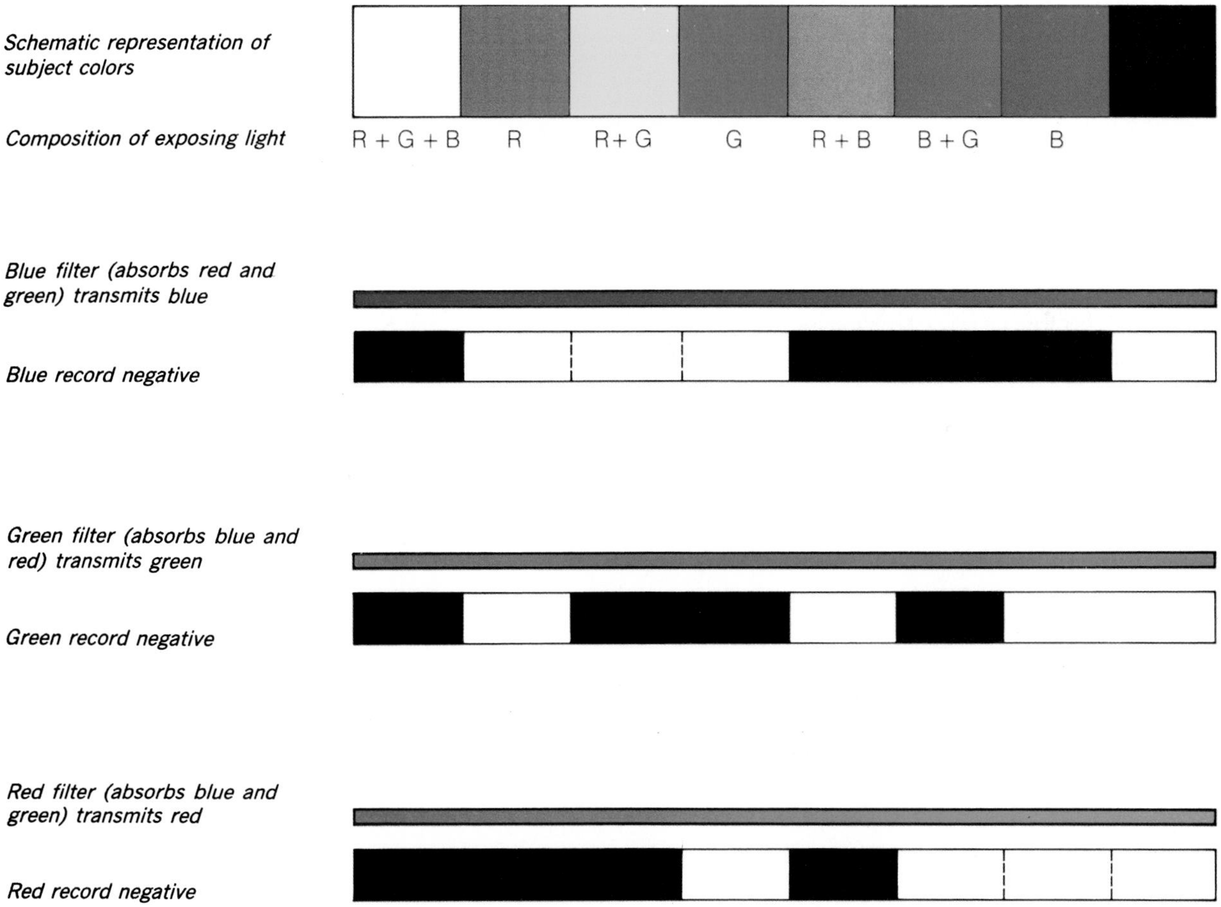

Schematic representation of subject colors

Composition of exposing light   R + G + B   R   R + G   G   R + B   B + G   B

Blue filter (absorbs red and green) transmits blue

Blue record negative

Green filter (absorbs blue and red) transmits green

Green record negative

Red filter (absorbs blue and green) transmits red

Red record negative

A positive image can be produced in color print material by separate exposures to each of the separation negatives. White exposing light is composed of relatively equal proportions of red, green, and blue. Light passing through the negative blue record and a blue filter exposes a positive image in the blue-sensitive layer of the print film. The green record, with a green filter, exposes a positive image in the green-sensitive layer. The red record, with a red filter, exposes an image only in the red-sensitive layer.

Printing a Positive Transparency from Separation Negatives

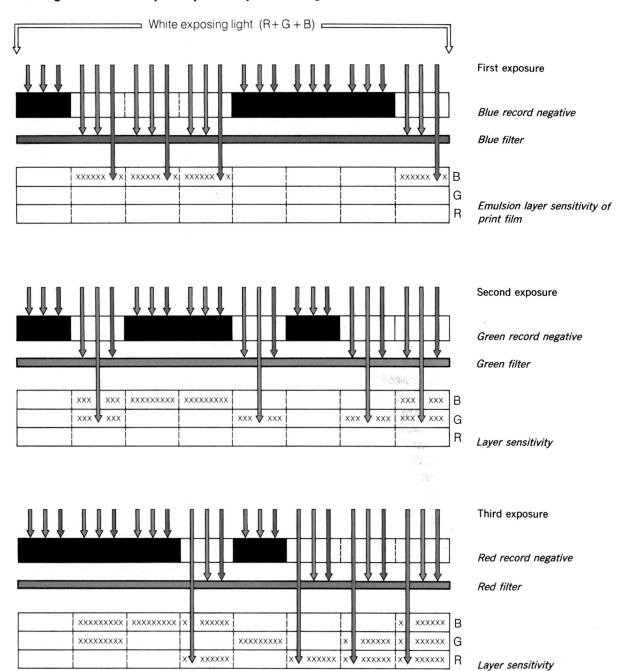

Color Separation Photography

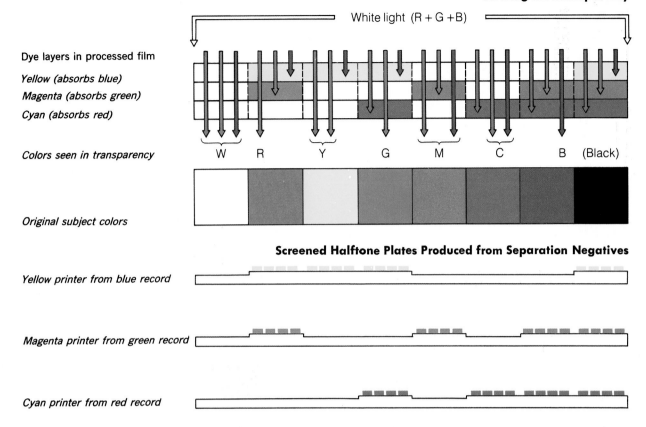

Dye layers in processed film

Yellow (absorbs blue)

Magenta (absorbs green)

Cyan (absorbs red)

Colors seen in transparency   W   R   Y   G   M   C   B   (Black)

Original subject colors

Screened Halftone Plates Produced from Separation Negatives

Yellow printer from blue record

Magenta printer from green record

Cyan printer from red record

The processed transparency has positive images composed of yellow, magenta, and cyan dyes. The dyes absorb some colors of white light; those that pass through combine to reproduce the original subject colors. If the print material has a paper base, light is reflected back up through the dyes; the final image colors are nearly the same as in the transparency—reproductions of the subject colors. In the dye transfer process, the same color dye image is created as cyan, magenta, and yellow matrices are individually pressed against a receiving sheet.

Similarly, a *blue record* is made by photographing the subject through the blue filter, and a *green record* by using the green filter.

This procedure is called color separation photography. If the original subject was an actual object, or a positive image, the three separation records form a set of *separation negatives;* if the subject was a color negative, they become *separation positives.* The accompanying diagrams show how color separations are achieved and how reproductions are made from them.

Color separation photographs can be exposed from actual subjects. The problem with this method is that if there is any movement whatsoever from one exposure to the next, the images will be out of register when they are printed together. For this reason only subjects such as architecture and still-life arrangements are suitable for direct photography. Most color separations are made from a color print, a transparency or slide, or a color negative as a subject.

The major uses of the separation process are in

Color Separation Photography

Color separation photographs can be exposed only from fixed subjects. Still lifes, architecture, and similar subjects are suitable for direct separation photography.

making plates or blocks for photomechanical reproductions, in making dye transfer prints, and in preserving records of color images for long periods of time.

Sharp-cutting separation filters, such as Kodak Wratten filters No. 29 (red), No. 61 (green) and No. 47B (blue), are filters that transmit only a narrow band of wavelengths. When separation negatives are made directly in a camera of a real subject (as compared to a photograph), broader band filters are usually used, such as Wratten filters No. 25 (red), No. 58 (green), and No. 47 (blue).

Printed Reproductions

The positive image in a color slide or print actually consists of cyan, magenta, and yellow dyes in the various emulsion layers. The same colors of ink can be used to create a full-color image in a printed reproduction. The inks are not mixed together; instead they are laid down in tiny dots, side-by-side and overlapping as required. The dots are so small that the human eye does not distinguish them, but they blend their colors together to form a composite image. You can see the dots in the color reproductions in this book by using a strong magnifier.

To make a color reproduction, there must be separate printing plates for each of the subtractive primary color inks (called process inks) and for black ink as well, which is used in normal four-color printing to improve the quality of the reproduction. The four plates are prepared from color separations made on black-and-white film. At an intermediate step in the process, the separation record for each plate is rephotographed through a halftone screen, which breaks the image up into the required dots. Because the printing inks create color effects subtractively (*See:* COLOR THEORY.), each plate uses an ink that is the complement of the color record used to prepare the plate. Printers call these inks red-, blue-, and yellow-printer inks, although they are really magenta, cyan, and yellow subtractive primary colors. The red record separation produces a cyan printer (plate); the green record produces a magenta printer; and the blue record produces a yellow printer.

When the plates are printed in proper registration on a single sheet of paper, the dots of the four inks create a full-color reproduction of the original subject. This method of halftone color reproduction is explained more fully in the article SCREENED NEGATIVES AND PRINTS. It is the major use of separation photography; without it colored photographic illustrations in books, magazines, billboards —any printed medium—would not be possible.

A mask is low-contrast, low-density film image (usually black-and-white), which is registered with the original image (usually colored) to provide contrast control and/or color correction. A sharp mask is made like a contact print; a soft mask is printed with a diffusing spacer sheet (matte acetate) between the original and the masking film.

Color masking is almost always used on a color transparency before the separation negatives are made, both to lower the contrast of the transparency and to correct for color imperfections in the process inks. They are not true subtractive primary colors.

Dye Transfer Process

Instead of printing plates, specially prepared gelatin matrix sheets can be exposed to the color separations and used to print dye, rather than ink, images. Exposure and special development of matrix films cause the gelatin to harden in proportion to the amount of light passing through the separation negative (or positive). Unexposed gelatin on the matrix film is washed away, leaving a "relief" image. Each matrix is placed in the appropriate cyan, magenta, or yellow dye, depending on whether it was exposed to the red, green, or blue separation record. One after another the dyed matrices are pressed against a receiving sheet, which absorbs the dyes to form the final full-color image. The matrices can be used to produce additional images simply by redyeing them.

This *dye transfer process* can produce the finest quality color photographic prints obtainable. It is superior to printed ink reproductions because the image is not broken up into halftone dots, and because the dyes are of greater purity than printing inks. It provides a great deal of control in adjusting color balance; two or more images can easily be combined by transferring from different sets of matrices. But it is more expensive and time-consuming, and demands extremely precise work. The entire procedure is explained in the article DYE TRANSFER PROCESS.

Preserving Images

The dyes in all color photographic materials are subject to change and fading with time even under the best storage conditions. But black-and-white silver images on film will not change over very long periods of time if they have been archivally processed and are stored properly. Because of this, black-

and-white separation records provide an excellent way to preserve color images. Whenever a new color image is required, it can be printed from the separations, using fresh color materials.

It is not necessary to use the dye transfer process to obtain the color image; conventional color print paper or film may be used. If each separation negative is printed through its own color filter onto the print material, it will expose only one emulsion layer. With the light passing through a blue filter, the blue record image will expose only the blue-sensitive layer in the print material. In the same way, with a green filter the green record image will expose only the green-sensitive layer, and with a red filter the red record will expose only the red-sensitive layer. When the paper or print film is processed, a full-color positive image is produced, just as if the original subject had been directly photographed. Again, exact registration of the three exposed images is essential to achieve the final result.

Fundamental Considerations

The techniques and procedures of color separation photography vary in detail depending upon whether the original is a color negative or positive and on what method of printing will be used. There are some things that are common to all situations, however.

The lens used to make the separations must be a flat-field design with good color correction. (For professional work, apochromatic lenses are desirable.) Most separation photography is from flat materials—prints, transparencies, or negatives—at magnifications of about 0.5:1 and larger. Conventional lenses are corrected for three-dimensional subjects and do not generally focus a flat subject with equal sharpness at the center and in the corners of the field at the close distances that produce large images. With a lens uncorrected for color, various color light rays come to focus at different points behind the lens. Most camera lenses have two-color (achromatic) correction. If a regular camera is used for separation work, one of the images may be a slightly different size when a filter of the uncorrected color is put in place. This is very difficult to observe visually; it usually becomes apparent only when an attempt is made to print from the separations. It makes it impossible to register the out-of-size image. Process lenses, used for photomechanical reproduc-

Yellow (red/green) positive plate made from blue negative filter

Magenta (blue/red) positive plate made from green negative filter

Cyan (blue/green) positive plate made from red negative filter

Black ink plate made from a modified filter

Color Separation Photography

Color separation photography is the basis of all printed color reproductions, such as this. Plates for three inks—cyan, magenta, and yellow—are made by photographing the original picture through a color filter which produces a negative record. When a positive plate is made from this negative, the colors in the plate will correspond to areas that did not contain the color of the filter used. An additional plate, a black printer, made from a modified filter, gives clarity and crispness to the final reproduction. Photo by Ted DeToy.

Color Separation Photography

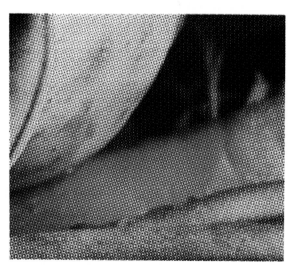

Cyan, magenta, yellow, and black inks are used to create a full-color image in a printed reproduction. As illustrated in the enlarged detail at left, the inks are not mixed together but rather laid down in tiny dots, side-by-side and overlapping as required. The dots are made by rephotographing the separation negative for each plate through a halftone screen. Photo by Ted DeToy.

Color Separation Photography

tion photography, are flat-field apochromats; they are preferred for separation photography.

Contrast and density must match, or be properly balanced, for all the separations. There are three factors involved: lighting, exposure, and processing.

Lighting must be absolutely even across a flat subject. Hot spots or lighting variations will cause uneven densities in each separation, and greater differences from one separation to another. This is partly because the contrast response of black-and-white emulsions is not the same to all colors of light.

Exposure must be balanced so that the densities and contrasts will match. Tungsten light is rich in reddish colors, deficient in blues. Therefore, the exposure through the red filter will be shorter than through the green or blue filters. It is essential to determine the true factor of each separation filter in relation to the other two filters, so that the exposure time can be adjusted to compensate. Often it is more effective to make tests to determine how much neutral density filtration should be added to the red and green filters to make them match the blue filter density. This will keep the exposure time and the lens aperture the same for all three exposures, and avoid any variations that might be caused by changing them.

Processing. All three films should be processed together to avoid the effects of any changes in the solutions, especially the developer. If lighting and exposure have been properly controlled, it is usually possible to give all three separations the same developing time. But if different times are required, each can be removed from the developer at the proper time and held in a stop bath until the others have completed development. In some applications of color separation photography a different emulsion or different developer may have to be used for one of the separations in order to achieve proper contrast control. This complicates the task of producing a matched set of separations. It is usual to photograph a gray scale alongside the subject so the negatives can be evaluated by eye or by comparison printing or, preferably, with a densitometer. Corresponding steps on the scale should have the same contrast and density in each of the separations. In most situations, the red and green filter negatives are developed for the same length of time, but the blue filter negative is developed longer to give it the same contrast as the other two.

Everything must remain in a fixed position throughout the exposure process. If the subject, the lens, or the camera back moves between exposures, the images will not register properly. This means that a sturdy camera support is essential, and that great care must be exercised in inserting and removing film holders. Not all holders keep film in precisely the same position at the back of the camera. For precision, the same holder can be used for all three exposures, reloading it each time. Registration film holders accept film sheets that have had holes punched along one edge; the holes fit over pegs in the holder so that each sheet is held in exactly the same position. The registration holes aid in aligning films for printing as well.

Separation records can also be made by contact printing from negative or positive images on film. And they can be printed by contact or by projection (enlarging). The qualities of separation records are often adjusted by using silver masks with the original subject to reduce or increase contrast, as required, and to correct for dyes or printing inks that are imperfect subtractive primaries. While color separation photography provides great flexibility and control in producing color images, it demands great care and precision in its execution.

• *See also:* COLOR THEORY; DYE TRANSFER PROCESS; MASKING; PHOTOMECHANICAL REPRODUCTION METHODS; SCREENED NEGATIVES AND PRINTS.

Further Reading: Southworth, Miles. *Color Separation Techniques.* Philadelphia, PA: North American Publishing Co., 1974; Wall, E.J. *The History of Three-Color Photography.* Belmont, CA: Pitman Publishing Corp., Inc., 1977.

Color Temperature

When a perfect radiator (*See:* BLACK BODY.) is heated, it gives off energy. At a certain temperature, the energy reaches the range of visible wavelengths and the radiator appears to glow deep red. As the temperature rises, additional energy of increasingly shorter wavelengths is emitted, and the color of the radiator changes through the spectrum. When virtually all visible wavelengths are being radiated, the material appears as pure white. The filament of a

SELECTED PRACTICAL SOURCES OF ILLUMINATION AND THEIR COLOR TEMPERATURES

Source	Color Temperature (Degrees Kelvin)	Mired Value
Sunlight (mean noon)	5400	185
Skylight	12000 to 18000	83 to 56
Photographic daylight*	5500	182
Flashcube	4950	202
Clear zirconium flash	4100	243
Clear aluminum flash	3800	263
500-watt (photoflood) approx. 34.0 lumens/watt	3400	294
500-watt (3200 K photographic) approx 27.0 lumens/watt	3200	312
200-watt (general service) approx 20.0 lumens/watt	2980	336
100-watt (general service) approx 17.5 lumens/watt	2900	345
75-watt (general service) approx 15.4 lumens/watt	2820	353
40-watt (general service) approx 11.8 lumens/watt	2650	377

*Condition of daylight which best represents that encountered in typical photographic situations.

light bulb can be considered to be a black-body radiator.

Using the above as a standard, any light emitted by a heated filament can be expressed in degrees Kelvin (K). The color temperature of the light is equal to the temperature at which the black body radiates the same color.

Color is a psychophysical effect, and all impressions of color can be created by the action of discontinuous as well as continuous spectra on the eye (*See:* COLOR THEORY; VISION.). "Color temperature" describes only the visual aspect of color. It is, therefore, a meaningful description of light only if the source produces energy continuously through the spectrum up to the point at which a given color is visible, in the same way a black body would. This is not true for all light sources, most notably fluorescent tubes. However, it is essentially the case for tungsten lamps, flash bulbs and tubes, most photographic light sources, and for most daylight condi-

tions. (See the accompanying table of sources of illumination and their color temperatures and mired values.)

Color films are designed to produce accurate color records with illumination of a specific color temperature: 5500 K (daylight-type films), 3400 K (type A films), or 3200 K (Tungsten films). If the light source differs from the film color balance, filters may be used to raise or lower the color temperature of the light to achieve an accurate rendering. Bluish filters raise color temperature; yellowish or amber filters lower color temperature.

Mired Values

To simplify the selection of filters, a unit called the microreciprocal degree, or *mired,* is used instead of the actual color temperature. (See the table of mired values of color temperatures.) A mired value is equal to 1,000,000 divided by the color temperature. For example, a 3400 K photoflood lamp has a

MIRED VALUES OF COLOR TEMPERATURES FROM 2000–6900K

K	0	100	200	300	400	500	600	700	800	900
2000	500	476	455	435	417	400	385	370	357	345
3000	333	323	312	303	294	286	278	270	263	256
4000	250	244	238	233	227	222	217	213	208	204
5000	200	196	192	189	185	182	179	175	172	169
6000	167	164	161	159	156	154	152	149	147	145

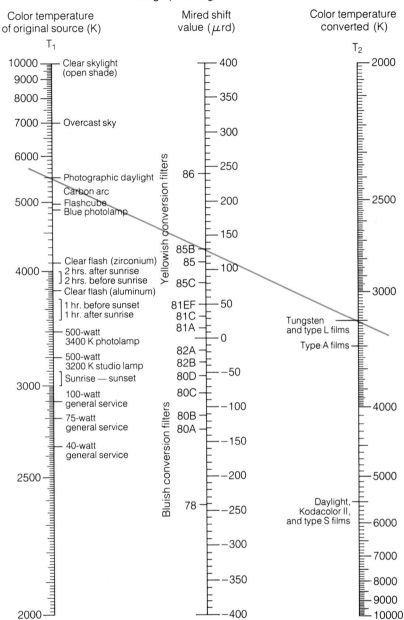

Color temperature of original source (K) T_1

Clear skylight (open shade)	10000, 9000
Overcast sky	7000
Photographic daylight	6000
Carbon arc	
Flashcube	5000
Blue photolamp	
Clear flash (zirconium)	4000
2 hrs. after sunrise	
2 hrs. before sunrise	
Clear flash (aluminum)	
1 hr. before sunset	
1 hr. after sunrise	
500-watt 3400 K photolamp	
500-watt 3200 K studio lamp	
Sunrise — sunset	3000
100-watt general service	
75-watt general service	
40-watt general service	
	2500
	2000

Mired shift value (μrd)

Yellowish conversion filters

400	
350	
300	
250	86
200	
150	
	85B
100	85
	85C
50	81EF
	81C
	81A
0	
	82A
-50	82B
	80D
-100	80C
	80B
-150	80A
-200	
-250	78
-300	
-350	
-400	

Bluish conversion filters

Color temperature converted (K) T_2

2000	
2500	
3000	Tungsten and type L films
	Type A films
4000	
5000	
6000	Daylight, Kodacolor II, and type S films
7000	
8000	
9000	
10000	

Mired nomograph for light-source conversion. To find the filter required for a particular conversion, place a straightedge from an original source (T_1) to a second source (T_2) as illustrated by the diagonal line. In the illustration, daylight illumination at 5500 K requires an approximate + 130 mired shift to convert type B illumination at 3200 K. Kodak daylight filter No. 85B with a mired shift value of + 131 meets this requirement.

mired value of $1,000,000 \div 3400 = 294$. Because the mired is a reciprocal factor, mired values decrease as color temperatures increase.

Filters can be assigned mired shift values equivalent to the amounts they raise or lower color temperature. It then becomes a simple matter of choosing a filter for color conversion or light balancing.

Subtract the mired value of the film's color temperature balance from the mired value of the light source. If the answer is a positive number, a yellowish filter with that positive mired shift value is required to lower the color temperature of the light. If the answer is a negative number, a bluish filter with that negative mired shift value is required to raise the color temperature of the light. To obtain higher shift values, two filters may be used; their mired values may be added together. As an example:

	Mired value
Light source (5500 K)	182
Film balance (3400 K)	−294
Required filter shift value	−112

Conversion Filters for Color Films. Conversion filters are intended for use over the camera lens to make significant changes in the color temperature of illumination. (See the accompanying table.)

Light Balancing Filters. Light balancing filters make *minor* adjustments in the color quality of illumination reaching the film in order to obtain cooler (bluer) or warmer (yellower) color rendering. They are intended for use over the camera lens. Where a color temperature meter is available to determine the color temperature of prevailing light, or where the color temperature is already known, the accompanying table can be used to convert the prevailing

CONVERSION FILTERS FOR COLOR FILMS

Filter Color	Filter Number	Exposure Increase in Stops*	Conversion in Degrees K	Mired Shift Value
Blue	80A	2	3200 to 5500	−131
	80B	1⅔	3400 to 5500	−112
	80C	1	3800 to 5500	−81
	80D	⅓	4200 to 5500	−56
Amber	85C	⅓	5500 to 3800	81
	85	⅔	5500 to 3400	112
	85N3	1⅔	5500 to 3400	112
	85N6	2⅔	5500 to 3400	112
	85N9	3⅔	5500 to 3400	112
	85B	⅔	5500 to 3200	131

*These values are approximate. For critical work, they should be checked by practical test, especially if more than one filter is used.

KODAK LIGHT BALANCING FILTERS

Filter Color	Filter Number	Exposure Increase in Stops*	To obtain 3200 K from:	To obtain 3400 K from:	Mired Shift Value
Bluish	82C+82C	1⅓	2490 K	2610 K	−89
	82C + 82B	1⅓	2570 K	2700 K	−77
	82C + 82A	1	2650 K	2780 K	−65
	82C + 82	1	2720 K	2870 K	−55
	82C	⅔	2800 K	2950 K	−45
	82B	⅔	2900 K	3060 K	−32
	82A	⅓	3000 K	3180 K	−21
	82	⅓	3100 K	3290 K	−10
	No Filter Necessary		3200 K	3400 K	
Yellowish	81	⅓	3300 K	3510 K	9
	81A	⅓	3400 K	3630 K	18
	81B	⅓	3500 K	3740 K	27
	81C	⅓	3600 K	3850 K	35
	81D	⅔	3700 K	3970 K	42
	81EF	⅔	3850 K	4140 K	52

*These values are approximate. For critical work, they should be checked by practical test, especially if more than one filter is used.

temperature to either 3200 K or 3400 K. To obtain color temperatures other than those listed, use the mired nomograph in this article.

• *See also:* BLACK BODY; COLOR THEORY; FILTERS; KELVIN; VISION.

Color Theory

Although we speak of objects as having various colors, in the strictest sense, color is not a physical attribute of an object. When energy of various wavelengths strikes receptor cells in the human eye, the mind identifies the sensation as "color" of a certain hue. The significant attribute of an object is how it emits, reflects, or transmits energy wavelengths within the range the eye can detect—the range of wavelengths that we call light.

Thus, color is a combined physical and psychological phenomenon produced by the complex interaction of light, the wavelength-affecting characteristics of objects, object surfaces, and the response of the human eye. The matter is additionally complex because not only can the eye identify the color of any isolated wavelength of light, it can also see a color by being stimulated by certain other wavelengths, none of which match the wavelength of the perceived color. It is this aspect of vision that makes color photography possible.

There are two ways in which the eye can be made to see a certain color. One is to use separate sources that produce key, stimulus wavelengths of light, and to present their output to the eye in the proper proportions so that the effect adds up to the intended color sensation. Colored light sources provide this type of color stimulus. The other way is to begin with all the visible wavelengths—white light —and to subtract all that are unnecessary, leaving only the required proportions of stimulus wavelengths to reach the eye. The color in objects that we see by transmitted or reflected light is representative of this second method.

The nature of light and the way the eye sees are more fully discussed in the articles LIGHT and VISION. This article discusses how wavelengths are added or subtracted to create color; the interaction between subjects and the light falling on them; and how colors are measured and identified.

The Nature of Light

Light is one of a number of known forms of radiant energy that travel in wave motions. These forms of energy travel at 300,000 kilometres (186,000 miles) per second in air, but they differ in wavelength and frequency. Wavelength is the distance from the crest of one wave to the crest of the next, while frequency is the number of waves passing a given point in one second.

Frequency is much more difficult to measure than wavelength, which can be determined with great accuracy. Hence, a particular type of radiation can customarily be identified by its wavelength as it travels in air.

The various forms of radiant energy form a continuous series of wavelengths known as the electromagnetic or energy spectrum. At one end are the extremely short waves of gamma rays emitted by certain radioactive materials, and at the other end are the waves of radio, the longest of which are miles in length.

Toward the center of the electromagnetic spectrum are the waves of light, which range from 400 nanometres (millionths of a millimetre) to 700 nanometres in length. These two wavelengths are not the actual limits of visible radiation, but since the eye is relatively insensitive at either extreme, they can be considered as the practical limits.

White Light

When all of the wavelengths between 400 and 700 nanometres are presented to the eye in nearly equal quantities, you get the sensation of colorless or "white" light. There is no absolute standard for white, because the human observer's visual processes adapt to changing conditions. The changes in the intensity of daylight with time of day and with different atmospheric conditions are frequently noticed. But, a less noticeable fact is that daylight varies considerably in color quality, that is, it contains different proportions of light of the various wavelengths. Similarly, tungsten light tends to be accepted as being white. It appears white even though, for the same visual intensity, it contains far less blue and far more red than daylight. This is apparent when the eye can make a direct comparison. In a room illuminated principally by daylight, a tungsten lamp appears distinctly yellow, because our eyes are adapted to daylight.

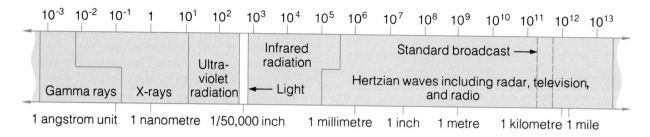

Wavelength in nanometres

10^{-3}	10^{-2}	10^{-1}	1	10^1	10^2	10^3	10^4	10^5	10^6	10^7	10^8	10^9	10^{10}	10^{11}	10^{12}	10^{13}

Gamma rays   X-rays   Ultra-violet radiation   Infrared radiation ◀— Light   Standard broadcast —▶   Hertzian waves including radar, television, and radio

1 angstrom unit   1 nanometre   1/50,000 inch   1 millimetre   1 inch   1 metre   1 kilometre   1 mile

Wavelength in nanometres. The energy spectrum is formed by a continuous series of wavelengths of radiant energy. The short waves of gamma rays are at one end of the spectrum, and the radio waves are at the other end.

The Spectrum

White light can be separated into its constituent wavelengths so that it can be analyzed. This commonly occurs in nature when sunshine, falling on the curved surfaces of raindrops, forms the familiar rainbow.

In the laboratory, this analysis can be performed by passing a narrow beam of white light through a glass prism. The resulting band of colored light, called the *visible spectrum*, will be seen. The principal colors that can be discriminated in the spectrum are red, orange, yellow, green, blue-green, blue, and violet.

In viewing a spectrum, its continuous nature becomes apparent; color shifts gradually as the wavelength of the light changes, and many more different colors can be distinguished in the spectrum itself than in the reproduction. The colors of an actual spectrum are physically the purest colors possible, because they are unaffected by mixture with light of other wavelengths. In a real spectrum, the broadest bands we see are red, green, and blue.

Filters

In order to understand how the human eye sees colors, consider the action of light filters, shown by the accompanying illustration. With a red filter in the path of the light proceeding from the prism to the screen, the blue, blue-green, green, and most of the yellow regions of the spectrum are missing. The

red filter has absorbed the rays giving rise to these sensations from the light that fell on it. The reason the filter looks red is simply that it filters out of white light all radiations except those giving rise to the sensation of redness. A green filter looks green because it transmits to a screen or to the eye only the middle, predominantly green region of the spectrum, and a blue filter looks blue because it transmits only the predominantly blue region of the spectrum. In the unfiltered spectrum, the red, green, and blue bands of wavelengths are the widest because these are the wavelengths to which the three sets of color-sensitive nerve endings in the eye are sensitive. This is why the red, green, and blue filters are used in the accompanying illustration.

Color Vision

Unlike a radio—which can be selectively tuned to a given wavelength—the human eye has no tuning mechanism. It responds simultaneously to all radiation within the visible band, regardless of wavelength. Light of one particular wavelength cannot be distinguished by the eye unless it is presented alone. For example, the eye identifies a certain green when it is seen in the spread-out spectrum, but is quite unable to isolate a green sensation from white light. Although the eye does not analyze the various mixtures of wavelengths it sees into separate colors, it can combine or synthesize certain discrete stimulus wavelengths into a complex color sensation.

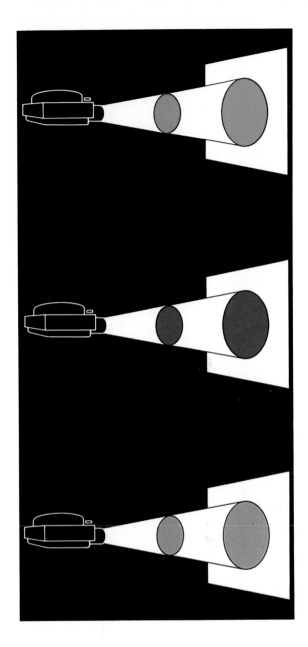

Almost all colors can be matched by suitable mixtures of red, green, and blue light. Hence red, green, and blue are known as the *primary colors* of light. The response factors in human color vision appear to relate directly to these three colors. The relationship may be described as follows: The light-sensitive elements of the retina are connected to the brain through a complicated network of nerves that form three light-sensitive systems: one responding to red light, one to green light, and one to blue light. When only one system is stimulated, the sensation is that of seeing a single, pure, primary color. When two of these systems are stimulated simultaneously, a composite color sensation results. For example, equal proportions of stimulus to the red and blue systems produce magenta. Unequal stimulus of the systems can produce the entire range of colors. The color "seen" depends on which systems are stimulated, and in what proportions. When all three systems are stimulated equally, the brain interprets the sensation as "neutral." When the equal stimulation is bright, the neutral is seen as white; when it is moderate, it is seen as a gray; when it is low in brightness, it is seen as very dark gray or black. These visual principles can easily be demonstrated.

Additive Color Mixture. The accompanying illustration shows the effect of projecting primary red, green, and blue light in partial superimposition. Where all three beams overlap, the effect is white because all three receptor systems of the eye are stimulated equally. Hence, for all practical purposes, white light can be thought of as a mixture of red, green, and blue light in nearly equal quantities.

That blue-green should be formed where the blue and green overlap is not surprising, nor is the formation of magenta from a mixture of blue and red light. In both cases, it is easy to trace the contributions made by the primary colors. That a mixture of red and green light should appear yellow is, however, surprising at first sight. This phenomenon is easier to understand if it is remembered that this

yellow is not the yellow seen in the spectrum, which is confined to a narrow band of wavelengths between the approximate limits of 575 and 590 nanometres. Here, a broad band includes substantially all the wavelengths of light except those in the blue region of the spectrum. Actually, by using (over two separate light sources) a green filter that transmits no light of wavelength longer than 575 nanometres and a red filter that transmits no light of wavelength

Color Theory

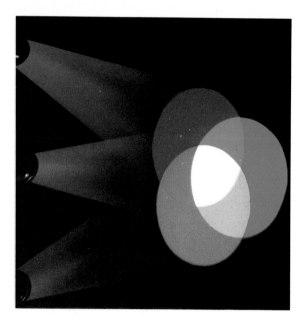

shorter than 590 nanometres, we can obtain the sensation of yellow without using any light of the wavelengths that appear yellow in the spread-out spectrum. The essential factor in seeing yellow is equal stimulation of the red and green receptors. It does not matter what wavelengths stimulate the receptors, provided their responses are roughly equal.

The yellow colors of reflecting surfaces seen in nature and in everyday life are due to the fact that the surfaces absorb blue light from the white light falling on them. Red and green light are reflected, and in combination they give rise to the sensation of yellow.

By mixing red, green, and blue light in varying proportions (that is, by varying their relative intensities), almost all colors can be produced, even the purples and magentas, which do not occur in the spectrum. Most colors of the spectrum (and those of nearly equal purity) can only be approximated, but any ordinary color can be matched exactly. There are two types of color match. One is a match in which the two colors contain light of the various wavelengths in the same proportions. The other is a match in which the component energies are different, but their effect on the visual receptor systems is such that the two colors *appear* the same. The distinction between the two types of color match is important, because the latter type is essential to the

successful operation of color photography. If it were necessary to duplicate the actual physical stimuli reaching the eye, reproducing a scene in color would be practically impossible.

Since matching a wide range of colors by using red, green, and blue light involves addition of the colored lights, the primary colors are often specified further as the *additive primaries*. The exact nature of the primaries is variable. Three wide bands of wavelengths, or even three single wavelengths, can be used. The only requirement is that when mixed, no two of the primaries may match the third.

In color photography, the three colors produced by mixtures of the additive primaries in pairs are of particular importance. These colors—blue-green (cyan), magenta, and yellow—are known as the *subtractive primaries*. Since each represents white light minus one of the additive primaries, they are the complements of the additive primaries. Thus, for example, cyan is complementary to red. That is, cyan being blue plus green, adding red to it makes a complete set of the primaries, which combined give colorless or white light. Similarly, magenta (red plus blue) is complementary to green, and yellow (red plus green) is complementary to blue.

Subtractive Color Mixture. A cyan filter transmits blue and green light, but absorbs red light; hence it subtracts the primary red from white light. Similarly, a magenta filter, which transmits blue and red light, subtracts green from white light; and a yellow filter, which transmits green and red light, subtracts blue from white light. These effects are shown in the accompanying illustrations.

Additive color mixture can be demonstrated with three projectors, one covered by a red filter, one by a green filter, and one by a blue filter. It is not possible to place all three filters over one light source because to a considerable extent the filters are mutually exclusive; that is, none of them would transmit the light passed by either of the other two. Therefore, any of the filters, superimposed over the light source, would cut out substantially all the light.

With cyan, magenta, and yellow filters, however, this is not the case. Since each of the filters

Color Theory

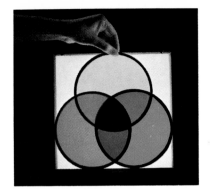

(Near right) In subtractive color mixture, cyan, magenta, and yellow filters (which act as pigments) superimposed combine to produce red, green, and blue. Where all three overlap, all color is subtracted, leaving black. (Far right) Cyan, magenta, and yellow watercolors. Cyan and yellow have been mixed to make green, just as they did when filters were used. Other colors obtained with these primaries are shown below.

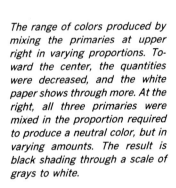

The range of colors produced by mixing the primaries at upper right in varying proportions. Toward the center, the quantities were decreased, and the white paper shows through more. At the right, all three primaries were mixed in the proportion required to produce a neutral color, but in varying amounts. The result is black shading through a scale of grays to white.

transmits about two-thirds of the spectrum, they can be superimposed over a single light source to produce other colors, as shown in the accompanying illustration. The combined subtractions of any pair give one of the additive primaries. For example, the cyan filter subtracts red light from white light, whereas, the magenta filter subtracts green. Where the two overlap, only blue light is left. Where all three filters overlap, the yellow subtracts the blue and all light is cut out.

To produce other intermediate colors by mixture of the subtractive colors, the relative strength of the colors must vary. This can be done with three series of filters, such as Kodak color compensating filters CC-C, CC-M, and CC-Y, containing various concentrations of cyan, magenta, and yellow dyes.

Using watercolors, for example, a large variety of colors can be matched by making appropriate mixtures of the three chosen primaries, commonly called "red," "blue," and "yellow." The "red," however, must really be a magenta and the "blue" must be a blue-green or cyan.

Suitable cyan, magenta, and yellow watercolors are shown in the accompanying illustrations. In the illustration of the cyan, magenta, and yellow watercolors, cyan and yellow have been mixed to produce green, just as they did when filters were used. The more comprehensive illustration shows the full range of colors produced by this particular set of primaries. Toward the center, the white paper shows through more and more as it is covered by less pigment, and the colors become progressively lighter. Also shown is a scale of grays obtained by mixing cyan, magenta, and yellow together in the proportion required to produce a neutral color, but in smaller quantities as the scale moves away from the black.

The range of colors that can be produced by subtractive mixture of three dyes is quite large and makes possible the modern processes of color photography that depend on the subtractive principle. In all such processes, the real function of the subtractive primaries is to control the red, green, and blue light to which the three visual receptor systems are sensitive. Cyan, which subtracts red light from white light, is used in various amounts to control the amount of red light reaching the eye. Similarly, magenta and yellow are used to control green and blue light, respectively. Thus, the dyes in photographic prints and transparencies act subtractively on the white light used for viewing or printing. The resulting wavelengths are combined additively by the response of the eye.

Color-Light Relationships. The six individual colors of a color circle representing the visible light spectrum—red, green, blue, cyan, magenta, and yellow—are single points on the continuously changing band of light. The additive primary colors (red, green, and blue) added together in approximately equal amounts, as with three projectors aimed at a screen, will produce white light. The subtractive primary colors (cyan, magenta, and yellow) added together in approximately equal amounts, as with three filters on a single light source, will absorb all color and produce black or shades of gray; that is, neutral density.

Each primary color on the light-spectrum circle is composed of equal amounts of its adjacent colors, and is complementary to the color directly across the center of the circle. Complementary colors, added together, also form neutral densities (see p. 497).

Production of Color

There are a number of different ways in which color can be produced. Those which are most important to the practical color photographer are described in the following text.

Radiation (Emission). Objects can be sources of colored light. They may give off visual energy when heated, when stimulated by electrical current (which heats a tungsten filament to a visible glow), or because of chemical action, as in phosphorescence.

Absorption. The colors of most ordinary objects as seen in white light are due to the fact that they do not absorb the same amount of light at each wavelength. The color of an object such as a green blotter is due to its having a physical structure that absorbs red and blue light. The surface of the paper is an irregular arrangement of translucent fibers that have been treated with the coloring material. The light penetrates into these fibers fairly deeply. Before the light is reflected to the eye of the observer, it has passed through several of the fibers, and the coloring material has absorbed the blue and red components of the original white light. Thus, whether the blotter is viewed by reflected light or whether it is held over a strong light source and viewed by transmitted light, it always appears green, and the color is due to the removal of light that is not green.

Other surfaces, whether rough or smooth, act in the same way. Light falling on them penetrates far enough to undergo the absorption that is characteristic of the surface and then reflects to the observer, causing the sensation of color. In the case of a surface covered with paint, the color is influenced by the absorption characteristics of the vehicle in which the pigment particles are suspended, the size of the particles if they are opaque (this is the usual case), and the color of the surface underneath if the particles are transparent as shown in the accompanying illustration.

Surface Characteristics. A few materials, chiefly polished metals like copper or brass, have the property of selective reflection at their front surfaces. This phenomenon gives rise to "surface" or "metallic" colors, as distinguished from the more common "body" or "pigment" colors. An example is gold, which has a surface quite unlike that of most non-metallic objects. Specular or mirrorlike reflections from gold are always of a characteristic color that indicates the selective reflection of yellow and red light. They are not white, as they would be in the case of most other objects such as a paint layer.

Color Theory

Scattering. The color of the blue sky is due to scattering of light by the atmosphere, as shown in the accompanying diagram. Variations in the density of the atmospheric gases act in such a way that they scatter light of the shorter wavelengths at the blue end of the spectrum much more than they scatter light of the longer wavelengths at the red end of the spectrum. When the air is dusty or contains water in the form of droplets or ice crystals, the particles scatter more light of the longer wavelengths. Thus the sky is bluest when it is clearest, and more neutral when it is less clear. If there were nothing in the atmosphere to scatter light, the sky would always be dark and the stars would be visible at any hour of the day or night. Above the earth's air blanket, the sky is always black.

Scattering of light by the atmosphere is also responsible for the reddishness of the sun when it rises or sets. When the sun is high in the sky, the direct rays pass through the atmosphere without noticeable subtraction of blue light by scattering. Early or late in the day, however, the rays of the sun strike the earth approximately at a tangent; consequently they must pass through a much greater thickness of atmosphere. Depending on the angle of the rays and the sizes of the particles present in the atmosphere, light of different wavelengths is scattered and the sun appears yellow, orange, or even a fairly deep red.

On a sunny day, distant mountains appear a hazy blue, lacking in detail, because the blue light that results from scattering in the atmosphere is superimposed on the light reaching the observer from the mountains themselves. Any distant object on the horizon is thus seen through a veil of blue haze, which strongly affects its appearance.

Some other colors in nature are due to the same cause. For example, blue feathers often contain not blue pigment but finely divided particles, which are suspended within a translucent framework and scatter blue light more effectively than light of other wavelengths.

Interference. Color can also be produced by the interference of light waves in thin films. Examples are to be found in a soap bubble or a film of oil floating on water. The light reflected from the top surface of such a film undergoes a reversal of phase (as a hump shaken into the free end of a rope fastened at the other end returns as a hollow), but the light reflected from the bottom surface does not undergo this type of change. With films that are extremely thin in comparison to the wavelength of the light, the two reflected rays interfere with each other and cause the film to appear very dark. If the films are somewhat thicker, waves of some lengths interfere, while waves of other lengths reinforce each other, giving rise to colors that vary with the thickness. The reflected light is variously colored, even

(Left) The specular reflection of white light from a smooth red surface is also white, but the diffuse reflection is red, because the light of other colors has been absorbed. (Right) At sunset, the path of sunlight through the atmosphere is longer than at noon, and increased scattering of blue and green light makes the sun appear reddish.

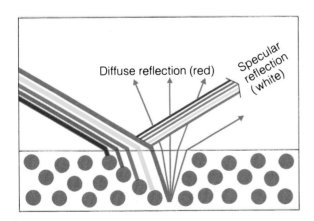

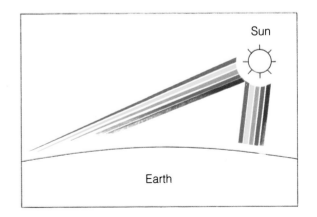

though the film is illuminated by white light and contains no differentially absorbing materials.

The color seen in the specular reflections from coated lens surfaces is due to interference. This interference reduces the amount of light reflected and increases the transmission of the lens.

Fluorescence. Molecules of fluorescent material absorb energy at one wavelength and reradiate it at another. The same principle is used in colored signaling fabrics, which can be seen from remarkable distances because of the intense coloration produced by fluorescent dyes. Fluorescent dyes are regularly used in the textile industry because they extend considerably the range of colors that can be made available in finished cloth. White fluorescent dyes used in photographic papers make the papers "whiter than white" when viewed under conditions where there is both white light and ultraviolet radiation.

Dispersion. Finally, color may arise from differences in the refractive or bending power of a transparent medium for light of different wavelengths. A rainbow and the spectrum formed by a prism are examples. The flashes of color seen in viewing a cut and polished diamond illuminated by a concentrated light source are also due to dispersion.

Spectral Reflectance and Transmittance

In the laboratory, the color of any surface (with the exception of one that fluoresces) can be specified in terms of its reflectance at each wavelength in the visible spectrum. The instrument used in making such determinations is called a *spectrophotometer.* Essentially, it consists of an optical system in which the light from a lamp is dispersed into a spectrum by a prism. One narrow band of wavelengths at a time is reflected in such a way that half of the beam of colored light is allowed to fall on the sample being tested, the other half on a standard white surface. In the automatic recording type of spectrophotometer, a photocell measures the relative intensities of the two halves of the beam after they have been reflected from the two surfaces. As the comparative reflectance of the sample is measured, the instrument draws a continuous graph, wavelength by wavelength.

In spectrophotometric determinations of reflectances, the light source must emit light of all the wavelengths at which measurements are to be made.

The reason for this requirement is obvious, considering that if no light of a given wavelength were available, the photocell in the instrument would have no way of measuring the relative reflectance of sample and standard at that wavelength.

Since the characteristics of human vision do not enter into the determination of a spectrophotometric curve, the curve can be considered as a purely physical measurement. Two samples that have identical curves will match in appearance under all viewing conditions. In the case of reflecting samples, it is also necessary that the surface texture be the same. *If two samples match in appearance under one set of viewing conditions, however, it cannot be assumed that their spectrophotometric curves are identical.* This statement follows from the fact that colors can be matched without matching the distribution of energy at each wavelength.

From the point of view of color photography, the converse is even more important: *In order to match visually, two samples need not have identical spectrophotometric curves.* Thus a color transparency that matches a certain area of the subject visually may not match it spectrophotometrically. The fact that a spectrophotometric match is not necessary enormously simplifies the problem of obtaining satisfactory color reproduction.

Effect of Light Source and Viewing Conditions

Since light sources vary in their distribution of energy throughout the spectrum, the distribution of energy after reflection from a given colored sample will also vary from one light source to another. In other words, the physical stimulus reaching the eye will vary. As a result, the visual sensation aroused in viewing the sample will depend on the character of the illumination. This effect is not so pronounced as might be expected, owing to a visual phenomenon known as *approximate color constancy*. However, the shift in appearance is quite noticeable with surfaces that are highly selective with respect to wavelength in their absorptions, or in other words, surfaces that show sharp peaks and depressions in their spectral-reflectance curves. It is also quite noticeable with light sources having energy-distribution curves of a similar character.

Certain types of fluorescent lamps are relatively so rich in some wavelengths and so poor in others that they exert a marked influence on the apparent colors of objects. Similarly, the appearance of fluorescent dyes is likely to change when the light source is changed. With the widespread use of fluorescent textile dyes, it is not uncommon to find fabrics that change color to a much greater extent than other objects.

Surroundings also affect visual judgment of a color. It is not possible to establish the relationship between the physical characteristics of a surface and the visual sensation it arouses unless the viewing conditions are specific. A standard set of conditions, recommended by the International Commission of Illumination (abbreviated CIE for Commission Internationale de l'Eclairage), has gained general acceptance for this purpose.

Color as a Sensation

It is not technically precise to ascribe color to an object, but rather it should be ascribed only to the light reflected from the object or to the visual sensation resulting from it. However, it is a convenience, and even a practical necessity, to assign colors to reflecting surfaces seen under customary types of illumination such as daylight or tungsten light. This refers to the capacity of a surface to modify the color of the light falling on it. We should remember that an object has no single characteristic color, because its appearance is affected by a number of factors, the most important of which are the quality and intensity of the illumination.

It may be said, for example, that the color of an object is red. This identifies the *hue* of the object— that is, whether it is red or yellow or purple. However, such a description is inadequate. In an effort to be more specific, it may be said that the object is light red or dark red, which describes the *brightness* of the color. This characteristic of a color is independent of the hue; two colors may have the same hue but differing brightness. It might also be said that the object is a dull red or a bright, vivid, or brilliant red. This describes *saturation*. The saturation of a given color may be regarded as a measure of the extent to which it departs from a neutral gray of the same brightness.

Thus any color perception has three characteristics, any one of which can be varied independently of the other two. In psychological usage, the correct term is *attributes*, because they describe sensations,

not the object or the physical stimuli reaching the eye.

While little difficulty occurs in detecting hue differences, confusion frequently occurs in judging brightness and saturation differences—it cannot be decided whether two colors differ only in brightness or whether their saturation is also different. This fact is of some importance in color photography, because it affects our judgment of color rendering. For example, an excessively deep blue sky in a color picture may give the impression of high saturation when the real difficulty is low brightness. If the reproduction of the sky is compared with a blue filter, the relatively low saturation in the photograph is immediately apparent. The confusion between saturation and brightness is typified by the frequency with which the word "bright" is used in everyday speech to describe a highly saturated color.

Color Constancy. The memory of the color of familiar objects causes that color to be seen under a wide variety of illumination conditions, even though the color of light reaching the eye from the object changes over a relatively wide range. This effect of memory on the visual apparatus is color constancy.

Systems of Color Specification

Terms such as pink, cherry, cerise, dusty pink, rose, scarlet, vermilion, crimson, and rust are all used to decribe various reds. The difficulty is that each term means one thing to one person and another to someone else. The need for an accurate means of describing color becomes acute when circumstances do not permit direct comparisons. There are two major systems of color specification and notation that answer most needs.

Munsell System. Essentially, this system is an orderly arrangement into a three-dimensional solid of all the colors that can be represented by actual surface samples prepared from stable pigments. The general shape of the solid is shown in the accompanying illustrations.

The various hues are spaced horizontally around a circle in such a manner that they appear approximately equidistant to a normal observer. The circle is divided into ten major hues, consisting of five principal hues (red, yellow, green, blue, and purple) and five intermediate hues (yellow-red, green-yellow, blue-green, purple-blue, and red-purple). Each of these ten major hues is number 5 of a

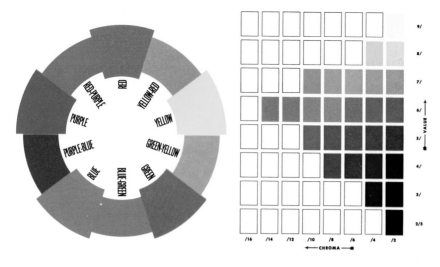

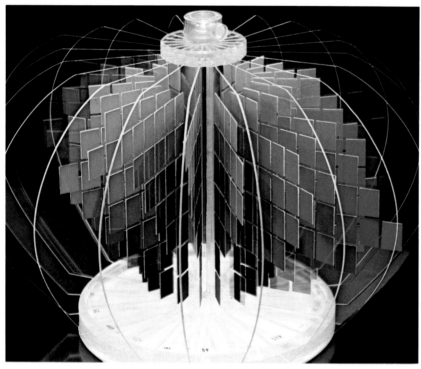

The Munsell System. (left) Hue circle showing the Major Hues. Each is No. 5 of a family of 10 adjoining hues. (right) Chart showing variations in value and chroma for 2.5 YR. (left) Color tree showing the three-dimensional relationship of hue, value, and chroma. Illustrations by Munsell Color Company.

hue series of 10 numbers. Thus the complete hue circle consists of 100 hues, 40 of which are represented by actual samples in the *Munsell Book of Color.* *

*Published by Munsell Color Company, Inc., 10 East Franklin Street, Baltimore 2, Md. (Available in several editions).

Extending vertically through the center of the hue circle is the scale of reflectances, known as *values* in the Munsell System. Numbered 10, at the top of the value scale, is a theoretically perfect white (100 percent reflectance); numbered 0, at the bottom, is a theoretically perfect black (0 percent reflectance). In between, there are nine value steps represented by actual samples. These steps appear

Color Theory

approximately equidistant in brightness under the specified illumination.

From a photographic point of view, the value scale deserves attention. It would seem that the midpoint of the scale should have a reflectance of 50 percent, that is, it should reflect 50 percent of the light falling on it. However, the eye tends to see as equal tone steps not equal differences in reflectance (for example, 10, 20, 30, and 40 percent, where there is a constant difference of 10 percent), but rather equal ratios of reflectance (e.g., 10, 20, 40, and 80 percent, where the ratio of each reflectance to the preceding one is 2). Under low levels of illumination, the ratio between dark steps must be greater than that between light steps in order to appear equal. The gray which impresses the eye as falling midway between white and black actually has a reflectance of about 18 percent.

Radiating out from the scale of values, which is the central core of the color solid, are the steps of saturation, known as *chroma* in the Munsell System. Here again the steps appear approximately equidistant to a normal observer. The numbers extend from 0, which is the neutral gray, to numbers as high as 16, depending on the degree of saturation attainable with a given hue at a given value level. Because of variations in attainable saturation with hue and value, the color solid is not symmetrical. For example, the highest chroma of red is 14, whereas the highest chroma of blue-green, opposite red, is only 6. Yellow reaches a maximum chroma of 12 at a value of 8; purple-blue, opposite yellow, reaches the same chroma but at a value of 3. However, the Munsell System has the advantage over some other systems that if a new pigment is produced that permits samples of higher saturations to be prepared, there is no difficulty in adding the new samples to the appropriate hue chart.

The *Munsell Book of Color* can be used to describe reflective colors by comparing them with the actual samples in the book. The arrangement in notation of hue, value, and chroma is H V/C. A certain blue, for example, might be identified as 5B 4/6. However, 5B is a major hue, and in the case of the major hues, it is customary to omit the 5. If no sample that matches the color exactly is found in the book, an intermediate notation can be estimated.

Because the Munsell System has relied on the judgment of observers in spacing the color samples when they are illuminated by a standard source, the steps in the Munsell scales of hue, value, and chroma correspond rather closely to our mental or psychological concepts of equal steps in hue, brightness, and saturation.

The *Munsell Book of Color* provides the method recommended by the American National Standards Institute for the popular identification of color. Tables have been published that give the equivalent specifications in terms of the technical standard system described in the following paragraphs.

CIE System. The recommendations of the International Commission on Illumination and the psychophysical system of color specification which is based on these recommendations have been adopted the world over as a basic standard.

By mixing three colored lights—a red, a green, and a blue—in the proper proportions, almost any color can be matched. All spectrum colors cannot be matched with real primaries, but the data obtained with real primaries can be transformed mathematically to arrive at a set of imaginary primaries with which all the spectrum colors could be matched. The fact that these primaries cannot be obtained experimentally does not detract from their value.

The CIE System, in effect, specifies colors in terms of the amounts of each of three selected primaries necessary to form a match with the sample in question. The color-mixture curves for the "standard observer" show the amounts of each of the three primaries required to match each wavelength of the spectrum.

The other essential of the CIE System is standardization on a few light sources, such as daylight and tungsten light. The spectral-energy distributions of the standard sources are accurately known and can be reproduced by well-defined means.

Given the "standard observer" and a standard light source, only the spectrophotometric curve of a sample is required in order to compute its color specification. Since the system is based on data accepted internationally, the specification means the same thing everywhere and is not dependent on the visual characteristics of a single individual.

The chromaticity diagram of the CIE System is shown in the accompanying illustration. This diagram is of particular interest because it forms what might be described as a map of all possible hues and saturations. The relationship of a given sample to all the colors can thus be visualized readily.

The horseshoe-shaped boundary represents the positions of the colors that have the highest possible saturations; these are the spectrum colors. The colored area represents the limits of saturation possible with a set of modern-process printing inks. Near the center of the colored area is the "illuminant point" for daylight, likewise the position of any neutral gray illuminated by daylight.

Since color as perceived has three dimensions—hue, brightness, and saturation—a two-dimensional chromaticity diagram cannot describe a given color completely. Actually, it provides indications of hue and saturation relative to other samples. The hue is indicated by the direction of a straight line drawn from the illuminant or neutral point toward the position of the sample. If this line is extended to intersect the curved line representing the spectrum colors, the hue can be specified in terms of the

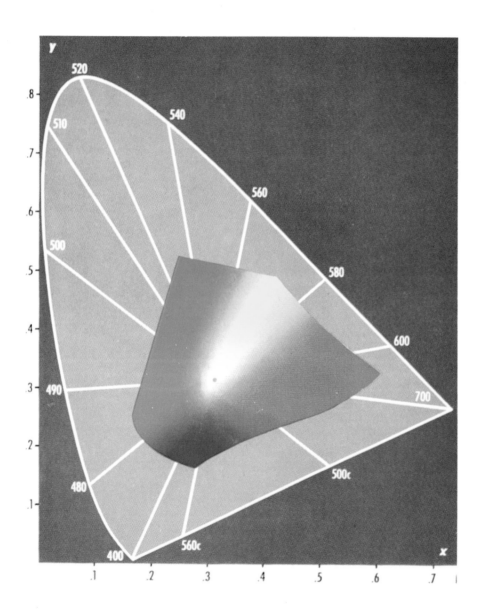

CIE Chromaticity Diagram. On this "color map," the horseshoe-shaped boundary line around the light gray area shows the positions of the pure spectrum colors. Some of these are identified by their wavelengths in millimicrons. The straight line closing the horseshoe shows the positions of the magentas and purples, which are complementary to the greens of the spectrum. The edge of the colored area shows the purest colors which can be printed with a typical set of modern process inks. Near the center of this area is the "illuminant point" for the standard light source equivalent to daylight; this is also the position of any neutral gray illuminated by daylight. By simple mathematics, the spectrophotometric curve of any color sample can be translated into values of x and y. The position of the color can then be plotted on the diagram to show its relationship to all other colors.

Color Theory

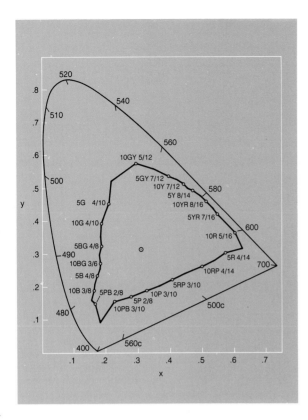
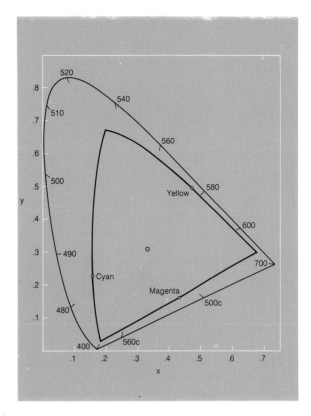

The diagram at the left shows the range of colors bounded by glossy Munsell samples, each of which has the highest excitation purity for the given hue. At the right is shown the range of colors that can be produced by mixing three subtractive dyes of the type used in Kodak color film.

wavelength at the intersection of the two lines. Such a specification is called the *dominant wavelength*.

The straight line at the bottom of the horseshoe represents the magentas and purples of maximum saturation. Since these colors do not occur in the spectrum, their hues are expressed in terms of the wavelengths of green light to which they are complementary.

As we move away from the neutral point toward the spectrum colors, saturation increases; that is, the colors become more pure. If the distance from the neutral point to the sample point is divided by the total distance from the neutral point to the spectrum line, a measure of purity is obtained. This is called *excitation purity* and is expressed in percent. A spec-

trum color is 100 percent pure, whereas white, gray, and black have zero purity.

To make the specification of color complete, we must also include the brightness aspect of the sample, which is expressed in terms of *luminous reflectance* or *transmittance*. In this usage, the word "luminous" indicates that the value takes into account the color quality of the light source and the visual response characteristics of the standard observer.

Luminous reflectance (or transmittance) is a weighted average of the spectral reflectances (or transmittances) of the sample. The weighting function is the product of the spectral distribution of the illuminating light source and the spectral sensitivity of the standard observer, multiplied wavelength by wavelength. The spectral sensitivity of the standard observer, which is called the *luminosity function,* has been standardized internationally and is part of the CIE System.

Values for luminous reflectance (or transmittance) range from 0 to 100 percent. With any given sample, the value can be noted beside the point at which the sample plots on the chromaticity diagram. Two samples that differ only in reflectance (or transmittance) thus plot at the same point and are distinguished by the figures beside it.

Since color is properly defined in both physical and psychological terms, color is a psychophysical concept, and the CIE System is a truly psychophysical method of color specification. As such, it does not always agree exactly with our purely mental (psychological) concepts of color. For example, the colors lying on a straight line between the illuminant point and the line representing the spectrum colors do not necessarily appear to have exactly the same hue. However, the CIE System is valuable in that it provides a scientific standard for the measurement of color. Its descriptive terms—dominant wavelength, excitation purity, and luminous reflectance or transmittance (or other appropriate photometric quantity)—are the psychophysical counterparts of hue, saturation, and brightness.

The accompanying diagram shows at the left the limits of saturation obtained with the pigments used in preparing the samples in the *Munsell Book of Color.* At the right are shown the limits of color reproduction obtainable with a set of three subtractive dyes of the same type as those used in Kodak color films. This illustration indicates that the subtractive dyes are very satisfactory in regard to the range of chromaticities that they are potentially capable of reproducing. Since the luminances corresponding to this range of chromaticities are not the same in different parts of the diagram, we should not expect a color film to provide good reproductions of colors at all levels of luminance even within this range of chromaticities. We obviously should not expect a film to provide good reproduction of colors having chromaticities that fall outside this range, as is the case with the saturated spectral colors. The appearance of a rainbow can be approximated in a color photograph only because most of the colors are less saturated than those of a pure spectrum. Some are due to mixtures of broad bands of wave-

lengths rather than narrow bands presented alone, and all the colors are desaturated by the surrounding skylight.

• *See also:* BLACK BODY; COLOR TEMPERATURE; LIGHT; VISION.

Further Reading: Bomback, Edward S. *Manual of Colour Photography.* Garden City, NY: Amphoto, 1972; Clulow, Frederick W. *Colour—Its Principles and Their Applications.* London, England: Fountain Press, 1972; Küppers, Harold. *Color.* New York, NY: Van Nostrand Co., Inc., 1973.

Combination Printing

Combination printing is the term used for making one print from two or more negatives. This can be done by simultaneous printing (often called "sandwiching negatives") or by successive printing of the negatives onto one sheet of paper.

The effect can look the same as photographs made by *montage,* that is, a photograph that is rephotographed from several images that have been placed together. For an explanation of this technique, see the article MONTAGE.

Simultaneous Combination Printing

This method of placing negatives together and exposing them simultaneously is used for producing interesting patterns, for ghosting effects, or for adding a subject to a very dark part of a photograph.

The negatives or transparencies are placed together, emulsion-to-emulsion, and exposed as one. One of the major problems you may encounter in doing this with slides is Newton's rings. To counteract this you can dust the film with a spray of fine talc. Brush off the excess talc and then mount the slides together. Fine talc is available from graphic arts suppliers. This technique can only be used when the subjects and blank spaces to be superimposed are in respective positions and require the same amount of enlargement. If the blank space where the subject is to be superimposed is very dense, or if the two negatives need to be enlarged by different degrees, you will have to print them separately.

Successive Combination Printing

Several negatives can be printed one after the other on one sheet of paper either to make a dis-

A straight-print scene exposed during the day, when there was enough light to use a high shutter speed to stop the action of the geese.

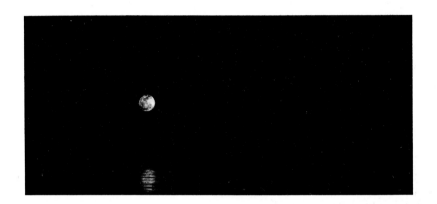

An internegative was made of this transparency of a full moon. Photo resulted from a short-time exposure made on Kodachrome II film with a 300 mm lens.

This combination print was made by sandwiching the moon negative and the geese negative. The resulting picture has a considerably lower print density level, creating the effect of dusk.

Combination Printing

guised addition of a subject to a photograph or to form a very complex image if desired. When you expose two or more negatives successively, if there is any overlapping, remember that you will have to reduce each individual exposure, or a very dark print will result. Successive combination printing is often used with masking and complementary shading to blend the images together. The technique is outlined as follows:

1. Put the negative with the blank space in the enlarger, and compose the picture on the easel. Put a sheet of white paper in the easel, and sketch the boundaries of the blank space. Remove the sketch.
2. Make a test strip to determine the exposure of this negative, note the position of the enlarger and the exposure, and then remove the negative.
3. Put the second negative in the enlarger and place the sketch on the easel. Compose this negative in the area indicated on the sketch. Remove the sketch and make a test strip. Be sure to record the position of the enlarger and the exposure.
4. Print the second negative onto a fresh sheet of paper. Dodge any areas of the negative that might overlap and print into areas of the first negative. Mark the paper so that you can place it back in the easel in the same position, and put it in a lighttight box. Remove the negative.
5. Place the first negative back in the enlarger in the same position that you used for step 1. You can use the sketch to help you recompose the picture. Place the exposed paper back on the easel in its original position, and print the first negative. If the blank area might turn out black, dodge it during this exposure.
6. Process the paper in the normal way.

To produce this combination print, the sand dunes were photographed on Kodak Plus-X pan film, and that negative was printed on Kodak commercial film to produce a positive image. The nude was then photographed against a black paper background. While printing the positive film of the sand dunes, the photographer dodged the bottom of the paper with a piece of cardboard. Then, the negative with the nude was printed at the bottom of the paper while the top was dodged. Photo by Gungor H. Demirezer.

Combination Printing

(Left) A file of cloud negatives such as this formation solves the problem of cloudless skies. A wide range of formations—backlighted, frontlighted, feathery, billowy—should be included so that you can match them appropriately to the foreground. (Right) This straight, cloudless print would benefit from the addition of a cloud formation.

(Left) A cloud formation adds considerable interest to this scene. (Right) Two Kodalith film negatives were masked to make the addition of the clouds possible. One negative is for the foreground area and the other is for the sky area of the picture.

For a description of this technique using color reversal film, see the sections "Multiple-Image Printing" and "Combination Printing" in the article COLOR PRINTING FROM TRANSPARENCIES.

The most common use for this technique is adding clouds to a cloudless sky, as described in the following section.

Adding Cloud Formations

The problem of color pictures with cloudless skies can be overcome easily in the darkroom. A color negative lacking cloud detail can be combined with a black-and-white negative having the desired cloud formation to make a much more pleasing color print. A file of black-and-white negatives hav-

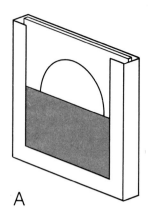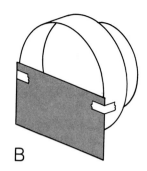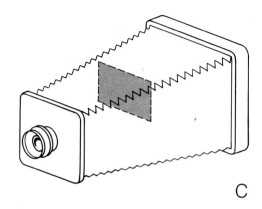

A   B   C

Vignetting methods to block-out ground area in making cloud negatives. (A) Card inserted in front of filter frame in holder. (B) Card taped onto lens shade. (C) Card at top of bellows, inside view camera.

ing a wide range of cloud formations can be built up as opportunities arise. The same system can be used for black-and-white printing; it is much simpler because you don't have to be concerned with color balance.

The cloud negative must be the same size or larger than the subject negative so its edges will not be in the picture when they are sandwiched together. If it is larger, it is easy to shift the subject negative to position the clouds wherever desired. However, the clouds must not be out of scale with other things in the picture, and the direction of the light must be the same in both images. The only detail in the cloud negative should be the clouds themselves. Horizon and ground elements are eliminated by masking them off when the clouds are photographed; the tone of the blue sky is eliminated by using a filter.

For masking with a 35 mm or roll-film camera, position a black card a short distance in front of the lens so that it blocks off about half of the lower portion of the picture area. An easy way to do this is to slip a card into a gelatin filter holder on the lens, along with the filter frame. Or you can tape a card onto a lens shade. The card must be positioned so that its edge is out of focus. (See the accompanying illustrations.)

To make large-format cloud negatives, you must use a view camera. Attach a black card to the inside *top* of the bellows (because the image behind the lens is inverted). Locate the card one-third to one-half the distance from the lens to the film plane. It should be large enough to vignette about half the negative area.

Position the camera on a tripod so that the horizon is obscured by the card. Photograph the cloud formation on a high-contrast panchromatic film. Suitable films include Kodak high contrast copy film for 35 mm negatives, and Kodalith pan film for sheet film sizes. Use a No. 29 (dark red) filter over the lens. To determine exposure, take an incident-light reading of the sky area you want to photograph, with the meter set to the normal ASA rating of the film. For a reflected-light reading, set the meter at one-half the normal ASA and point it at the brightest part of the cloud area. To compensate for the filter, multiply the meter-indicated time by the filter factor of 25, or use a lens aperture 4⅓ stops larger than the meter calls for.

Process the film for full-scale tonality in the clouds, using a normal developer (such as Kodak D-76 diluted 1:1, or HC-110 at working dilution D). Do not use a high-contrast developer.

To prepare for printing, position the color negative, base-side-down, on the cloud negative. Allow the unexposed, vignetted area of the cloud negative to extend under the subject to the bottom of the

Combination Printing

color negative. If necessary, turn the cloud negative over so that the direction of the light on the clouds is the same as on the subject. The negative combination should print with a normal filter pack, but with about 20 percent more exposure. Some burning-in may be necessary to emphasize the cloud effect.

With this method of printing clouds into a sky, the resulting cloud will always be white or light tones of sky blue, regardless of the color it was when photographed.

• *See also:* BACKGROUNDS, ELIMINATING; COLLAGE; COLOR PRINTING FROM NEGATIVES; COLOR PRINTING FROM TRANSPARENCIES; MONTAGE; SPECIAL EFFECTS.

Be careful not to make this artistic mistake—a naturally impossible backlighted foreground and frontlighted clouds.

In this combination print, the scene and the clouds are both frontlighted correctly, but there is still something wrong—there are no clouds in the reflection.

Commencement-Day Pictures

Photographing commencement is not the sort of thing you can try again if your first attempts aren't successful. So it's important to be sure that your camera and flash work properly. A daylight-type color film will let you shoot indoors with electronic flash as well as outdoors, with or without flash, without corrective filters.

The significance of the day justifies complete picture coverage, so take plenty of pictures.

Ceremonies vary from school to school: Some exercises are held outside in stadiums; others take place in chapels or field houses. But there are com-

The significance of commencement day calls for extensive picture coverage. Color film will capture rich details such as the colors of the visitors' clothing, or the vivid and dramatic tones of the mantles worn by professors and graduate students which signify their particular disciplines.

Try to get photographs of various stages of the graduation ceremony. Here, a high-angle view of the entering graduates shows the size of the class and the location of the activities.

mon elements to most graduation ceremonies. Whether you are a relative or a friend of the graduate, here are some of the things you should be sure to photograph:

1. Take a picture of a sign or marker identifying the school. Such a picture can be a kind of title for the pictures that follow.
2. There is generally some sort of processional for the graduates. Try to photograph the graduates walking *toward* you. This makes it easier to stop the action without a blurred image. Get as close as you can.
3. When ceremonies are held outside, take at least one picture of the entire graduating class. If the ceremonies are held inside, there may be enough existing light for acceptable pictures if you have an adjustable camera. Do *not* try distant flash pictures. They won't be successful in large interiors because near and far subjects will not be illuminated equally. And if you have a simple camera, the far subjects will not receive enough light and will photograph as black.
4. The most important pictures are the ones you take after the ceremonies, when there is time to pose the graduate and select a good camera angle. Look for plain, uncluttered backgrounds, such as a plain wall, grass, blue sky, or foliage. *Don't* get telephone poles, knots of people, or other distracting elements in the background. Take several pictures from about 15 feet to show the graduate with members of the family. Then move in close for pictures from the waist up. Other things to photograph can include a close-up of the graduate's diploma, the graduate with friends and relatives, and some pictures of the school's landmarks.

After the ceremonies is the best time for taking photographs of the graduates with their families or friends. Look for locales with uncluttered backgrounds; get close enough to eliminate surrounding elements that might be distracting.

Lighting

Bright sunlight can cause harsh shadows and squinting expressions. If the day is hazy or overcast, you have excellent lighting for close-up pictures of people. If the sun is bright, turn your subject's back to the sun. Then fill in shadows on the face with light from an electronic flash unit or a blue flashbulb. This technique of fill-in flash works even with simple cameras as long as you stay close—within the range recommended by the instruction manual.

Another way to avoid harsh lighting is to put your subject into an area of open shade—next to a building, for example. You need an adjustable camera for such pictures. There's not enough light for simple cameras unless you use flash and stand close to the subject.

To avoid a difficult exposure situation, never pose groups of people partly in sunlight and partly in shade. Place them all in sunlight or all in shade so that they are illuminated evenly.

(Above) Semi-formal photographs of the graduates may be taken in settings which indicate their major fields of interest. (Right) Even among a crowd of well-wishers, an individual can be singled out. Use a long lens and a wide aperture to create a shallow depth-of-field that eliminates distractions in foreground and background.

Commencement-Day Pictures

Commercial Photography

Commercial photographs are illustrations of subjects that are to be promoted or sold. The subject may be the product itself, or it may be a product or service that can only be illustrated indirectly. In any case, a commercial photograph will be used for advertising, promotion, or sales display. And it will probably be used as a printed reproduction in catalogs, brochures, displays, and advertisements.

One of the primary attributes required for success in commercial photography is versatility. Many advertising photographers specialize—for example in fashion or small-product photography. But the commercial photographer or studio must be capable of doing many different kinds of photography. The techniques called for will depend upon the subject and the nature of the problem. They may range from glamour treatment of models, to some kinds of scientific and industrial or highly technical photography. The equipment and films used also will vary

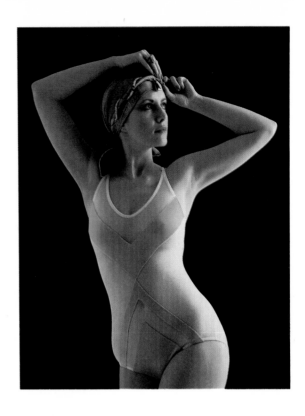

One of the primary requirements for success in commercial photography is versatility. One week may call for location shooting in a factory, restaurant, or office. The next may bring a variety of studio assignments such as these. (Above) Fashions modeled for a manufacturer's brochure and magazine display. Photo by Bob Clemens. (Left) Product study for a department store catalog. Photo by John Pemberton.

Product illustrations for magazine and billboard advertising provide considerable opportunities for the commercial photographer. Photo by S. Kelly.

according to the nature of the assignment. However, the commercial photographer is usually required to produce large-format color transparencies. This gives the client maximum flexibility, for black-and-white reproductions can be made from color originals when necessary. The commercial photographer must deliver work that follows the specifications of the client exactly, and that is technically excellent in all respects.

• *See also:* ADVERTISING PHOTOGRAPHY; BUSINESS METHODS IN PHOTOGRAPHY; FASHION PHOTOGRAPHY; FREELANCE PHOTOGRAPHY; MODELS AND MODELING; PRODUCT PHOTOGRAPHY; SELLING PICTURES; SILVERWARE AND JEWELRY, PHOTOGRAPHING.

Commercial Processing

Commercial processing laboratories process films and make prints on a very high-volume basis. Laboratories that service the depots in drugstores, shopping plazas, photographic shops, and similar places where amateurs turn in film for processing and printing are known as photofinishing laboratories. Laboratories that service businesses and industrial corporations that do not maintain their own processing departments, and clients such as advertising and public relations firms that may require hundreds of copies of various prints or slides are usually called professional laboratories. The largest organizations process both still and motion-picture materials in color and black-and-white, and offer a variety of other services such as copying, diazo and blueprint reproduction, and microfilming. Small organizations may offer only a single, or a few, services. Labs that provide individualized processing services for professional photographers are called custom laboratories, and their type of operation is described in the article CUSTOM LABS. Custom labs may use some of the volume processing methods described in the following text.

Because high volume is essential for business profit, all operations are carried out by automatic processing and printing equipment. Roll films are either clipped at each end to individual rods that are handled in hangers in groups of twenty-five or more, or are spliced together into long rolls. Sheet films are placed in multiple holders, or in open-mesh-compartment baskets, and handled in large groups. The hangers or holders are automatically transported from one solution to another, each contained in a tank of many gallons capacity within the processor. Continuous rolls are pulled over guiding rollers through the solutions and into a drying chamber. Speed of movement, temperature, and the time in each solution are controlled by automatic timers. Solution level and chemical replenishment are also monitored and controlled automatically.

Human operators are largely concerned with seeing that the machines function without interruption, and with analyzing the quality of the processing at regular intervals. Quality is monitored with control strips. These are test strips of film exposed under strict conditions, usually by the film manufacturer, and stored at -18 C (0 F) to avoid latent image changes. A typical color process monitoring control strip contains a gray scale and color reference patches. A strip is processed at specified intervals along with the regular run of materials, and key densities in the strip are read and plotted on a monitoring graph. In this way, changes in processing results become apparent before they go outside the limits of acceptable variation, and corrections can be made in the chemical content of the solutions or the timing of various operations.

Prints are made on rolls of paper 250 or 500 feet long. Negatives are fed into continuous-operation contact printers or fixed-magnification enlargers.

Some printing enlargers may make simple enlargements, while others may make "packages" of prints. Package printers utilize beam splitters and clusters of lenses to produce, for instance, four small prints from a negative with a single exposure. Built-in analyzers read negative density and color balance and adjust exposure and filtration as required; some machines use a human operator/observer at this point, but many do not. High-intensity light sources cut exposure time to a few seconds. Completely exposed paper rolls are machine-processed, and the prints are automatically cut apart as the roll emerges from the drying chamber.

Document copying, slide duplication, and other services are similarly automated.

The product of a commercial processing lab is a standard one. Films are given uniform processing; prints are made to a certain average level of quality. The nature of the equipment and the volume of work handled do not permit special processing or individual printing of a single order or picture. Commercial processors specialize in providing good quality output in large numbers, with great speed and efficiency, and at low cost.

• *See also:* CUSTOM LABS; PROCESS CONTROL STRIPS.

Compensating Developer

A compensating developer is a developer that has the property of holding back the growth of highlight densities while shadow details continue to develop. Usually, such a developer is based on a Metol formula of low alkalinity and is very sensitive to the restraining action of soluble bromides. As the emulsion is developed, wherever large amounts of silver are formed, equally large amounts of bromide are released, which tends to restrain further development in such areas. This action is typical in highlight areas. In the shadows, little silver is formed and little bromide released, thus development continues unchecked.

Obviously, agitation must be minimal; if the developer is strongly agitated, the free bromides will be washed out into the solution instead of remaining in the highlight areas of the film. Developers such as the Kodak developer D-23 and the Windisch Metol-sulfite formula—which is similar but of even lower alkalinity—have a useful amount of compensating action. They are often used to develop flash exposures, to avoid blocking up of highlights. Thin-emulsion films do not retain the bromides as well as thicker-emulsion films, so compensating developers do not work as well with modern thin-emulsion films.

•*See also:* DEVELOPERS AND DEVELOPING; FORMULAS FOR BLACK-AND-WHITE PROCESSING.

Composition

Photographic composition is the selection and arrangement of subjects within the picture area.

Some arrangements are made by placing figures or objects in certain positions. Others are made by choosing a point of view. You may move your camera a few inches or a few feet and change the composition decidedly. Some chance shots may turn out to have good composition, but most good pictures are created. How do you create a picture? First, you become familiar with some principles of composition. Then you will realize that most pictures with good composition are the result of careful and sensitive looking—and sometimes patient waiting. It's not as hard as it may sound. Keep in mind your feelings about the subject as you try to observe the following things.

A Strong Center of Interest

Finding a strong center of interest helps you identify what the real point of the picture will be. You may want to include a secondary subject, but make sure that it doesn't detract from your main subject.

Avoid putting the center of interest in the center of your picture unless you want a formal, symmetrically balanced effect. Sometimes, placing the main subject smack in the middle of the picture looks static and uninteresting. If that is the case, try placing the center of interest according to the "rule of thirds": Divide the picture area into thirds, both vertically and horizontally; then place the center of interest near one of the four places where the lines intersect. This isn't a sure-fire way to succeed, but it offers a way to start looking for alternative picture arrangements.

You should also look for ways to emphasize the center of interest and to make it stand out from the background. If the center of interest has a full range of tones, while the background is more subdued, the

The center of interest should be visually strong. Here, the graceful curve of the flower and stem allows the subject to be centered against a plain background without becoming static and formal. Photo by John Fish.

(Above) This photograph is completely self-contained in a single subject, encompassed by the graceful lines of the extended leg, the curved back, and the arms and hands. The skirt, which is the lightest tone in the photograph, contrasts pleasingly with the darkest tone of the hair. Photo by John Fish. (Right) A small boy, almost dwarfed by the high, dark walls of the barn, becomes the center of interest at the angle formed by the sunlight coming in through the door.

center of interest will stand out. If the center of interest is light and the background dark, not only will the subject stand out, but it will separate visually from the background. If the background and the center of interest have about the same tonality, the center of interest can be made to stand out by back- or rimlighting.

Angles

When you find a subject, first impressions are often quite perceptive. Follow your immediate impulses and take a picture. But don't stop with that. Walk around the subject and look at it from all angles; look for the best angle to shoot from. Photographing from a low angle provides an uncluttered sky background outdoors. However, in bad weather you may want to shoot from a high angle. Overcast skies can look bleak. If that's the mood you want, fine; if not, choose an angle that keeps the sky out of the picture. On the other hand, the soft, diffuse light of a lightly overcast sky gives excellent effects

on close-ups of faces. The camera angle is one of the factors that determines the effect of the lighting. Look to see how this changes when the subject is placed in different angles to the sun.

Consider the horizon line; the sense of space, distance, and perspective are affected by its location in the picture. You can have the horizon low to accent spaciousness—especially nice if you have some white, fluffy clouds against a blue sky—or high to suggest closeness.

Closeness

Beginning photographers often look through the viewfinder and start backing away from the subject. This is not only an unsafe way to travel, it can dilute a picture. When you look through the viewfinder, move toward the subject until you have eliminated everything that does not add to your picture. Although you can crop your picture later if you plan to enlarge it, that is almost always a salvage operation. It's always better, when you take the pic-

Shadow is the most important compositional element in this picture. The dividing line between light and dark areas is the center of interest in this photograph, emphasizing the repetition in the men's poses and the almost perfect positive-negative effect of their clothes and coloring.

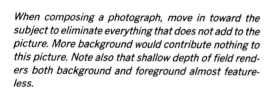

When composing a photograph, move in toward the subject to eliminate everything that does not add to the picture. More background would contribute nothing to this picture. Note also that shallow depth of field renders both background and foreground almost featureless.

ture, to concentrate on exactly how much to include and what to eliminate.

In terms of expressiveness, close-ups convey a feeling of intimacy; long shots suggest airiness and depth.

Lines

Dominant lines should lead attention into the picture, not out of it. You can find a line in almost anything, such as a road or a shadow. The road will always be there; it's just a matter of choosing the right angle to make it run into the picture. A

shadow, however, is an ever-changing thing. There may be only one time in the day when it is just right. So if possible, be patient and wait for it to be where you want it to be. Remember that shadow shapes in a picture form part of the composition.

Backgrounds

The background can make or break a picture. It can add to the composition and help set the mood of a picture, but it can also be very distracting if it is cluttered. Before you snap the shutter, stop for a minute and look at the background. Is there a tele-

Composition

Strong forms fill space with visual energy; cropping too closely amputates the forms, with disturbing results. Foreground-to-background space is as important as that moving up–down and left–right.

In scenic pictures, the presence of people in the field of view may improve the image. Here, the solitary climber adds scale and dimension to the scene. Photo by J. Michalson.

phone pole growing out of your subject's head? Beware of an uncovered trellis or the side of a shingled house when you take informal portraits or groups, because prominent horizontal or vertical lines usually detract from your subject. Foliage makes a better background. A plain background, such as blue sky, is almost always a safe solution. Remember, look beyond the subject—because your camera will.

Add Interest

In scenic shots, it is often a help rather than a hindrance to include people who may be in the field of view. If they look at the scene—not at the camera —and are at least 25 feet from the camera, they will seldom claim undue attention. But if you believe *obvious color* is essential in color pictures, have your foreground figures wear colorful clothing, preferably red or yellow.

Frame scenics with an interesting foreground, such as a tree or a branch. Watch the depth of field so that both the foreground and the scene will be in focus. It is very distracting to have an out-of-focus foreground.

Composition

In essence, composition is simply the selection and arrangement of objects within the picture area. Your own experience will teach you a great deal about this subject. When you look through the viewfinder, look to see the picture that is actually there. Don't try to find some picture that you have seen before. Instead, look to find a new experience and the most expressive way to show it to someone else.

Further Reading: Clements, Ben, and David Rosenfeld. *Photographic Composition.* Englewood Cliffs, NJ: Prentice-Hall, Inc., 1974; Feininger, Andreas. *Principles of Composition in Photography.* Garden City, NY: Amphoto, 1973; Jonas, Paul. *Photographic Composition Simplified.* Garden City, NY: Amphoto, 1975; Litzel, Otto. *Litzel on Photographic Composition.* Garden City, NY: Amphoto, 1974; Wolchonok, Louis. *Art of Pictorial Composition.* New York, NY: Dover Publishing, Inc., 1969.

 # Contact Printing

Contact printing is the procedure of exposing photographic print material while it is pressed in contact with the negative that is being reproduced. It is commonly used to make proof sheets of 35 mm and roll films (*See:* CONTACT SHEET.), and to make proof and finished prints from large-format negatives. Contact prints may be made with either black-and-white or color materials. With suitable material, the procedure can be used to make positive transparencies, and duplicate negatives or transparencies. It is widely used for these purposes in various stages of photomechanical reproduction processes, in engineering drawing reproduction, and in nearly every other specialized photographic field.

Contact printing is the simplest and most economical method of photographic printing. It can be done with a sheet of glass, a piece of print material,

and a light source. Large-volume work and close printing control are easier if a contact printer is used. With large negatives, you can get same-size prints at a lesser cost using a contact printer than if you were to use an enlarger, lens, and paper easel of comparable quality to produce the print.

In terms of print quality, contact prints can surpass enlargements in tonality because there is no scattering of image-forming light, as there can be in the projected beam of an enlarger. Contact prints also usually look sharper because there is no lens in the printing system to add its aberrations to the image-making process and because details that may be slightly out of focus—but just below the eye's ability to detect that condition—are not enlarged so that their unsharpness becomes apparent. On the other hand, negatives may contain many times the amount of detail that can be seen in a contact print, and that will only become apparent in enlargements.

The major limitation of contact printing is that only same-size prints can be produced. With the small-size negatives commonly made today, such prints are useful only for proofs. If a large contact print is desired from a small negative, it is necessary to first make a duplicate negative the size of the desired print. Since this entails the same lenses involved in making an enlarged print, and is more costly, the enlarged print method is usually chosen. Most photographers use both contact and projection (enlarging) printing in the darkroom. Especially with negative sizes larger than 4" × 5", contact printing provides useful prints without the considerable expense of a large-format enlarger.

Equipment and Materials

There are three arrangements commonly used for contact printing: a glass and pad, a pressure

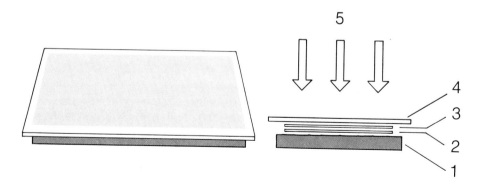

This contact printing arrangement is a sheet of glass on resilient padding. (1) Padding (2) Print material, emulsion-side up (3) Negative, emulsion-side down (4) Glass (5) Exposing light

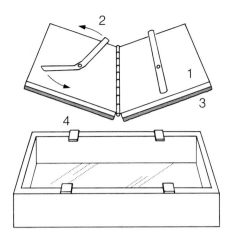

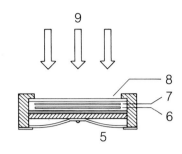

A pressure frame with glass forms another type of contact printer. (1) Hinged back (2) Pivoting leaf springs (3) Resilient padding (4) Locking tabs for springs (5) Back locked into frame (6) Print material, emulsion-side up (7) Negative, emulsion-side down (8) Glass (9) Exposing light

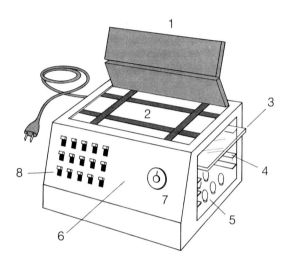

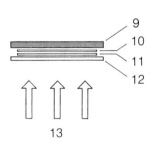

A commercial contact printer. (1) Double-hinged, padded locking cover (2) Glass printing stage with adjustable border masks (3) Adjustable glass shelf inside (4) Shelf supports (5) Lamps (6) Control panel (7) Timer (8) Switches (9) Cover (10) Print material, emulsion-side down (11) Negative, emulsion-side up (12) Printing-stage glass (13) Exposing light

printing frame, and a contact printer. (See the accompanying illustrations.)

Glass and Pad. For occasional proof printing, a sheet of glass and a supporting pad are all that are necessary. The glass should be at least two inches larger on all sides than the size of the print material to give a border for handling and for placing weights or applying pressure during the exposure. Double-strength window glass is suitable, but quarter-inch plate glass is less likely to break, and its weight is an asset in keeping negatives flat. The glass must be free of bubbles, flaws, and scratches. For color printing it should be "water white" or "crystal" grade; otherwise slight filtration may be required to counteract a color tinge in the glass. The edges should be beveled and the corners slightly rounded by a glazier to prevent cuts during handling and to reduce the chances of edge-nicking. Or they can be covered with tape, which should be waterproof to stand up under repeated washings.

The pad should be as large as the glass, or nearly so. If it is too small, an edge may break off if too much pressure is exerted. The pad provides a resilient surface to press the print material and negative together under pressure from the glass. The composition, sponge rubber, or plastic foam pads used as noise cushions under typewriters are excellent for this purpose. Or a one-half-inch stack of sheets of

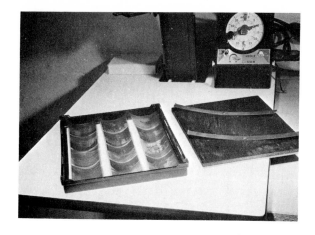

built-in timer. In the simplest printer, only one light intensity is available, and all lamps are switched on and off together. In more sophisticated printers, there may be a great number of small exposing lamps that can be individually switched in or out of the overall exposure control circuit. This permits reducing overall intensity, or providing different intensities to various parts of the image. Many printers have adjustable blades for masking off the printing area on the glass, and many have an adjustable glass shelf between the exposing lights and the printing stage to assist in burning-in and holding-back as described in the section on procedures. The pressure cover is covered with a pad or a rubber sheet with many small rubber "fingers" to even out the pressure.

Light Sources. Illumination is built into contact printers. For printing with a frame or a glass and pad setup, any easily controlled lamp can be used. In most darkrooms, it is convenient to use the enlarger as a light source. An overhanging lamp can also be used. A safelight fixture with the filter removed and the fixture connected to a printing

newspaper can be used. The sheets should be trimmed and taped together so that folds do not cause increased thickness at one side.

Pressure Printing Frame. A pressure printing frame is like a picture frame with a removable hinged back. Leaf springs on the back lock it into place and exert pressure against the glass in the frame. For precision work such as dye transfer printing and photomechanical reproduction, frames are available with register pins that ensure that all copies from the same negative can be assembled in exact alignment. The hinged back permits opening one side to inspect exposure when using printing-out paper. It also makes it easier to adjust the alignment of the negative and the print material when the frame is being loaded. Masks of red plastic or black paper can be inserted to reduce the exposure area and provide print borders if desired.

Pressure print frames work well in small and moderate sizes. For large contact prints, vacuum printing frames are made that hold large negatives in close contact with the contact printing paper.

Contact Printer. For large-volume work and controlled printing, a contact printer is most efficient and convenient. Essentially, it is a glass-top box with exposing lights and a safelight (for arranging the negatives and print material) inside, and a hinged pressure cover over the glass. Switches on the front control the lights; they may be coupled to a

For even, overall illumination, the distance of the contact printing light source must be at least twice the diagonal of the area being exposed.

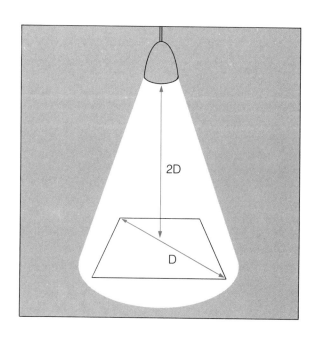

timer makes a convenient arrangement. A printing frame can be set on edge vertically in front of a desk lamp or a similar source. With suitably dense negatives, the frame can be placed in direct or indirect sunlight; in this case a lighttight covering is required to avoid unwanted exposure when taking the frame to and from the printing location.

In two types of contact printing, it must be possible to adjust the light source with filters: when selective-contrast black-and-white materials are used, and when color prints are made. Filtration is easy to accomplish when an enlarger is employed as a light source. With a contact printer, it is necessary to have filters that cover the entire exposing area.

Print Materials. Any photographic material can be exposed by contact printing. However, films and enlarging papers have great light sensitivity, and it is sometimes difficult to reduce the intensity in a contact printer to obtain exposures long enough to be controlled accurately. Contact-speed papers have slower, silver-chloride emulsions. Because the light source is usually so close to the papers—especially in a contact printer—the papers produce proper exposures in about the same time as enlarging papers do in projection printing. If there is a great deal of printing to be done, it is worthwhile to stock contact-speed papers. For occasional printing, and to obtain prints of the same tonality and coloration as their enlargements, most photographers simply use enlarging paper with reduced illumination.

Printing-out papers such as Kodak studio proof paper are very slow. They are suitable for printing by sunlight, or ultraviolet or arc lamps. Printing-out papers do not require development; a reddish-brown image appears as exposure progresses. The print exposure must be carried to greater than normal depth, because the tones will lighten considerably in fixing and washing. For further information, see the section on procedures and the references at the end of this article.

Negatives. Good quality proof prints can be made from negatives that are intended for enlarging. (For condenser enlargers, the black-and-white negative contrast index should be about 0.45, or a density range of 0.8; for diffusion enlargers, the contrast index should be about 0.56, or a density range of 1.05.) Negatives that have the same density range as those made for diffusion enlargers are usually suitable for contact printing. For further explanation,

see the following articles: CALLIER EFFECT; CONTRAST; CONTRAST INDEX; and NEGATIVES.

Procedures

The glass must be clean and dust-free. The negative is placed with its base side against the glass and its emulsion facing the emulsion of the print material. This provides proper left-right orientation of the image and maximum sharpness. If a film, rather than a paper, is being exposed, it must be backed with black paper so that reflected light will not add unwanted exposure. The printing area should be masked down to the size of the negative being printed, although this is not important unless you want white borders.

Constant pressure must keep the negative and print material firmly in contact over their entire surfaces during the exposure; any separation will result in unsharpness in the image at that point.

When an enlarger is used as a light source, it should be adjusted so that the projected light just covers the printing area. There should be no negative in the carrier. The lens aperture can be adjusted to give the required light intensity, as determined by test exposures. Single-lamp light sources must be located a distance from the printing frame or glass that is at least twice the diagonal of the print area. This will provide even intensity across the area. Greater distances than this provide longer exposure times.

Exposure is determined by making a test print and covering portions of the printing area in progressive steps, just as in making a test strip for enlarging. If the negative has a scattered variety of tones, it is better to expose several strips successively at different times, all placed to cover the same portions of the image.

Burning-in and holding-back can be accomplished just as they are in enlarging—with cards, hands, or various devices placed between the light source and the negative-print sandwich. It is not so easy, however, to control printing this way as in enlarging, because it is difficult to see exactly where in the image the shadow or additional light is falling. These techniques are virtually impossible when contact printing small negatives.

In a contact printer, pieces of tissue paper torn to the shapes required to shadow various areas can be laid on the interior glass shelf. Two or more thicknesses of paper can be used to decrease the light to a suitable intensity. Alternatively, the glass shelf, or a sheet of plastic laid on it, can be drawn on with lipstick to create various patterns of light reduction. Graded-contrast printing papers are not sensitive to red light; the density of the lipstick determines the degree of light reduction. Some workers even use handfuls of sawdust scattered about to build effective densities in areas that are to be held back.

Contact prints on conventional materials are developed, fixed, toned, and otherwise finished by standard procedures. Printing-out paper does not require development. It must be fixed in a plain 30 percent hypo solution (300 grams of sodium thiosulfate in water to make 1 litre). An acid fixer must not be used; it will bleach the image. Image color can be improved by treatment in a gold chloride solution such as Kodak gold protective solution GP-1.

• *See also:* BURNING-IN; CALLIER EFFECT; CONTACT SHEET; CONTRAST; CONTRAST INDEX; FORMULAS FOR BLACK-AND-WHITE PROCESSING; NEGATIVES; PRINTING-OUT PAPERS; TEST STRIPS.

Further Reading: Editors of Time-Life Books. *The Print.* New York, NY: Time-Life Books, 1971; Feininger, Andreas. *Darkroom Techniques,* Vol. 2. Englewood Cliffs, NJ: Prentice-Hall, Inc., 1974; Hertzberg, Robert. *Elementary Developing and Printing.* Garden City, NY: Amphoto, 1973.

Contact Screen

Contact screens are a special type of halftone screen used in the photomechanical reproductions of pictures. They are made photographically on film and have multiple graded dots on them. They are used in direct contact with a lith-type film and break the continuous-tone image of the picture into different-size dots. There are magenta and gray contact screens, and positive and negative screens, with a variety of dot spacings. A 65-line screen (65 lines of dots per inch) is relatively coarse and is used to make halftones to be printed in newsprint paper, while a

135- to 150-line screen produces halftones to be printed on fine coated paper stock. With fine screens, more of the detail in the original picture is retained in the reproduction.

• *See also:* PHOTOMECHANICAL REPRODUCTION METHODS.

  ## Contact Sheet

Most roll films and 35 mm films can be proof-printed on one piece of photographic paper by cutting the film into strips and arranging them side-by-side for a single contact printing exposure. The length of the strips and their arrangement depend on the film size and the picture format. Sheet films may be grouped for printing in the same way. The resulting *contact sheet* provides a record of every negative.

Contact sheets can be made from black-and-white or color negatives, on either contact or enlarging paper. An entire roll of most formats can be printed on one 8" × 10" sheet. However, most processing labs use 8½" × 11" paper in order to accommodate 36-exposure lengths of 35 mm film (see illustrations). This is the same size as standard letter paper, so it can be stored easily in file folders and ring binders.

The films can be exposed by placing them in a contact printer, in a contact frame, or simply under a sheet of glass, using any convenient light source, such as an enlarger. (*See:* CONTACT PRINTING.) If enlarging paper rather than contact paper is used, the light intensity must be reduced because of the greater paper speed.

To determine exposure, place a single strip of negatives on a narrow piece of paper and progressively cover it at intervals, just as in making a conventional test strip. If there are negatives of different densities, include the strips containing them so that the two or three different required exposures can be determined from a single test. Choose an exposure that is just enough to make the clear film borders

The best solution for printing a 36-exposure roll of 35 mm film is to use 8½" × 11" paper. It accommodates an arrangement of six 6-frame strips or five 7-frame strips plus the extra frame. Using 8" × 10" paper would require a separate sheet for the 36th frame, which might become separated from the others.

next to a normal-contrast negative print black. If the majority of the negatives are of higher or lower contrast than normal, use a paper grade or a selective contrast filter that will compensate and produce normal-contrast images. An under- or overexposed contact sheet is useless because details become obscured and make it impossible to judge the true quality of the images. Low-contrast paper grades are often used for making contact sheets because they have a greater exposure latitude than the higher contrast grades and will accommodate the variation in densities of different negatives.

To make a contact sheet, arrange the negatives under an appropriate safelight for the photographic paper to be used so that their emulsions will face the emulsion of the printing paper. If possible, group all strips requiring the least exposure at one side and cover them with an opaque card. Start the exposure and remove the card when there is just enough time left to print the thin negatives. It is easier to adjust timing this way than to try to cover some negatives after the exposure has begun.

If it is not possible to separate the frames that require a different exposure, make the contact sheet with an exposure that is appropriate for the greatest number of images. Then make separate prints of the variant frames on other pieces of paper, and staple

or tape them in place after the processed prints are dry. It is usually important to identify the proof sheets. When negatives do not completely fill the paper area, mask off one edge to produce a white area on the face of the contact sheet in which the roll or file number, or other identification, can be written. Alternatively, you can use a self-adhesive label on the face of the sheet. More extensive information can be written on the back of the dried contact sheet.

Unferrotyped F surface and semi-gloss surface conventional papers are relatively easy to write on. However, water-resistant papers present more of a problem. Markers with fine tips and waterproof ink (solvent type) offer one solution, while self-adhesive labels offer another.

Enlarged Proof Sheets

The images from small-format negatives are often difficult to evaluate on a contact sheet without a magnifier. So-called "enlarged contact sheets" provide bigger proof images that are convenient for the photographer and are especially useful in showing work to clients. These proofs are not "contact sheets"; they are made by grouping negatives in the carrier of a large-format enlarger. A glass-type carrier (or two pieces of glass) is required to prevent the strips from sagging out of focus. The spaces between

ROLL-FILM CONTACT SHEETS

cm	Picture format (inches)	No. of frames per 120 or 620 roll*	Arrangement (no. of strips)	Frames per strip	Paper size (in.)
6 × 4.5	(2¼ × 1¾)	16	4	4	8 × 10
6 × 6	(2¼ × 2¼)	12	4	3	8 × 10
6 × 6	(2¼ × 2¼)	12	3	4	8 × 10
6 × 7	(2¼ × 2¾)	10	3 + 1 frame extra†	3	8 × 10
6 × 9	(2¼ × 3¼)	8	4	3	8 × 10

*220 film has twice as many frames and would require two sheets to print an entire roll. 70 mm film is generally used in long camera loads; more than one sheet would be required for any number of frames greater than listed for each format.
†Extra frame could be printed separately and stapled to sheet.

the strips of film should be masked off so that scattered light will not degrade the images. Thin, black masking tape is useful for this purpose and will also hold the strips of film in place. Nine 35 mm, or two 6 × 6 cm (2¼″ square) negatives can be grouped in the opening of a 4″ × 5″ carrier. The images will be enlarged 2× if the proofs are printed on 8″ × 10″ paper, or 2.75× if printed on 11″ × 14″ paper. Up to thirty-five 35 mm frames can be grouped in an 8″ × 10″ enlarger to give 1.4× images on 8″ × 10″ paper, or 2× images on 11″ × 14″ paper.

• *See also:* CONTACT PRINTING; TEST STRIPS.

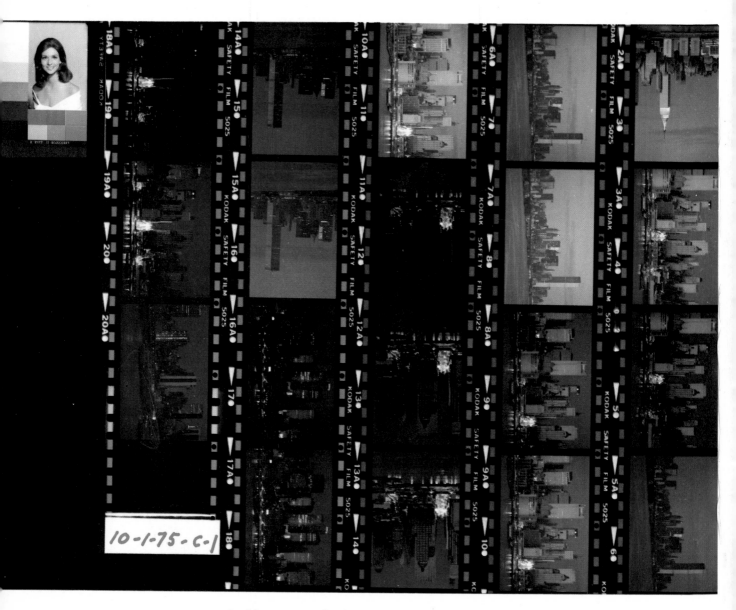

A 20-exposure roll of 35 mm film can be printed on a single 8″ × 10″ sheet. Picture in upper left-hand corner is from a ring-around which the contact-printed pictures must match in color balance and density. If certain frames require different exposures, expose the contact sheet for the majority of images and make separate prints of the variant exposures. (For further information on using the ring-around, see the articles on Color Printing from Negatives and Ring-around.) Photos by Bob Nadler.

Contact Sheet